Strategic Failures in
the Modern Presidency

The Hampton Press Communication Series
Political Communication

David L. Paletz, Editor

forthcoming

Strategic Failures in the Modern Presidency

Mary E. Stuckey
University of Mississippi

HAMPTON PRESS, INC.
CRESSKILL, NEW JERSEY

Printed in the United States of America

Library of Congress Cataloging-in-Publication Data

Stuckey, Mary E.
    Strategic failures in the modern presidency / Mary Stuckey.
       p. cm. -- (The Hampton Press communication series)
    Includes bibliographic references and indexes.
    ISBN 1-57273-100-1 (cloth). -- ISBN 1-57273-101-X (pbk.)
    1. Presidents--United States--Case studies. 2. Communication in politics--United States--Case studies. 3. Rhetoric--Political aspects--United States--Case studies. I. Title. II. Series.
JK516.S78 1996
808.5'1'088351--dc21   96-44486
                                                            CIP

Hampton Press, Inc.
23 Broadway
Cresskill, NJ 07626

Contents

Acknowledgments

I am grateful for the support and assistance of numerous scholars, all of whom gave generously of their time and wisdom. Frederick J. Antczak, Larry Berman, G.R. Boynton, Bethami A. Dobkin, Robert Hariman, Kathleen Kendall, Matthew Kerbel, John Nelson, Laurie Rhodebeck, Theodore O. Windt, and John W. Winkle, III, all deserve much more than a thank you for their personal support and professional acumen. Their assistance and insight are responsible for most of the book's merits.

Hall Bass, Ryan Barilleaux, Barbara Burrell, Janet Martin, and Matt Moen have all been patient and supportive friends and allies. I drink yet another toast to them.

The University of Mississippi, through a variety of summer grants, travel support, teaching reductions, and a sabbatical in Spring 1995, gave me the chance to work on this manuscript. My colleagues and students maintain a challenging intellectual environment. Laura Harper and the staff at the University's government documents center were as helpful in this project as they have been in times past, which is saying a good deal.

I received boundless help from the staff of a number of presidential archives: Greg Cummings and Kate Sewell at the Ronald Reagan Library; Allen Fisher and Linda Hanson, archivists at the Lyndon B. Johnson Library; Kathleen Grant of the National Archives' Nixon Presidential Material Staff; Jim Herring, archivist at the Jimmy Carter Library; Robert Parks, archivist at the Franklin D. Roosevelt Library; and Sam Rushay, archivist at the Harry S. Truman Library. All were generous with their time and unfailing in their capacity to provide information.

Part of the research was funded by the Gerald R. Ford Foundation travel grant program. I owe special thanks to William McNitt, archivist at the Library, and to the archival colleagues there.

The staff at Hampton Press is exemplary. David Paletz, the series editor, was my best reader. Barbara Bernstein is eminently professional. The reviewer's insights were thorough, valuable, and greatly appreciated.

No book would every be completed without the help of family and friends. Ellen Gardiner and Greg Shelnutt provided encouragement and ice cream when needed. Gary Grigsby always made me laugh, even if it was long distance. Gary Miller provided many a welcome diversion, and more than a few good lunches. Ira Strauber gave me a reason to turn on my computer every morning. Fred Antczak was, as always, unfailingly supportive, kind, and generous. John Winkle was there when I needed him, which is saying a good deal. Cory and Ron Lewis and the folks at "Phil's Stab 'N' Go" reminded me of why I like Oxford. Jennifer and Jim Beese, Joe and Karen Dolan, Chuck and Linda McCarty, Indra and Susan Obeyesekera, Raba Gunasekera and Niromi Wijewantha, and the Pamelas Kennedy all gave me necessary refuge from my work. Special thanks are due once again to my family.

This book is for Michael, Jennifer, and Melanie, with the affectionate awareness that nothing I can give them will ever be enough.

Introduction
A Theory of Presidential Strategies

Presidents, whether by calculation or instinct, approach their office and its tasks strategically. To be president is to be given the opportunity to place one's mark on history. Presidents therefore try to control as much of the political history in which they are embedded as they can, thus assuring themselves that the mark is to their liking. Political events, however, are difficult to control, and strategies designed to facilitate that control often fail. This book focuses on these presidential strategic failures.

Strategic decisions are important not only because, as a consequence of their strategies, presidents either succeed or fail to get what they want in an instrumental sense, but also because their strategies provide constraints on them as they seek to define themselves in relation to the electorate. Ineffective use of the tools of presidential persuasion can lead presidents to particularly limited constructions of their public selves. Thus, although this book is about strategic presidential political communication, in a larger sense it is also about presidential ethos and how it is shaped, fused, and transformed, often unintentionally, by the instrumental use of persuasive appeals.

The modern presidency is an extraordinarily fluid institution and depends greatly on the individual occupying the office. At any given time, the presidency is an office that is defined by the president, who operates within an environment determined by past presidents,

present institutional and political configurations, and the expectations of
the electorate. Presidential communicative patterns thus provide a valuable perspective into how the presidency is shaped and how it operates
strategically within the larger political system.

Americans expect their politicians to be effective communicators
and are quick to punish presidents (and presidential aspirants) who are
found wanting in communicative skill. Defining the parameters of that
skill is a singularly difficult analytic task. It is relatively simple to
describe an event after it has occurred and to derive sound reasons for a
president's persuasive success or failure from that description. But to
predict, in advance of an event, whether a particular rhetorical strategy
will succeed or fail is a much more difficult endeavor.

Partially this difficulty is a function of the rhetorical task itself.
Many different elements (audience, occasion, the speech itself, etc.) combine in any rhetorical event, and a speaker has, at best, only incomplete
control over any of those elements, which combine and interact in complex and endlessly variable ways (Burke 1966). Predicting the outcome
of these varying interactions is a risky proposition indeed.

Success and *failure* are, of course, slippery terms. A presidency
that is seen as a failure at one point may be reevaluated in a more favorable light at a later date, such as in the cases of Truman and Eisenhower;
other presidencies, thought at one time to be successful, may later be
considered less successful as perspective and information are added, as
seems to be happening with Reagan. In addition, normally adept presidents can have strategic failures and still survive, even prosper, as did
Roosevelt following the court-packing fiasco. And presidents generally
considered woefully deficient communicators remain nonetheless capable of stunning persuasive success, as was Jimmy Carter in his accomplishment of the Camp David Accords. Like all factors influencing a
presidential administration, communication interacts with other important personal and institutional factors. Governing is largely, although
never merely, communicative. Thus, by examining discrete instances of
governance through a communicative lens, important elements of the
governing process are illuminated. Consequently, *success* and *failure* are
used here primarily in an instrumental rather than in an ethical or a con-
stitutive sense; they mean simply that the president accomplished the
goals of a particular strategy.

It is important to note that no political event is exclusively communicative. I do not pretend to derive complete analyses of every aspect
of the case studies presented here, for they are all complex combinations
of political, institutional, and personal factors. Focusing on the strategic
communicative choices surrounding these events offers a valuable perspective on both the events themselves and on the presidency as well.

This book is not an attempt to correct the conventional wisdom about any particular president or set of presidents, nor is it an attempt to describe the rhetorical style of any president or set of presidents. Rather, it is an effort to categorize and analyze discrete instances of failed presidential attempts to define themselves and their policies in ways that would be positively received by their audience(s).

Presidents operate within an institutional environment that is relatively stable but not rigid. Congress, for example, is always a factor in presidential calculations. But it is not always the same sort of factor. Individual members, constant or temporary alliances among individual members, committee and subcommittee composition can all affect presidential goals in ways that can vary remarkably as time and circumstances change. This institutional flexibility allows for a certain dependence on the skill of individual presidents, creating both opportunities for and constraints on presidential leadership. Contemporary presidents are expected to "lead," but they are given relatively wide latitude in how they define their leadership tasks (Jones 1994).

Those definitions are central to this book. Presidents define themselves as leaders in response to situations, events, and the interplay of those situations and events with the members of other institutions. These definitions influence both the presidents' chances for instrumental success as well as their options for the future. Both political and communicative skills are critical in determining presidential success or failure (Barber 1977). Rhetoric is thus an instrument of presidential power. It is, however, a specific *kind* of instrument. Rhetoric functions more like a musical instrument than a hammer. Unlike a hammer, for instance, that allows people to accomplish tasks with greater ease than they would otherwise enjoy, rhetoric is performative. Although public political speech is, like a carpenter's tools, directed at a specific goal, rhetoric also affects the public character of the speaker in relation to the audience, something that a carpenter's tools cannot accomplish, no matter how well or poorly they are used.

ELEMENTS OF STRATEGIC THINKING

In an insightful article, Robert Hariman (1989) identified four key elements that have concerned theorists of strategic thinking since Aristotle. First, all strategists assume a world that is composed of capable adversaries who struggle over scarce resources. That is, for strategic thinking to be necessary in the first place, there must be an element of competition between worthy adversaries over some desirable—and scarce—property. If adversaries are not worthy, strategy is not necessary; if there is enough for all, again, no strategy is needed.

The second element of strategic thinking is that strategies are essentially reactive. All strategies are attempts to modify another's attempt to modify the environment, what William Riker (1985) calls *heresthetic*, which "involves orchestrating a situation such that other people want or are impelled to join them even without persuasion" (ix). Command is a direct attempt to alter or direct the behavior of others. Strategy is an indirect attempt to modify others' behavior by influencing the context in which that behavior occurs, to influence choices by influencing the meaning of possible options.

Third, there are no universal rules for strategic thinking. No one strategy or set of strategies will always work. Strategies are situational; they depend on success for an appropriate blend of circumstance and action. No single action or set of actions will be equally effective in all circumstances. Because human affairs are always contingent, an adept strategist is able to maneuver through those changes, remain focused on the goal, and thus avoid the traps and snares set by others. Riker (1985) says, "the heresthetician is a battlefield strategist, an opportunist, not a closet planner and ideologue" (34).

Finally, all strategists and strategic thinkers must deal with the role of virtue. For classical theorists such as Aristotle, there is a tension between skillful maneuvering and virtue. Aristotle reconciled this tension by declaring that arguments supported by truth were, by definition, rhetorically stronger arguments (Hariman 1989). Machiavelli elided the tension by focusing not on virtue and vice as ethical choices, but on the political uses of choosing vice or virtuous conduct. (Hariman 1989). More contemporary theorists, such as Clausewitz, argued that it is good strategy to articulate good or virtuous behavior (Hariman 1989).

This, of course, is exactly what the president does. Like a good general, the president must unite the political with the ideal, engage in behaviors that further goals while representing the best in American culture. Politics is, after all, the art of the possible, even in a shining city on a hill. What presidents want to do, as well as who presidents want to be, is always constrained by their perceptions of what they can in fact do or who they can in fact be.

PRESIDENTIAL STRATEGIES

Given that theoretical context, then, it is possible to derive a clear theory of presidential strategic behavior. Such a theory must be grounded in definition. Strategies are situationally grounded, purposeful adaptations of individual style and preferences (character) to accommodate institutional expectations (role) and promote a specific, policy-oriented goal.

Strategies are situationally grounded. Like all of us, presidents make their choices in a certain context and in response to specific exigencies (Bitzer 1980). Some elements of that context are relatively stable: personal and partisan preferences, institutional alignments, and so forth. Yet the presidential situation is not completely predictable. Sometimes, whether because of perceived crises, fortuitous institutional circumstances, or other factors, presidents have more latitude for action in some situations than in others (Burns 1978; Skowronek 1988). In the aftermath of Vietnam and Watergate, for instance, neither Gerald Ford nor Jimmy Carter could afford to appear "imperial," whereas in the wake of Ford's and Carter's "failed presidencies," Reagan and Bush floundered when they appeared "imperiled." Furthermore, Bill Clinton must constantly address governance with reference to the issue of "gridlock" and the Democratic promise to end governmental stalemate. The political context is composed of the prevailing partisan structure of the national government and the polity as a whole, the personal prestige and generalized ethos of the president, and the issues dominating the national political agenda.

The variables of the institutional environment interact with this political context. The institutional environment is comprised of the organizational structure of Congress and the executive branch (such as committees, subcommittees, and the partisan balance) their modes of interaction, and the bureaucratic structures that the president encounters as part of the daily routine. This context is a powerful factor influencing how the president attempts to accomplish the administration's goals. Certain procedures must be complied with, and specific paths followed. None of the modern presidents operated within a strong institutional environment, which means that although they were not particularly constrained by institutions, they were also relatively unsupported by those institutions, creating both opportunities and risks for presidential leadership.

The media interpret these political and institutional factors and help create and organize public expectations. They are not a neutral conduit of information, but structure the kinds of information that are available and the ways that the information will be transmitted (Alger 1989; Bennett 1988; Entman 1989; Graber 1989).

Context is individual as well as institutional. Presidents develop personal relationships and personalized ways of managing professional relationships. This web of interpersonal relations forms an important part of the presidential situation. For example, presidents who have served in Congress have detailed knowledge of the legislative process that other presidents lack. These legislatively experienced chief executives also bring baggage from their congressional years with them to the White House. Both Johnson's reputation for legislative skill and Ford's for relative legislative anonymity formed part of the context of their presidencies.

Strategies are purposeful adaptations of individual style and preferences (character). Presidents, like people in general, bring to their work certain styles and preferences. And, like most people, they find that these styles and preferences can—and do—conflict with those of others, and in ways that may prevent the accomplishment of important tasks. Generally, presidents have been in public life for a long time; they have left a trail of their personae behind them that a voracious media are pleased to trace and report on. Presidents are faced with the question of how to present themselves in such a way that they retain at least some semblance of their "real" (or at least their "historical") selves, while adapting those selves to meet the exigencies of the moment.

Presidential images are not flat constructions that depend on a small selection of characteristics. They are complex and multitextured constructs. The process of adapting these images is less one of constant creation and recreation and more one of choosing which aspect of a previously created character to emphasize or invent.

Strategies are designed to accommodate institutional expectations (role). This book is confined to modern presidents, those who have been in office since Franklin Roosevelt, when public communication became an integral part of the presidency. At the same time, the relationship between the president and Congress became increasingly problematic. Partly, this is due to the changing role of the political parties. Many of the modern presidents have governed with a Congress controlled by the opposing party. The party system remains important as an organizational structure within both houses of Congress, and leadership in both Congress and the executive branch has been complicated by tension that has not been ameliorated by the party structure (Neustadt 1990).

This interbranch tension has made governance more difficult for both members of Congress and for the president. Cooperation between the branches has become increasingly important and less common as the president has assumed a greater role in proposing legislation, setting the legislative agenda, and so on. At the same time, the impetus for cooperation has diminished. As expectations of the federal government have increased and surpassed the government's institutional ability to respond, there is more political capital to be made out of scapegoating other people or other institutions than there is to be made out of attempting to cooperate.

The strain between branches puts the president at an increasing disadvantage vis-á-vis Congress. For whereas Congress as an institution is reviled by the American people, individual members continue to earn the approbation of their constituents. Presidents, on the other hand, are held individually responsible for most of what occurs during their tenure in office (Bond and Fleisher 1990). This appearance of responsibility can work to the president's advantage, as when George Bush reaped the public relations benefits of the fall of the Berlin wall and the end of the Cold War. This tendency of holding presidents accountable for nearly every event can also hurt the president, however, as Jimmy Carter discovered during the energy and hostage crises, and George Bush discovered with a failing economy.

There is some difference of opinion regarding when the "rhetorical presidency" and the strategies involved with "going public" became an important part of the institution, and cases have been made for both Woodrow Wilson (Tulis 1987) and Franklin Roosevelt (Ryan 1988). Despite the controversy over their origins, there is widespread agreement on how the office has changed as a result of these strategies. Samuel Kernell (1986) considers "going public" to be an institutional adaptation to the exigencies of the information age and the need on the part of the electorate to have information more tightly organized and compactly presented. As a strategy, "going public" involves the invocation of the mass public as a way of forcing compliance from Congress.

Initially, "going public" appeared to provide presidents with increased strategic maneuverability vis-á-vis Congress, but in becoming part of the institution, public politics also constrain the president as a result of the need to exhort an increasingly alienated and cynical electorate (Stuckey 1991). As political parties have weakened, presidents turn to the mass media as the least confining means of communicating with the public (Grossman and Kumar 1981). They find that their preferences and policies are forced to intersect with the organizational requirements of the media, and that these requirements do not always favor presidential goals (Paletz and Entman 1981). Lacking the baseline support of the parties, presidents are increasingly atomized as political actors and are extraordinarily dependent for their political survival on events they cannot completely control yet are held increasingly accountable for. This has led to tremendous fluctuations in the public perceptions of the office, from president to president, and even within presidencies (Edwards 1983; Hart 1987). Institutionally, it has led to particularly difficult relations with Congress.

The combination of these political, institutional, and presentational elements has led to increased public expectations of the office of the presidency and the individual who is president (Rockman 1984). These increased expectations allow for greater latitude in some spheres of action while constraining the president in others (Stuckey 1991).

Although the president is now "allowed" to be more active in all spheres of public debate, and although the public sphere has been enlarged since the inception of the modern presidency, this also means that the president is responsible for more areas of public life and must act—or be perceived as acting—on a wider variety of issues. Ignoring any one of these issues can be problematic in terms of public support. As these issues become ever more complex, and as the public becomes ever more fragmented into a variety of publics each with its own agenda, presidential action on policy has tended to devolve into presidential speech on policy areas. Furthermore, the president's relationship with the mass public has become more critical to success in the office (Edwards 1983; Kernell 1986; Lowi 1985; Ryan 1988; Tulis 1987; Windt 1977).

Just as presidents tend to encourage high expectations among the electorate, they also encourage Congress to abrogate their responsibilities to the executive branch. Presidents seek to maximize their power personally and institutionally (Neustadt 1990). Initially, it appeared that increasing the president's scope of activity was a viable way to accomplish this. However, as expectations exceed ability to meet those expectations, the prestige of the office is threatened, and, with it, the prestige and power of the person occupying the office becomes more tenuous.

Strategies promote specific, policy-oriented goals. Presidents engage in strategic behavior primarily because they are interested in influencing the policy process. The goal may be, for example, to pass a specific piece of legislation, to block a specific piece of legislation, to block legislation while appearing to support it, or to support it while appearing to block it. Strategies are designed to further the president's policy goals through the use of persuasion based on adapting the president's public character to the presidential role.

STRATEGIC FAILURES

Presidents can control very little of the importance attached to their strategies. The elements of situational and institutional expectations cause particularly thorny problems for presidents and lie well beyond their ability to manage. Presidents have considerably more control over the adaptations of character to role, of ethos to expectations. When strategies fail, they fail because of poor adaptations. There are four main kinds of strategic failure, of imbalances between the requirements of character and the expectations of role: slippage, singularity, mismanagement, and overreaching.

Slippage

When there is a slippage between character and role, failure generally results. Presidents are expected to be honorable people, even if that is not always important in the conduct of the office. But a person of questionable integrity is always in danger of demeaning the office; demean it too extensively or too publicly, violate the public trust, and scandal will result. Truman was accused of financial impropriety, Nixon of illegality, and Reagan of excessive patriotic zeal. In all cases, there was a gap between what was expected of the man and what was required of the office.

Singularity

The presidency is a plural office, one that involves the chief executive, White House staff, and executive bureaucracy. Presidents sometimes forget that their staffs are extensions of themselves, that the behavior of those staff members can—and does—affect the perception of the president's character and how adapts to the requirements of the presidential role. Singularity is the problem engendered by the assumption that only the actions of the chief executive affect the perception of the presidential character and its fitness for the presidential role. Nixon's nominations of Haynesworth and Carswell, like Reagan's nomination of Robert Bork and Bush's nomination of John Tower, all indicate the perils of singularity.

Mismanagement

Singularity is not the only potential problem when presidents face Congress. In matters of legislation, a failure to understand the situation and its institutional requirements can affect the perception of presidential character and its fitness for the role of president. An important part of that role entails managing the administration and through it, obtaining desired legislation. Presidents who fail in their procedural understanding forget that they must act as presidents, and tend to focus exclusively on the character aspect of their public being. This is always a mistake. Franklin Roosevelt discovered this during his failed attempt to purge Congress, as did Gerald Ford as he tried to pass WIN (Whip Inflation Now) legislation, and as did Jimmy Carter as he struggled to insure passage of his energy plan.

Overreaching

Presidents occasionally go beyond overreliance on character (slippage) and come to believe that character and role are in fact identical. This is when overreaching results, for these presidents come to believe that they are the only ones who can see the national interest, understand what that requires, and act accordingly. This failure of perspective is a problem unique to successful presidents, who have some reason to believe that they are, as president, invincible. Roosevelt in the court-packing fiasco, Truman during the steel mill crisis, and Johnson in Vietnam all discovered that overreaching is surely, if not always swiftly, punished.

CONCLUSIONS

Examining presidential communicative failures can help us to learn more about the conditions and strategies necessary for presidential success. It is not sufficient to note and/or to deplore the expansion of our expectations regarding the chief executive. We must either derive ways for presidents to meet those expectations or to curtail them without doing irreparable harm to the presidency, the national government as a whole, or the polity they serve. The book is organized with these ideas in mind.

The first chapter, "Slippage: Public Failure," analyzes three cases of presidential misdeeds, all of which resulted in part from the president's inability to design a personal image of his character that was consonant with the expectations of the presidential role. The Bureau of Internal Revenue scandal during the Truman administration, Watergate, and the Iran-Contra affair are the cases studied. The extent of the damage each created for the president concerned had more to do with the context in which the scandal was embedded and how that context affected the strategic adaptation of character to role.

Chapter 2, "Singularity: Failed Appointments," extends this theme by examining how presidents failed to understand the presidential role as including the characters and actions of the presidential staff. This is a particular problem for presidents early in their administrations, when the president's character is most likely to be open to interpretive challenge. Richard Nixon's difficulties getting first Clement Haynsworth and then G. Harrold Carswell confirmed as Supreme Court Justice, Ronald Reagan's similar problem with Robert Bork, and George Bush's failure to have John Tower confirmed as Secretary of Defense are examples of how not to approach the appointments process.

Chapter 3, "Mismanagement: Failed Congressional Relations," deals with the problems presidents have as a result of their failure to recognize the importance of the presidential role as manager of legislation and the administration. The Constitution pits the Congress and the executive branch against one another; presidents have accommodated themselves to this institutionalized conflict with varying degrees of success. Franklin Roosevelt and his attempted purge of Congress, Gerald Ford and his "Whip Inflation Now" campaign, and Jimmy Carter's energy plan are examples of presidents who adapted poorly to the organizational needs and institutional mores of working with Congress.

Chapter 4, "Over-Reaching: Personal Failure," studies the strategic difficulties that otherwise successful presidents are prone to create for themselves. These presidents are victims of their own communicative and political success, for it leads them to act as if their character is equivalent to the presidential role. Franklin Roosevelt and the "court packing plan," Harry Truman and the seizure of the steel mills, and Lyndon Johnson and Vietnam provide examples of presidents who failed to realize the limits of their power and authority.

Finally, Chapter 5, "The Best Laid Plans," offers conclusions about the nature of presidential strategic failures and applies the theoretical framework developed in the book to the early years of the Clinton administration.

All these chapters focus on rhetoric as an instrument of presidential power. It is important to bear in mind that the kind of failures to which any given instrument is susceptible informs us not only about the failures themselves and those who perpetrated them but instrumental failures also enlarge and qualify our sense of available instruments, about how those instruments themselves are affected by their (mis)use or are sharpened for some purposes but misshapened for others. This book is about presidential strategic communication and what it reveals to us about the limitations and possibilities of the political and communicative choices open to presidents as they affect a president's ability to govern in the short term as well as make a more lasting mark on history.

1

Slippage: Public Failure

Scholars and pundits have long been interested in "the presidential character," as James David Barber (1977) has labeled that most elusive of attributes. Particularly since the inception of television, Americans have become fascinated with the private lives and "real" motives of the chief executive. Consequently, presidents and their advisors work diligently to provide us with information about who exactly the president "really is." But this information is created, adapted, and treated by "spin doctors," to provide a specific image of the president. That image, in turn, becomes a shell for the president—sometimes providing protection, at other times confining and constraining him.

Despite the appearance of constant and intense media scrutiny, it is only rarely that scandal actually cripples a president, rarer still that scandal destroys one. It is, in fact, possible to argue that although many presidents, and the members of many presidential administrations, have been guilty of improprieties, presidential indiscretions are most often overlooked. Scandals are most likely to erupt and damage a president when there appears to be a conflict between the public image of the president—character—and the public expectations of the president's behavior—role.

In general, the public has very broad expectations of the president—he should be strong, trustworthy, and so on (Greenstein 1974; Hinckley 1990; Hodgson 1980). But the precise definition of *strong*, or *trustworthy*, can change with the temper of the times. Presidents can thus

13

exert some degree of control over the perception of their character as consonant with the demands of their role as president. When they do this successfully, their misdeeds and those of their aides are likely to be perceived as largely immaterial to the presidential task.

The cases that appear in this chapter were not among those overlooked improprieties; they all involved issues that came to center on the character of the president and his ability to assume the role of chief executive. Consequently, they all had the potential to fatally affect a presidency: The Bureau of Internal Revenue (BIR) scandal helped to further erode Truman's standing; the bundle of events and issues that have become lumped under the rubric of "Watergate" destroyed Richard Nixon's presidency; and the events surrounding the Iran-Contra scandal damaged Ronald Reagan's effectiveness in his last years as president.

Although only one of these scandals can be credited with doing fatal damage to a president, they all had the potential to do so. What then makes a president vulnerable to scandal? Two elements seem to be crucial: the president's political past as it is interpreted as providing information relevant to his present character, and the interplay of that past with the relevant political context as it affects the perception of his ability to play the presidential role. Harry Truman, for instance, was tainted by his past connection to Missouri machine politics and was thought likely to engage in the unsavory behavior associated with "cronyism." That past made him vulnerable to the accusations associated with the BIR scandal, a vulnerability that was heightened by widespread doubt that he was capable of filling the shoes left empty by Franklin Roosevelt. He did survive the scandal, however, for he was not seeking reelection in 1952, and, importantly, the context favored both sitting presidents and Democrats.

Richard Nixon, on the other hand, entered the White House with a reputation for political ruthlessness, a reputation that did not serve him well as he faced a hostile Congress and a national media that were not invested in protecting the presidential image. That combination, added to the level of personal culpability disclosed by the White House tapes, allowed him no hope of recovery.

Politically and institutionally, Ronald Reagan was situated between the examples represented by Truman and Nixon. Although the Iran-Contra affair involved, among other things, a struggle for power between Congress and the executive branch, and between Republican and Democratic policy goals, and he thus had less overt institutional support than did Truman, Reagan's challenge to Congress and the bureaucracy was conveyed in a less blatantly hostile way than was that of Nixon. He thus faced less personal animosity than did Nixon.

Additionally, the legacy of Watergate and the subsequent "failed presidencies" of Ford and Carter had become part of the context in which Reagan operated. In the absence of definitive evidence of personal wrong-doing such as that offered by the Watergate tapes, ending the Reagan presidency as Nixon's had ended was not politically practical, even if it was politically desirable.

In all these cases, the actual presidential misdeeds were less important than how they were interpreted in light of the president's character. Truman and his cronies, Nixon and his plumbers, Reagan and the contras, all these were relationships that highlighted aspects of the presidential character. Furthermore, the degree of failure involved in each case reveals how those aspects of character were interpreted by the relevant audience(s).

HARRY TRUMAN AND THE BUREAU OF INTERNAL REVENUE

The Political/Institutional Context

Harry S. Truman became president on Franklin Roosevelt's death, April 12, 1945. At the time of his death, Roosevelt had been president for 12 years and was so completely "the president" that Truman had difficulty establishing his right to the office. As James Pfiffner (1988) notes, the president is given *authority* on inauguration day; *power* must be consciously developed by the president during the days that follow. After his inauguration, Truman did indeed attempt to seize power, bringing World War II to a successful conclusion and making the decision to drop atom bombs on Hiroshima and Nagasaki. However, power was never unambiguously held by Truman. He was thwarted in his attempt to seize the steel mills during a strike. He faced opposition from Congress, particularly in the persons of Senators Fullbright and McCarthy. He had difficulty controlling the military, most prominently in his confrontation and subsequent firing of General Douglas MacArthur. Never a man to retreat from a fight, Truman found himself often embattled.

Partially, this was due to Truman's somewhat abrasive personal style. That style, immortalized in the slogan "Give 'em hell, Harry!," energized his supporters and enraged his detractors. This was particularly important given the institutional and political context of the Truman presidency.

The New Deal of the 1930s and 1940s created an explosion in the size and complexity of the national government (J. Hart 1987). While government functions and staff multiplied, the bureaucratic apparatus organizing those functions and that staff remained static. Procedures concerning control and supervision were inadequate for the tasks assigned to them, creating a situation fraught with potential for abuse.

Compounding the administrative difficulties caused by burgeoning government, the Democrats had been in office for two decades. Democrats controlled the presidency, both Houses of Congress, and the bureaucracy. The Supreme Court was comprised of Justices committed to the New Deal/Fair Deal agenda. Yet that agenda was beginning to show signs of enervation. Roosevelt had enlarged the scope of the national government and established his role at the center of that government. Truman lacked Roosevelt's personal magnetism as well as Roosevelt's grasp of administration. He occupied the same institutional position as Roosevelt without being able to exhibit Roosevelt's power and control. As an administrator, Truman relied heavily on his staff and was deeply loyal to "his people." He had a tendency to surround himself with good friends rather than able administrators; a situation that in an earlier administrative age would have caused few significant problems and less comment. In the institutional context of the early 1950s, however, it created both problems and comment.

These problems were exacerbated by the fear of domestic communism caused by the Korean war. These fears were heightened by revelations concerning the Philby spy ring and the controversy over the trial and execution of the Rosenbergs. The country appeared threatened by communism at home and abroad, and Americans wanted desperately to feel protected and in control (Ferrell 1983). Truman (1950a, 1950b, 1951a) was adept at outlining the threat, but less able to convey reassurance. Truman, squarely placed in the middle of "the mess in Washington," absorbed the brunt of the anger created by Americans' fear and frustration. That anger was apparent in the Bureau of Internal Revenue (BIR) scandal of 1951-1952.

The Events of the BIR Scandal

Scandal was a particular problem for Truman because of his prepresidential career. His associations with a Missouri political machine caused some suspicion concerning his sense of honesty in the past. His tendency to invite "the boys" over to the White House for a friendly game of poker contributed to the image of a "hick" politician who played by a rather free-wheeling set of rules. His specific trouble with scandal began as early as 1950, when a Senate investigatory committee heard evidence connecting Truman's military aide, General Harry Vaughn, to the "five percenters," then under investigation by the committee. (The "five percenters" were a group of public relations men who earned a 5% commission for information on how to obtain government contracts and other favors.) Truman supported Vaughn and refused to fire or otherwise punish his aide, thus creating an appearance of sanctioning corruption when it concerned his close associates. One citizen wrote Truman, asking him not to "let weak friends, unskilled in sound governmental practices, do damage that can never be repaired" (Lee 1952).

Truman's troubles with Vaughn may have been easily forgotten, but in 1951 the Senate Banking and Currency Committee began hearings on improprieties concerning the administration of the Reconstruction Finance Corporation. During the hearings, allegations were made concerning E. Merl Young, a protege of White House staffer Donald Dawson. Again, Truman "staunchly supported his aides" (Koenig 1956: 72). In the face of these revelations, the BIR scandal resonated much more deeply than it would have alone.

The events of the scandal are straightforward, if somewhat farcical. In 1947, Senator John J. Williams (R-DE) made public charges that a Wilmington tax office cashier was guilty of embezzlement. After some years of investigation of this and related matters, a subcommittee of the House Ways and Means Committee began hearings on March 19, 1951. The committee became known as the King Committee after its Chair, Cecil King (D-CA).

Among revelations concerning collection offices in St. Louis, Boston, New York, and San Francisco came testimony from Abraham Teitelbaum, one of the late Al Capone's defense attorneys. Teitelbaum accused Theron Lamar Caudle, the Assistant Attorney General in charge of the Tax Division, Charles Oliphant, General Counsel for the BIR, and Jess Larson, chief of the General Services Administration, of using their administrative positions to eliminate individual tax problems for a price (Phillips 1966). These disclosures, and the variety of officials accused, fed the impression that the Truman administration was rife with corruption (Dunar 1984).

Early on, Truman promised to cooperate with the King Committee. However, as they began to demand extensive documentation, Truman's irascibility asserted itself. He decided to deal with the requests on a case-by-case basis. This decision assured Truman continual—and irritating—reminders of the Committee's activities.

By Autumn 1951, it became apparent that Truman needed to muster some response to the series of charges stemming from the committee's investigation (Bell 1951; Biddle 1951). Upon returning from a vacation in Key West, he decided on two courses of action. The first was to reorganize the BIR and establish rule changes and reforms to inhibit misconduct (a decision that eventually led to the creation of the Internal Revenue Service). The second was to begin investigations of his own to uncover past violations (Dunar 1984). To this end, and following a December press conference during which he promised "drastic action," Truman decided to appoint an investigatory commission.

Originally, Truman wanted a three-man commission, composed of Alger Hiss's prosecutor, Judge Thomas A. Murphy; the Reverend Daniel Polling; and Chicago attorney, Justin Miller. For reasons that remain controversial, the commission dissolved before its first meeting. Truman then assigned Attorney General J. Howard McGrath to the investigation. McGrath was a singularly poor choice. Prior to his appointment as Attorney General, McGrath had been Chair of the Democratic National Committee. Putting such a committed partisan in charge of an investigation of this nature seemed to signal an impending whitewash (Phillips 1966). The King Committee responded to McGrath's new responsibility by broadening their investigation to include the Justice Department.

Meanwhile, McGrath, seeking for reasons of his own to limit the investigation, asked Newbold Morris, a New York liberal Republican with no investigatory experience, to head up the executive branch investigation (Dunar 1984). Morris "was a compulsive talker before the news media and gloried in appearing on weekend television specials" (Hechler 1982: 203). Unsurprisingly, then, Morris managed to antagonize nearly all of Washington in a remarkably brief period of time.

The most immediate reason for this antagonism stemmed from Morris's questionnaire. This questionnaire devolved from his experience in New York and was an attempt to locate improper monies through extensive financial inquiries. The result was a document that very probably involved invasion of privacy and was so offensive that Truman was widely reported to have said, "If someone asked me to fill it out, I'd tell them to go to Hell" (Phillips 1966: 413). One staffer characterized the Morris investigation in the following manner:

> In the two months that Morris has been Special Assistant to the Attorney General, no investigative efforts have been instituted other than the delivery of the questionnaires to the Department of Justice. Morris is apparently miscast in his role, as he is not an investigator by personality, is not a good administrator, talks too much and obtains more publicity than is necessary or desirable. (Hansen 1952)

The hostility Morris engendered became apparent as a Senate committee heard allegations that Morris's law firm arranged an illegal sale of oil tankers to China; Morris's partner directly implicated Morris. Appearing before the committee, Morris denounced the Senators, telling them that they had "diseased minds" and were "seeking character destruction" (Dunar 1984: 115). Although such accusations are common-place today, in the political context of the 1950s they appeared harsh and unwarranted.

By late March, the tension between McGrath and Morris became intolerable, and McGrath fired Morris on April 2. Truman, concerned by the image of incompetence this was generating, fired McGrath on April 3 and appointed James McGranery Attorney General. The mass firings and seeming inability to find an investigator who was not himself guilty of some impropriety underlined the apparent corruption much more clearly than any Republican attack could have done (*New York Times* 1966). This impression of shady dealings amateurishly executed and poorly hidden helped render the Republican charges of rampant corruption and incompetence credible, and significantly contributed to the Democratic defeat in the November election.

Truman's Strategy

Coming on the heels of earlier scandals, by the time the BIR scandal became an issue, Truman was already on the defensive. Yet, even a defensive president in the early 1950s had much more power vis-à-vis the press than do presidents today. For one thing, the expectation of presidential speech was much lower. These days, "Presidents are not only speaking more often, they are speaking to a greater variety of audiences" (R. Hart 1987: 10). Truman was expected to speak primarily to Congress. Presidents rarely spoke to the country, and only on issues of great moment. His press conference announcing McGrath's replacement was the first press conference ever to be filmed for later television presentation. This relationship to the media and to the country meant that Truman had more latitude in choosing both the content and the timing of his response to the allegations than would later presidents.

Truman did receive considerable mail from citizens outraged at his tendency to "appoint men to high office whose honesty and loyalty to our government is questionable" (Christie 1952), many of which were also published in various newspapers. However, even in responding to criticism, Truman's stature as president gave him a certain credibility vis-à-vis other governmental actors.

Even given the president's relatively strong rhetorical position, Truman was eventually forced to respond to the substance of the charges, which meant that he had to address the issue of whether he condoned corruption among his close associates. In a letter to Representative Bennett concerning Bennett's concern over the apparent improprieties and his suggestion that Truman establish a code of ethics for the executive branch, Truman attempted to seize the moral high ground:

> Unless a man is fundamentally sound ethically, you can't teach him what to do as a public servant. There is only one code that is fundamental in the lives of the people who make up the free countries and that code is found in the Twentieth Chapter of Exodus and in the Fifth, Sixth, and Seventh Chapters of the Gospel according to Saint Matthew. There is one Commandment that seems to have been thrown out of the window by some of our Congressional colleagues, and that is the one that cautions us, "Not to bear false witness against our neighbor" and the one which was named number Two by the Master in the Saint Matthew Code of Ethics is "love thy neighbor as thyself."
>
> All of the hearings and all of the conversations will not produce a code of ethics. It has to be in a man's heart to start with. (Truman 1951b)

This attempt did little other than to further alienate members of Congress, who appeared to resent Truman's assumption that he had a superior claim to moral understanding, and to insist that he respond directly to the allegations.

Typically, Truman chose to respond to the specific question by addressing the larger issue. On March 29, 1952, a few days before replacing McGrath, Truman gave a speech on the issue of corruption in government (Koenig 1956: 73-75). He first located himself as the enemy of corruption: "I stand for honest government. I have worked for it. I have probably done more for it than any other President. . . ." He then underscored that position by detailing his motivation. This was an effective technique, for it allowed listeners to integrate this side of Truman into the understanding they already had of Truman as president. "I hate corruption not only because it is bad in itself, but also because it is the deadly enemy of all the things the Democratic party has been doing all these years. I hate corruption everywhere, but I hate it most of all in a Democratic officeholder; because it is a betrayal of all that the Democratic party stands for."

As anyone who had ever heard Truman speak knew, the Democratic party and its goals were important to Truman; he was a party man to the core. By putting the issue of corruption into the context of partisan politics, Truman could thus persuasively make the case that he was, in fact, honestly against corruption, for it crippled the party that he loved.

Truman then expanded the definition of morality and corruption to include those who were accusing him as well as the actual malefactors. He said, "I think it is just as immoral for the Congress to enact special tax favors into law as it is for a tax official to connive in a crooked tax return. It is just as immoral to use the lawmaking power of the government to enrich the few at the expense of the many as it is to steal money from the public treasury" (Koenig 1956: 73-75). This had two effects. First, Truman reminded lawmakers that, in Truman's eyes, at least, they who lived in glass houses should be very careful about throwing stones. Second, Truman reminded the audience that he was on their side—the side of the many as opposed to the few—and that the Republicans in Congress were most clearly on the other side. Truman underlined both of these points with allusions to the Teapot Dome and other Republican scandals of the 1920s as well as Republican support for Andrew Mellon.

Just to make sure that the point had been made, Truman then launched into a vituperative attack on the Republican party: "And where have the Republicans been in this fight for morality in government? Do they come out and vote with us to keep the special interests from robbing the public? Not at all. Most of them are on the other side" (Koenig 1956: 73-75). Truman thus implicitly argued that the entire "mess in Washington" scenario was created and magnified by the Republicans to secure partisan advantage in the upcoming election. It is an argument that reflects Truman's tendency to divide people into two groups: those who were "with" him, and those who were not (Dunar 1984).

It was also the kind of argument that created as well as reflected the partisan split. By dividing people into two opposing camps, the president forced them to react as if those camps were the important issue. Republicans who were inclined to support the president might well have been enraged at his accusations. Democrats inclined the other way were reminded that in an election year the party's fortunes often reflected those of the presidential candidate. They might well have decided that Truman's behavior and image were bad for the party. If Truman suffered at the hands of committed partisans, he largely had himself to blame, for he insisted on drawing the dividing line.

Discussion

Truman's strategic problem centered on his tendency to view politics as a personal enterprise in an era when government was rapidly becoming bureaucratized. He understood governmental processes to involve personal loyalty and personalized leadership. Although he believed that, on the one hand, the office was more than the person who occupied it, he also believed that for the office to be effectively and efficiently managed, personal ties to the president were necessary. Truman had little patience with people who did not share his understanding of the world and little tolerance for perspectives that were not his own. He thus initially surrounded himself with people he felt comfortable with, those he could trust personally. He failed to realize that people who were trustworthy on a personal level were not always those who deserved the public trust.

The BIR scandal was less a problem of competence and corruption than it was a failure to recognize that the political, legal, and institutional culture of postwar Washington was fundamentally different from the political and institutional culture that Truman knew and understood. As political scientist and Truman aide Harold Seidman (1970) said:

> I never had a feeling that Truman had—I don't think that Truman was a philosophical thinker. He did not think in these terms. He was a pragmatist. On the other hand he was a pragmatist who had a very keen sense of the office of the Presidency and the protection of the office of the Presidency. . . . And he was sensitive to attacks on, or measures which would impair the institution.

His personal methods of "doing business" were not necessarily dishonest in Truman's eyes. They simply appeared dishonest given the parameters of the political culture in which he governed. Truman never managed to reconcile his personal character with the role requirements of the political and institutional environment, and he thus remains a president of profound contradictions. He is remembered less for the scandals than for the honesty and forthrightness he so eloquently portrayed. Yet the knowledge of the scandals and other instances of questionable administrative skill keep that remembrance from being unambiguously positive.

Truman was not unique in his inability to fit personal style to institutional context, nor is he unique in being the subject of subsequent reevaluation. In both, Truman has something in common with Richard Nixon. Truman and Nixon were politically educated in one culture and governed during another. Neither of them were able to fully comprehend the difficulties that this created for them. Yet as Watergate suddenly made the redemption of Truman possible in that the nation came to value honesty and "plain speaking," so recent events on the world scene have made the emergence of yet another "new Nixon" inevitable. In order to understand this parallel, it is necessary to examine the "old Nixon" as president.

RICHARD NIXON AND WATERGATE

The Political/Institutional Context

Richard Nixon assumed office at an extraordinarily complicated time in the nation's history. As he took the oath of office in 1968, Nixon (1969) asked that "we all lower our voices," a plea that was ignored by both the president and the public as student protests against the war in Vietnam escalated, civil rights advocates became increasingly militant, and the nation seemed to be, in the phrase of one scholar, "coming apart" (O'Neill 1971). Nixon presided over such diverse events as the "opening" of the People's Republic of China, illegal bombings of Cambodia, the Kent State riot, urban and black and student unrest, continued stalemate with the Soviet Union, and economic difficulties at home. Nixon sought to maintain order and a sense of stability in a time of national and international convulsions. His methods, however, explicitly contradicted those goals.

As president, Nixon stood at an intersection of a variety of political and institutional factors. The American party system, weak, but still an important source of support, provided Nixon with a narrow victory in 1968 (43.4% of the popular vote) and a Democratic Congress. Although the Democrats held clear majorities in both Houses, many of those Democrats were Southern and conservative. They were more likely to agree with Nixon on issues such as law and order, civil rights, and foreign policy than were Democrats from other regions. Given the divided nature and structural weaknesses of the political parties, coalition building was a complex process that varied by issue. Nixon could not be sure of support on any given issue at any given time (Seligman and Covington 1989).

Nixon's problems with coalition building extended beyond Congress to the bureaucracy (DiClerico 1990). In this, he was not alone among presidents, but he was unusual in the degree of control that he attempted to assert over the administrative branch. Nixon felt that career bureaucrats owed their political and personal allegiance to the New Deal and to the New Deal agenda, and that these bureaucrats perceived Nixon as hostile to that agenda. As a response to this bureaucratic hostility, Nixon centralized policymaking and other bureaucratic functions in the White House staff, minimized the role of the Cabinet, downgraded the standing of Cabinet Secretaries, and circumvented routinized executive branch procedures (Campbell 1986; Nathan 1975; Wayne 1978). This in turn resulted in a politicalization of the civil service (Berman 1979; Campbell 1986).

More importantly for Nixon, if not for the presidency as an institution, Nixon's treatment of the cabinet departments created no small degree of resentment among bureaucrats and among their allies on the Hill. Nixon was neither charismatic nor compelling, and even Republicans who supported his positions had occasional difficulty in supporting him personally. In a polity in which mediated communication and personalistic appeals were beginning to displace partisan and policy-oriented coalitions, this lack of personal support made the resentment Nixon created all the more dangerous for him politically.

This political danger was exacerbated by Nixon's political style. Foremost in importance was Nixon's antagonistic relationship with the national media. Nixon tended to blame all of his image problems on the media and could be quite bitter toward them:

> The press knows very well where I stand, but they realize that in some cases my position may be publicly popular. Consequently, they treat the stories in a way that my position does not appear to be strong one way or another. . . . What our opponents in the media will try to do whenever possible is make it appear that RN is vacillating on an issue, that he will not take a strong position one way or another, that he is dodging a public position, etc. . . . Now they are out to get us and we simply have to start growing up and being just as tough, ruthless, and unfeeling as they are or they will sink us without a trace. (Nixon 1971)

A man who viewed issues in dichotomous terms, Nixon was more comfortable with the battle of campaigning than with the negotiating necessary for governance (Windt 1990). Nixon and his aides believed that he had been elected to accomplish certain objectives, and anyone who stood in the way of those objectives not only opposed Richard Nixon, but the democratic process and "America" as well. Believing this, he could then also believe that he could justify any method used to combat and destroy his opponents. As Nixon himself said in the famous interview with David Frost, "when a president does it, that means it is not illegal" (quoted in Berman 1987: 57). During the 1970s, considerable controversy was generated by this belief.

Essentially, Richard Nixon was obsessed with his image and devoted considerable time and energy to dissecting and devising ways to improve or alter it (Colson 1972; Haldeman 1994). In early 1970, for example, H.R. Haldeman, Nixon's Chief of Staff, noted in his diary:

> P had me in for a couple of hours at lunchtime, got into long harangue about his revised views on PR. Now feels he was completely wrong in his original concept about building mystique and

image. Realizes this is impossible when press is against you. Roosevelts etc. only succeeded because they had the press with them (not sure that's true). Feels we should give up the struggle and just present our case via the P on TV. Realize Nixon will never have a good public image, so don't try. I think he's partly right, but that's no reason not to keep trying. But it would work a lot better if he would quit worrying about it and just be President. (1994: 167)

However, Nixon was unable to "quit worrying about it and just be President," because his concept of the presidency was tantamount to his conception of his image. Throughout 1970, he had Haldeman draw up lists comparing Nixon to FDR and Wilson, lists of Nixon's strengths (divided into the categories of guts, head, and heart), and lists of his weaknesses (e.g., calculating, lacking in humor), as well as devise means of addressing these image issues (Haldeman 1970). By December 1970, this obsession had gone to even more ridiculous lengths as Nixon was worried about his image as "too PR conscious" (Haldeman 1994: 214). It was an image he well deserved. Early in his presidency, Nixon had gone so far as to designate "White House Anecdotalists," whose job it was to attend routine and ceremonial meetings with the president, looking for items of public and personal interest, and to write up those items for consumption by the media (see Butterfield 1971).

This obsession created an extraordinary defensiveness regarding that image: Even in private conversations, Nixon was apt to refer to himself as "the President" or as "The Commander-in-Chief" (*Transcripts* 1973b). This tendency reveals a man who was himself uncomfortable with the connection between his character and the role of president and one who attempted to adopt his perception of the role as his character. Unfortunately for Nixon, the presidential role is well-defined only in its limits; in trying to enact the role without regard to his character, Nixon violated those limits.

The Events of Watergate

The complicated series of events called "Watergate" comprise a pattern of systematic abuse of governmental power for political purposes. "Watergate" did not begin with the break-in of Democratic headquarters at the Watergate apartment complex, but long before. It was not merely the break-in and the cover-up that led to Nixon's difficulties; those were merely the grounds for formal charges. Although some argue that Nixon only unleashed his efforts to "get" his enemies after the furor over Cambodia and the failure of the Carswell nomination (Magruder 1974), there is evidence that Nixon's penchant for political scullduggery had been indulged in very early during the Nixon administration (White 1975; Wills 1979).

The first clear sign of abuse of power for overtly political reasons, for instance, came on May 12, 1969, only four months after Nixon's first inauguration. Following newspaper revelations that the Nixon administration was engaging in secret bombings of Cambodia, the first of 17 "national security" wiretaps of administration aides and reporters was installed. This was a typical presidential response to leaking, the bane of every president's existence (Lasky 1977); however, it is indicative of the tactics the Nixon White House was willing to consider a relatively routine aspect of "politics as usual."

In September 1970, a CBS reporter named George Natason, reporting on the recent elections in Chile, said, "the victory is not Dr. Allende's alone, however. As one observer remarked, Chilean democracy has also won by letting a Marxist win" (Strachan 1970). This touched off a series of memos involving John Brown, Patrick Buchanan, Alexander Butterfield, Larry Higby, Jeb Magruder, and Lyn Nofziger, in which the identity of the reporter was demanded ("it is requested that you submit a report on who the reporter was who made that statement"), and action against the errant reporter was ordered ("Let's get something going with regard to this guy. Perhaps you will want to work through Kissinger or State on this project"; Strachan, 1970). The amount of time and effort spent on one reporter's interpretation of a Chilean election illustrates the prevailing ethos in the Nixon White House.

The establishment of the White House "Opponents List" is a more frightening indication of that same ethos. Members included prominent journalists, those who had contributed more than $25,000 to a Democratic campaign, members of the National Democratic Dinner Committee, all contributors to Edmund Muskie, and assorted heads of corporations, academics, and "politicos." Labor unions were also favorite targets. In at least one White House aide's opinion, however, singling out individual members was not beneficial, because labor was so strongly against Nixon in general (Bell, 1971). Members of the "Opponents List" were not to be invited to White House functions and were to be excluded from all commissions and other honors controlled by the administration.

The "politicos" on the list were entitled to special attention:

> We should decide who we believe will be the significant presidential candidates, have someone monitor them, analyzing their backgrounds and approaches, in order that a continuing program be maintained to discredit them. This should probably be done by the RNC with appropriate liaison here. The others are part of Congressional Liaison's daily problems, or Bob Powers with the Blacks. (Bell 1971)

The "Huston Plan" provides another, more well-known indication that Nixon was willing to expand the boundaries of previous presidential actions and abuses. Designed by White House aide Tom Huston and discussed openly in Attorney General John Mitchell's office (Dean 1977), the Plan expanded and authorized domestic intelligence-gathering. Despite Huston's warning—in writing—that elements of the Plan were "clearly illegal," Nixon approved the Plan on June 23, 1970. He rescinded that approval five days later (Woodward and Bernstein 1976).

The next important event occurred on July 23, 1971, when the *New York Times* began publishing the *Pentagon Papers*, a collection of classified documents illegally smuggled out of the Pentagon by an employee named Daniel Ellsberg. These documents indicated, among other things, the extent of presidential lying and manipulation concerning American military activities in Vietnam during the Johnson administration. Their publication added fuel to the growing antiwar movement and enraged the Nixon White House. On September 3-4, 1971, White House aides E. Howard Hunt and G. Gordon Liddy supervised a burglary of Ellsberg's psychiatrist's office in an effort to find damaging evidence that could be used to discredit Ellsberg. The burglary turned up nothing.

During the next year, Nixon's aides supervised and/or authorized a variety of illegal or marginally legal political activities aimed at discrediting, harassing, and discouraging Nixon's political opponents (Bernstein and Woodward 1974). These efforts culminated on June 17, 1972, when five men were arrested for attempting to break into and install listening devices in the headquarters of the Democratic National Party, located in the Watergate apartment building. No immediate connection to the Nixon White House or to the Nixon campaign was publicly apparent.

On June 19, White House Press Secretary Ron Zeigler refused to comment on a "third-rate burglary attempt" and denied White House involvement in or knowledge of the break-in. Later that same day, White House Counsel John Dean told Nixon's chief domestic advisor, John Ehrlichman, that he had information linking Liddy and the Committee to Re-Elect the President (CREEP) to the break-in. On June 20, Nixon and Mitchell met to discuss the arrests. Later that day, Nixon met with his Chief of Staff, H.R. (Bob) Haldeman, for further discussion of the arrests. Months later, crucial portions of the tape of that conversation were "accidentally" erased, creating the infamous "eighteen and a half minute gap." Nixon and Haldeman met again, on June 23, and formulated a plan to use the CIA to halt the FBI investigation of the burglary, on "national security" grounds. The cover-up was officially underway.

After connections between CREEP and the Watergate burglars became impossible to hide, Mitchell resigned from Nixon's campaign. Throughout the summer of 1972, the FBI continued to investigate. Members of CREEP and the White House continued to lie to the FBI and attempted to thwart the investigation. Nonetheless, on September 15, Hunt, Liddy, and the five Watergate burglars were indicted.

The cover-up successfully contained the scandal through the election. On November 7, 1972, Richard Nixon and Spiro Agnew were reelected by a landslide (60.8% of the popular vote and 97% of the electoral vote). The resulting exultation was short-lived however, as January 1973 brought the trial of the Watergate burglars and convictions for all participants. Hunt began pressuring the White House to insure that he would be "taken care of" in exchange for his silence.

So little did the White House enjoy the election results that Charles Colson, one of Nixon's closest aides, remembered being "gripped by this sort of sensation that all of a sudden the Presidency has changed. The election's been held; it's all over; everybody's been asked to resign. And it's almost like we lost the election" (Colson 1988).

On February 2, Judge John Sirica, who had presided over the Watergate trial, publicly stated that he was "not satisfied" that the full story was disclosed at the trial, and that more people ought to be questioned. Sirica got his wish; on February 7, the Senate voted 70-0 to establish a Select Committee charged with investigating the burglary and possible cover-up. The Committee, which became known as the Ervin Committee after its Chair, Senator Sam Ervin (D-NC), was granted full investigatory powers.

This combination of events exerted powerful pressure on the Nixon White House; pressure that was all the more frustrating given the recent and enormous electoral mandate. The 1972 election results confirmed Nixon's belief in the inherent rightness of his position and seemed to provide justification for his actions and those of his aides. Still, Nixon had to respond to the pressure. On February 27, he met with Dean and discussed the cover-up. The tape of this conversation was later subpoenaed, but it was never found.

The two met again on March 21. Dean informed the president that there was "a cancer growing on the presidency," and that "a lot of these people could be indicted." The discussion included ways to keep the burglars quiet and maintain the cover-up, including "hush money" and pardons. Nixon replied, "We could get that. . . . If you need the money . . . get a million dollars. And you could get it in cash" (*Transcripts* 1973c). Blackmail had entered the Oval Office.

By Spring 1973, the cover-up began to unravel. Reporters had followed the trail of money left by questionable campaign contributions and the even more questionable uses to which the money had been put; members of the CREEP staff had testified before a federal grand jury; and all investigative roads led inexorably to the Nixon White House. The question on everyone's mind that Spring, succinctly stated by Senator Howard Baker (R-TN), was "What did the president know, and when did he know it?" On April 30, Bob Haldeman and John Ehrlichman resigned. John Dean was fired. Kleindienst was replaced by Elliot Richardson and Dean by Leonard Garment.

By now, however, Nixon's credibility was strained, and the whole-scale firings were seen as desperate scapegoating rather than a serious attempt to recognize and solve a serious problem. Nixon was helped neither by his public displays of belligerence nor by the beginning, on May 17, of the televised Ervin Committee hearings. On May 18, Nixon, in an effort to salvage some credibility for the executive branch, named Archibald Cox Special Prosecutor to investigate Watergate. Any positive effect created by this decision was mitigated on May 22, when Nixon publicly denied knowledge of the break-in or the resulting cover-up, but acknowledged authorizing the Huston Plan and his attempt to use the CIA to halt the FBI investigation. Nixon again cited "national security" as the motivation for his actions.

Things deteriorated rapidly. In early June, Nixon began listening to the tapes of his conversations with Haldeman, Mitchell, and Dean, although he kept the tapes secret from investigators and refused to allow even his own attorneys to listen to them. The pressure on Nixon escalated in late June, as John Dean testified before the Ervin Committee, and the question of the extent of Nixon's involvement in Watergate was prominent news in all the major newspapers (Buchanan 1973). The worst blow fell in July, when White House aide Alexander Butterfield, in the midst of a routine interview with members of the Committee staff, disclosed the existence of a White House taping system.

It is impossible to overestimate the importance of the Watergate tapes. Without them, there would surely have been no impeachment proceedings, no resignation, and much less public information about the Nixon presidency. Knowledge of the tapes provided both the Ervin Committee and the Special Prosecutor with a way to demand evidence from the president. Cox lost no time; on July 23, a week after the Butterfield interview, he subpoenaed tapes of nine Nixon conversations. Two days later, Nixon refused to surrender the subpoenaed tapes on "national security" grounds.

By summer, editorials were systematically calling for the release of the tapes, with *Chicago Today* going so far as to say:

It's not clear what historical purpose could be more important than settling perhaps the greatest governmental crisis in our history, or why Mr. Nixon prefers to have scholars of the future solve a problem that is crippling the administration right now. . . . What is clear is that Mr. Nixon does not want to release the tapes, and right or wrong, there is only one conclusion most people will draw from that. It is Mr. Nixon knew of the coverup long before he said he did, and has been concealing evidence about [it] . . . the only possible effect of all this on the presidency is to cripple it further. (Waldron 1973)

On October 10, Vice President Spiro Agnew resigned after pleading no contest to the charge of income tax evasion, thus adding to Nixon's public credibility problems and increasing public perceptions about the culpability of the Nixon White House. Even worse from Nixon's point of view, on October 12, the United States Court of Appeals upheld Sirica's decision to mandate the surrender of the subpoenaed tapes.

The tension created among the courts, the Congress, and the executive branch became intense, and the attention focused on Watergate paralyzed the national government. On October 20, Nixon decided to go on the offensive. He called Elliot Richardson and told him to fire Cox and abolish the Special Prosecutor's office. Richardson refused, and then either quit or was fired. Nixon then asked Deputy Attorney General William D. Ruckleshaus to fire Cox. Ruckleshaus also refused and then quit. Nixon then appointed Solicitor General Robert Bork Attorney General; Bork fired Cox, and the FBI sealed the Special Prosecutor's office and files. If Nixon thought he was ending the Watergate problem by firing Cox, he could not have been more mistaken. The events of October 20 became instantly memorialized as "The Saturday Night Massacre" and touched off a firestorm of protest. On October 22, the House Judiciary Committee began an inquiry to determine whether the president had committed impeachable offenses. Nixon was forced to respond to these events. On November 1, he appointed Leon Jaworski Special Prosecutor.

By then, Nixon had lost most of the people who owed their loyalty to him personally, rather than to the institution of the presidency, the executive branch, or the government as a whole. On November 3, Nixon's attorney's advised him to resign and thus avoid impeachment. He refused.

The next few months were a maze of legal battles, presidential intransigence, and increasing doubts about Nixon's political position. On March 1, 1974, the Watergate grand jury indicted Bob Haldeman, John Ehrlichman, John Mitchell, Robert Mardian, Charles Colson, Gordon Strachan, and Kenneth Parkinson on charges related to the Watergate cover-up. Richard Nixon was named by the grand jury as an "unindicted co-conspirator." This last was not announced to the public, but a copy of the report and a briefcase full of evidence was given to Sirica. The grand jury also informed Sirica that they wanted to make a submission to the House Judiciary Committee.

Meanwhile, public and prosecutorial attention focused on the tapes. On April 11, the House Judiciary Committee, considering impeachment proceedings, subpoenaed 42 tapes; a week later Jaworski subpoenaed an additional 64 tapes. On April 29, Richard Nixon announced, in a nationally televised address, that he would supply the Judiciary Committee with edited transcripts of the subpoenaed tapes and would also make those transcripts public.

On April 30, 1,254 pages of transcript were released. This partial compromise was immediately overshadowed by White House Counsel James St. Clair's announcement that Nixon refused to surrender tapes and documents subpoenaed by the Special Prosecutor. On May 24, Jaworski appealed to the US Supreme Court for a ruling on the tape issue. On May 31, the Supreme Court agreed to decide the case.

Nixon again took the offensive. This time he initiated a public relations blitz designed to bolster his standing as president and drive Watergate from the headlines. On June 10, Nixon left for a Middle East tour and returned on June 19. He left again on June 25 for a summit meeting in Moscow. There was considerable public concern over Nixon's health and the risk he took in traveling with phlebitis.

The concern was short-lived. On July 24, the Supreme Court, in an 8-0 decision, ruled that Nixon was obligated to surrender the subpoenaed tapes. Importantly, the Court was unanimous; Nixon had no way to maintain legitimacy and defy the ruling. He was running out of options.

Nixon's options were reduced again on July 27, when the House Judiciary Committee passed, by a vote of 27-11, the first article of impeachment against him, which charged the President of the United States with obstruction of justice. Two days later, on July 29, the Committee passed the second article of impeachment on a vote of 28-10, which charged the president with abuse of power. The next day the Committee passed the third and final article of impeachment on a vote 21-17, which accused Nixon of violating separation of powers by refusing to comply with House subpoenas.

On August 5, Nixon conceded the inevitable, and made the tapes of his June 23, 1972 conversations on the break-in and cover-up public, thereby definitively answering the question "What did the president know and when did he know it?" Three days later he announced his intention to resign, and at 12 noon on August 9, 1974, Richard M. Nixon became the first president in American history to resign the office of the presidency.

Nixon's Strategy

Watergate was a political failure for which political and communicative coping strategies needed to be devised. Nixon's approach to the Watergate crisis was complicated and evolutionary. His response to the accusations leveled against first his staff, then his closest aides, and finally himself consisted of denying the charges, then admitting the truth of some, while asserting that those charges were made for political reasons to discredit him. He also insisted that Watergate was a matter for the courts and thus outside the realm of legitimate media interest or public concern. In addition to boosting his stature by calling on legal and constitutional arguments, Nixon also identified himself personally with the presidency as an institution. When no other options were left to him, he offered himself as a sacrifice to the office and the country.

Deciding when and how to respond to accusations of wrongdoing are difficult decisions for a president to make—to respond too soon may put the president on the defensive and lend credence to the accusations. But to refuse to answer persistent accusations can have the same effect. The difficulty comes in deciding when the accusations must be addressed and then how to address them. Both the timing and the content of the presidential response are vital.

As soon as the burglary occurred, Nixon began denying White House involvement to the public and, in some cases, to his aides and advisors (Colson 1988). On June 22, a week after the initial arrests, Nixon held an impromptu press conference, his first in three months. At that press conference, Nixon categorically denied any knowledge of or involvement in the break-in. On the subject of domestic surveillance, Nixon said that such behavior "has no place whatsoever in our electoral process or in our governmental process" (*New York Times* 1974: 136). Except for this instance, nearly all denials came from Nixon's Press Secretary or from one or another of his aides. The prevailing opinion was, as Nixon said to Dean, that "I do think that you've got to remember, as you sure do, that this is mainly a public relations thing, anyway" (*Transcripts* 1973a). In public, Nixon preferred denial-by-avoidance and steadfastly refused to enter into debate of the subject of the Watergate burglary.

An important exception to this rule was an August press conference, when Nixon argued that it was not making mistakes that mattered, "what really hurts is when you try to cover it up." He also said that both parties had been guilty of "technical violations" of the campaign finance laws, thus admitting some culpability. The truly important "revelation," however, was that his counsel, John Dean, had conducted an investigation and had found that, "no one in the White House staff, no one in this

Administration, was involved in this very bizarre incident." John Dean later testified that this was the first he had heard of the so-called "Dean investigation" (*New York Times* 1974: 150-151).

Nixon's next important response came on April 30, 1973, when he announced the resignations of Haldeman, Ehrlichman, and Attorney General Richard Kleindeinst and the firing of Dean. Nixon (1973a) called Haldeman and Ehrlichman "the two finest public servants it has been my privilege to know," but distanced himself from Dean and dismissed him with a brief, "the counsel to the President, John Dean, has also resigned." Nixon was by now forced into a position where he had to react to the charges made by others rather than make them himself against others, as he could have if the "Dean investigation" was real. This reactive posture undermined the ethos of the "New Nixon" as a man above politics, concerned with the great issues of war and peace. Nixon again appeared crassly political, dominated by political events: "Once more, Nixon gave the public an opportunity to drift back toward the belief that his political intelligence was derived from shiftiness and craftiness instead of wisdom and vision. The persona was being res-culpted and his own hand held the chisel" (Harrell, Ware, and Linkugel 1987: 285).

As the image of the "New Nixon" deteriorated in the public's minds, leaving the residue of the old Nixon in its place, Nixon had to respond to the claim that he was personally involved in Watergate. That response came on May 22, 1973. He admitted to the buggings, the Huston Plan, and other unsavory activities of his aides. Nixon also tried to separate those activities from other, to him unrelated, activities of those involved in national security operations. The distinction was a fine one, and Nixon was in too weak a position to draw it convincingly. From this point on, Nixon was on the defensive. As the televised Watergate hearings began, Nixon's legitimacy progressively eroded.

In a nationally televised address, that August, a year after the initial break-in, Nixon (1973b) publicly recognized the tenuousness of his position: "But as the weeks have gone by, it has become clear that both the hearings themselves and some of the commentaries on them have become increasingly absorbed in an effort to implicate the President personally in the illegal activities that took place." His person-al character was reduced to his role as president. Where some presidents err by taking their character as the benchmark for the presidential role (see Chapter 5), Nixon saw the role as the only relevant measure of his character. He thus indicated that the charges had to be addressed because they were undermining his position as president.

It is important to note that those doing the undermining were, in Nixon's view, maliciously assaulting the president for partisan reasons. Nixon (1973b), on the other hand, was not politically motivated, but acted only because the Constitution demanded it: "It is my constitutional responsibility to defend the integrity of this great office against false charges." He clearly indicated that he was obliged to speak rather than allow his opposition to discredit him and the office he represented.

The public did not accept Nixon's interpretation: an ABC phone poll from August 9, 1973, showed that 46% of those surveyed believed that the president was aware of the break-in; 55% believed that he was part of the cover-up; and 29% believed that the president was not involved. ABC also cited another poll indicating that 65% of those polled believed that the Ervin Committee was out to get the truth rather than to persecute the president (Zeigler 1973). Nixon was not winning the battle for public opinion.

He continued to assert his status as president by trying to deflect attention away from Watergate and on to other matters, a strategy that reflected, at least in part, the advice of his pollster. He was quoted by Alexander Haig, Chief of Staff since Haldeman's resignation, in a memo to the president on August 18, 1973, as saying:

> He now believes that we have turned the corner and established a base for successfully moving out of Watergate. It is his strong view . . . that now is the time for hyperactivity on the part of the President. He believes an early press conference and your involvement in governmental business will do the trick. (Haig 1973)

The strategy of "hyperactivity" as a means of asserting Nixon's status as president was composed of two tactics. The first was to ignore Watergate and continue business-as-usual in an indirect attempt to affect the national agenda. Whatever the president does is news; if the president could fill the news with non-Watergate-related events, then Watergate would vanish from the papers and from the public mind. On August 20, 1973, for instance, Nixon (1973c) held his first press conference in five months, saying that Watergate was "water under the bridge," and, although he accepted all of the blame for creating the political climate that made Watergate possible, he thought it was time to turn to the "people's business."

Because of all the various investigations, however, Nixon faced too much competition in his agenda-setting efforts. He therefore turned to the second tactic, a combination of legal and constitutional arguments to defend his position and undermine that of his opposition. He argued for separation of powers, executive privilege, and national security throughout the summer of 1973. On September 5, for example, Nixon (1973d) made an argument defending executive privilege and his right to withhold the tapes based on the importance of trust in the presidency. He said, "Confidentiality once destroyed cannot . . . be replaced." The argument here was that if Nixon made the tapes public, his ability to discuss options with aides, alliances with foreign leaders, and strategy with members of Congress would all be destroyed. Legally, Nixon argued that he had a right to protect the president's privacy.

In this, Nixon displayed a striking confluence between the person of the president (character) and the office of the presidency (role). His personal privacy was identical to the president's official privacy. This rhetorical identification of the man with the institution intensified as the pressure on him mounted. He referred to himself in the third person, as "The President"—"The President wants" or "The President thinks." This identification served a clear and powerful political function. Persecuting plain old Richard Nixon from Whittier was one thing. Impeaching the President of the United States was quite another. Nixon capitalized on this through his trips abroad, by making statesmanlike speeches on national television and by referring with greater frequency to past presidents in his public speeches. The vilification of Abraham Lincoln during the Civil War was a favorite topic in this regard (Nixon 1974a, 1974b).

Lincoln had been maligned, criticized, martyred, and reincarnated as an American hero. Nixon may well have seen the same process operating in regards to his own political career. On departing for his last trip abroad, one month before his resignation, he said:

> It will be a difficult trip from the physical standpoint . . . it will also be a difficult trip from the standpoint of the diplomacy involved. . . . But I can assure you that on this long, difficult, and very important journey, that when we sometimes may feel tired, that we will never be discouraged, and we will always be heartened by the memory of this luncheon that we are having today. (Nixon 1974b)

The theme of martyrdom also appeared in one of his final speeches as president: "I would have preferred to carry through to the finish, whatever the personal agony it would have involved, and my family unanimously urged me to do so. But the interests of the Nation must always come before any personal considerations" (Nixon 1974c).

To the end, Nixon attempted to preempt the judgments of others and to govern the public interpretation of his actions (Windt 1990). He presented himself not as an invidious and vicious man who abused the awesome power of the presidency, but as a president who suffered nobly for his people and was finally destroyed by his petty but powerful opposition. However, as one political cartoon, depicting Nixon wearing a crown, buttering bread with "executive privilege" and captioned "Tastes so good, I feel like a King!" (Williams 1973) indicates, Nixon's words had lost all their credibility: The statesmanlike "New Nixon," never firmly established, had been replaced by the political and untrustworthy "old Nixon," grasping for power that was not legitimately his. During Watergate, Nixon had rendered too many statements "inoperative," changed too many stories, attempted too many inconsistent explanations. By the end, he was a president without personal or political support anywhere in the government, a president whose options had all run out.

Discussion

Nixon's chief problem with Watergate was not the break-in, the dirty tricks, or the various acts of political and personal corruption identified with his administration. The root of Nixon's problem was that he could not seem to distinguish the person of the president from the office of the presidency. As the interview with David Frost indicated, Nixon felt himself to be above the law. Just as Vietnam made the limits of American military power clear, Watergate provided evidence of the limits of presidential political power.

Nixon was certainly not the first president to expand the perquisites of office to include personal and political gain. But few other presidents (Lyndon Johnson was one) had so great a burden in their past political ethos as did Nixon. That ethos made it easier to believe in his culpability. Nixon's lack of partisan and structural support from Congress and the bureaucracy compounded his ethical difficulties with political opposition. The national upheaval created by Vietnam and the civil rights movement made an assertion of law as an expression of stability particularly important. The partisan structure of Congress and the difficulty of creating a workable and stable governing coalition made Nixon a viable locus for that expression of stability and exertion of law.

Nixon's political past complicated his attempt to be president. He was always hesitant in the role, always comparing himself to other presidents, always checking to insure that he had received the proper respect. He knew that there were grave doubts concerning his ability to fulfill the presidential role; he thus worked overtime to create the "proper" image. But the image was, necessarily, contrived. In protecting his personal character while attempting to reveal personal characteristics appropriate to the role, Nixon came across as created, contrived, and hollow. Slippage between the man and the office was all but inevitable.

On taking the Oath of Office, Gerald Ford (1974) said, "Our long national nightmare is over. Our Constitution works. Our great republic is a government of laws and not of men. Here, the people rule." This is the lesson popularly assumed to derive from Watergate. Even after Nixon, it was easy to assume that the system was fully functional: It was just presidents such as Johnson in Vietnam and Nixon in Watergate that abused the system—the problem was not with the structure, but with the people who staffed the structure. The events of the Iran-Contra affair cast the optimism of that assumption into serious doubt.

RONALD REAGAN AND IRAN-CONTRA AFFAIR

The Political/Institutional Context

When Ronald Reagan became president in 1980, the office that appeared "imperial" under Richard Nixon and Lyndon Johnson seemed "imperiled" (Crovitz and Rabkin 1989). Gerald Ford and Jimmy Carter, both presidents who failed in their bids for reelection, were thought to have presided during the fall of the office from its days of power to a time when the president could accomplish little or nothing. The bureaucratic frameworks that were created under FDR because "the president needs help" became a structural impediment in realizing the presidential agenda.

Ronald Reagan promised to change all that. Running on a platform of "getting government off the backs of the American people" (Reagan 1980b), Reagan vowed to reverse the trend of increased bureaucratization, reduce the regulatory burden, and restore the primacy of the private over the public realm. During the 1980 presidential campaign, for example, he said:

> Together, let us make this a new beginning. Let us make a commitment to care for the needy, to teach our children the values and the virtues handed down to us by our families, to have the courage to defend those values and the willingness to sacrifice for them. Let us pledge to restore, in our time, the American spirit of voluntary service, of cooperation, of private and community initiative, a spirit that flows like a deep and mighty river throughout the history of our nation. (Reagan 1983)

These promises became the focus of Reagan's first year in office. Saying that his top three priorities were "the economy, the economy, and the economy," Reagan established an impressive legislative record during that first year (O'Neill and Novak 1987). Although Reagan advocated many of the same ideas espoused by Richard Nixon a decade earlier, the animosity these ideas created in the bureaucracy and Congress had difficulty finding expression during Reagan's administration. Reagan, both charming and telegenic, was able to deflect much criticism through humor, appeals to inclusion and exclusion, references to American values, and an anecdotally based communicative style (Erickson 1985; Stuckey 1990, 1991a).

Institutional and political factors also contributed to Reagan's initial success. A president with a clear agenda who is willing to lead usually finds that Congress is willing to be led (Kellerman 1984; Kernell 1986; Neustadt 1990). The importance of polls, presidential popularity, and other elements of the "permanent campaign" (Blumenthal 1980) have increased since Johnson's and Nixon's time to first help produce, and then sustain, the politics of "going public" (Kernell, 1986).

As explicitly governmental institutions weaken, extragovernmental institutions step in to fill the public space thus vacated (Hallin and Mancini 1984). In the context of American politics, the strongest of these institutions is the media (Ranney 1983). Utilizing the media as powerful allies during the first term, Reagan's people began to take it for granted during the second. Having already "proven" that a solid strategy and controlled access could defeat the liberal agenda of the national media, they appeared to take media meekness as a prerogative. This was particularly true of foreign affairs issues.

The president has long been the dominant player on the foreign policy scene. Ronald Reagan took this foreign affairs primacy to a new level (Barilleaux 1988; Stuckey 1990). From the presidential point of view, this was a very rational decision—presidents have some control over foreign policy, individual initiative and drive are often rewarded, and results are clearly discernible and often immediate. As presidents contend with a polity whose continual plaint is "what have you done for me lately?," foreign policy and even presidential wars are an increasingly attractive reply, particularly given the tradition of congressional acquiescence to presidential foreign policy dominance (Koh 1990).

Foreign policy had long been a key element of Reagan's personal agenda. During the 1980 campaign, for instance, Reagan (1980a) promised to "Bring America back" and restore the primacy of the United States as a world power. His opposition to the Soviet Union and international communism was as unrelenting as it was well known. Once in office, Reagan constructed his public image and that of his presidency primarily on foreign policy issues (Stuckey 1990).

Although Reagan gloried in the symbolic possibilities inherent in speaking on foreign policy, he was the first modern president to take little personal interest in the details of foreign policymaking (Mayer and McManus 1988). Reagan's inattention left a gap filled by his aides, engendering competition that restricted consultation and the flow of information (Ledeen 1988; Mayer and McManus 1988: 53; Regan 1988). The competition between advisors and Reagan's practice of setting ideological goals with little or no direction as to the means of accomplishing those goals made the Iran-Contra affair possible (Arnson 1989; Henderson 1988; Tower, Muskie, and Scowcroft 1987). The rhetorical primacy given foreign affairs by Reagan and the media made the Iran-Contra revelations particularly important and particularly difficult for Reagan to deflect.

The Events of Iran-Contra Affair

The series of actions and activities that have become known as the Iran-contra affair are extraordinarily complex, even when placed alongside the intricacies of Watergate. The events of the Iran-Contra affair involve American relations with Iran, Nicaragua, Saudi Arabia, and Israel (to name just the major countries) and several different people within and outside of the Reagan administration. The affair took place over at least a five-year period. Much of the evidence was destroyed, many details remain classified, and many irreconcilable versions of events remain. What follows is a brief summary of some of the more important highlights.

The story begins on November 14, 1979, when the United States, in response to the Iranian takeover of the American embassy in Teheran and the capture of American embassy personnel, imposed an arms embargo on Iran, hoping to exert pressure on the Iranian government to open negotiations with the United States. There were no discernible results.

Also in 1979, a group of Nicaraguan revolutionaries overthrew the Nicaraguan government and deposed its leader, General Anastasio Somoza. The revolutionaries then divided among themselves, each accusing the other of "betraying the revolution." The faction that remained in power, the Sandinistas, were led by Daniel Ortega. The Sandinistas instituted a socialist government and maintained strong ties to Cuba and the Soviet Union. They and their government were opposed by another faction, the Contras, at various times led by Eden Pastora, Adolfo Calero, and Edgar Chamorro.

Both factions were accused of human rights violations, connections with drug dealers, and other unpleasant involvements and connections. Neither side was unambiguously defensible. Many of those Americans opposing Contra aid did so not because they strongly supported the Sandinistas, but because they disapproved of the United States funding another country's civil war. Many of those Americans who advocated funding the Contras did so not because they approved of everything the Contras stood for or did, but because they feared the expansion of Soviet communism in the Americas.

The controversy over aiding the Contras reached a peak on December 22, 1982, when the U.S. Congress passed what has become known as the Boland Amendment, sponsored by the Chair of the House Intelligence Committee, Edward P. Boland (D-MA). This amendment, which allowed American support of the Contras, but not for "the purpose of overthrowing the Government of Nicaragua," was a compromise between the House, which had voted to halt funding, and the Senate, which supported a CIA role in funding the Contras. Rather than eliminating controversy over contra aid, the Boland Amendment exacerbated it, thus beginning a long battle in Congress, and between Congress and the president, over funding.

Meanwhile, the Reagan administration had other concerns as well as the Nicaraguan problem. Among other events, on October 17, 1983, Robert C. (Bud) McFarlane replaced William Clark as Reagan's National Security Advisor. That December, the United States began "Operation Staunch," urging allied governments to stop transferring arms to Iran.

However, Nicaragua continued as a irritant and gradually consumed increasing amounts of the administration's attention. In January 1984, the United States placed "harmless" firecracker mines in Nicaragua's harbors, hoping that this would frighten insurance companies, thus indirectly amounting to a blockade. In Spring 1984, President Reagan, annoyed by congressional intransigence, told McFarlane to "fund the contras any way you can" (National Security Archive 1987: 66).

That summer, and partially as a result of the harbor mining, Congress strengthened the Boland Amendment, this time specifically banning the CIA "or any other agency or entity involved in intelligence activities" from "directly or indirectly" spending money to support the Contras (Mayer and McManus 1988: 80). Oliver North, a Marine assigned to the National Security Council (NSC), then decided, without benefit of legal advice, that this directive did not apply to the NSC because the NSC does not explicitly engage in intelligence gathering.

North then began developing a variety of ways to provide the Contras with funding, circumventing the intent, if not the letter, of the Boland Amendment. In December 1984, for instance, the Sultan of Brunei contributed $10 million to the Swiss bank account controlled by North (National Security Archive 1987). By Spring 1985, Saudi Arabia agreed to give the Contras as much as $1 million a month.

In April 1985, Congress again rejected a White House appeal for Contra aid, but the votes were becoming increasingly close and the debate increasingly acrimonious. Less than a week after the vote, Daniel Ortega, in a fit of public relations insanity, flew to Moscow to request Soviet aid and strengthen their relationship. No one was surprised when the House approved $27 million in humanitarian aid in June 1985.

On June 14, 1985, TWA flight 847, scheduled to fly from Athens to Rome, was hijacked and taken to Beirut. An American Navy officer was shot and his body dumped on the tarmac at the Beirut airport. The remaining hostages were released on June 30. Ali Akbar Rafsanjani, head of the Iranian Parliament, played a major role in the negotiations. The TWA hijacking was important for several reasons. It focused American attention on the issue of terrorism and, by extension, on the fate of U.S. hostages in captivity in Lebanon. The hijacking also provided evidence that the Iranians, when they chose, could affect events in Beirut. Finally, the safe release of most of the TWA hostages seemed to indicate that by playing an active role the United States could affect the outcome of terrorist situations. The Reagan administration was not blind to any of these "lessons."

On July 20, President Reagan was hospitalized and subsequently operated on for intestinal cancer. During his recuperation, he gave McFarlane explicit approval to open negotiations with Iran through Israeli contacts. On August 20, 96 TOW missiles were delivered to Iran via Israel. No hostages were released then, but on September 15 Benjamin Weir was freed after an additional 408 TOW missiles were delivered to Iran.

On October 17, The cruise ship *Achille Lauro* was hijacked; Leon Klinghoffer, an American confined to a wheelchair, was murdered by the hijackers. On October 12, in a plan inspired by Oliver North, American fighters forced the hijackers' escape plane to land in Italy. Four of the hijackers were arrested by Italian authorities, although their leader, Abul Abbas, was released. The Reagan administration was jubilant, having finally "won" a round with terrorists (Bradlee 1988). The *Achille Lauro* incident provided strong support for an interventionist policy in dealing with terrorism and, for the first time, established the credentials of Oliver North.

At North's urging, and with his superiors' knowledge and support, the United States continued to ship arms to Iran. On November 14, 1985, 19 HAWK missiles were delivered; no hostages were released. On December 4, McFarlane, "physically and emotionally exhausted" (Bradlee 1988: 321), resigned as National Security Advisor and was replaced by his deputy, Vice Admiral John Poindexter, on December 5. One of Poindexter's first acts was to ask Reagan to sign a presidential "finding" retroactively authorizing the shipment of HAWK missiles.

Presidential "findings" are an important element in national security procedures. A "finding" is a formal presidential determination authorizing the initiation of covert action by the American government. "No such operation can be undertaken unless the President 'finds' that it is important to the national security. The purpose is to establish presidential accountability for all such operations" (Cohen and Mitchell 1988: 12-13). The procedure concerning "findings" was established by Congress in 1980 in an attempt to establish some congressional control over covert actions. There is a presumption that all such "findings" will be signed prior to the initiation of covert action, or, at the very least, will be reported to Congress "in a timely fashion" (Cohen and Mitchell 1988: 13). The December 5 "finding" did not comply, in spirit or in letter, to this presumption. Even worse, that December also saw the profits from the first round of arms sales being diverted to the Contras. This "neat idea" of Oliver North's nearly destroyed the Reagan presidency.

The pattern thus established continued through 1986. That January, Reagan signed two more "findings" authorizing further arms sales to Iran. By April, the Contras were establishing air supply routes with the diverted funds. By June, Congress funded the Contras again, voting $70 million in military aid and $100 million in total aid. The day after the vote, hostage Father Jenco was released. On August 8, 240 HAWK missile parts were shipped to Iran.

By late 1986, the Iran-Contra affair became news. The first revelation came on October 5, 1986, when Eugene Hasenfus was shot down over Nicaragua while he was flying a Contra resupply plane and discussed his activities on Nicaraguan television. On October 7, Reagan publicly and categorically denied any U.S. role in Contra supplies. On October 18, both the UPI and *Newsday* published information linking Oliver North, his associate Richard Secord, and the American embassy in Costa Rica to Hasenfus, creating many embarrassing questions and bringing the president's credibility into question.

Hostage David Jacobsen was released on November 2, and Reagan issued a statement announcing the release along with an assertion, "We have been working through a number of sensitive channels for a long time. Unfortunately, we cannot divulge any of the details of the release because the lives of other Americans and other Western hostages are still at risk" (Press Secretary 1986a).

Any positive publicity, however, was undermined by a story released in the Lebanese magazine *Al-Shira'a*, disclosing the arms sales to Iran and adding details about a trip McFarlane had paid to Iran, bringing a Bible signed by Ronald Reagan as a gift to Iranian officials. Given Reagan's public animosity to these same officials and his adamant opposition to selling arms to Iran, the story was doubly damaging.

On November 6, both the *Washington Post* and the *Los Angeles Times* headlined stories on the arms sales. They revealed that there had been more than one deal, that there was some Israeli involvement, that there was a connection to the hostages, and that both Secretary of State George Schultz and Secretary of Defense Caspar Weinburger were on record as having opposed the deal. Reagan's only response to the charges was to state that they "have no foundation."

The Reagan White House tried to contain the media, asking them to be careful about what they reported, for the hostages' lives were at stake, and refusing to comment on stories and allegations, "because it doesn't—you know, we don't think it serves the interests of the safety of the hostages to comment on these stories" (Speakes 1986a: 3). The White House also stated that the media coverage had already made it harder to release the hostages (Speakes 1986b). That this strategy also served the interest of the White House was obvious to everyone.

On November 13, Reagan gave a televised address in which he again denied all American involvement. It was not a convincing address, and both *Newsweek* and ABC found little public support for the president's position (Mayer and McManus 1988: 303). Press Secretary Larry Speakes (1986c: 3), facing a hostile media corps, had to assert, "Everything the President did, including the—condoning that shipment, was in his opinion, done in the best interest of the United States, United States foreign policy, and that was the sole criterion for making his decisions in this entire matter." In other words, Ronald Reagan is president, he knows how to be president, his character is what is important, be done with it. The media were not convinced.

On November 21, in response to public and congressional pressure, Reagan authorized Attorney General Edwin Meese to investigate. Oliver North and his secretary, Fawn Hall, began to destroy evidence. On November 25, the diversion of funds was disclosed, with a statement by Reagan saying that he was, "deeply troubled that the implementation of a policy aimed at resolving a truly tragic situation in the Middle East has resulted in such controversy" (Press Secretary 1986b). Poindexter was forced to resign, and Oliver North was "reassigned." Frank Carlucci was named to succeed Poindexter as National Security Advisor.

These staffing changes appeased neither Congress nor the public. On December 1, 1986, CBS released a poll showing that Reagan's approval had fallen from 67% in November to 46% in December—the largest drop of any president in a single month's time. That same day, *Time* reported Reagan calling North a "hero," which further undermined the president's position and added to the confusion—if North was a "hero" why was he fired? If he was fired, how could he be a "hero"? The Reagan administration seemed unable to resolve the plethora of contradictions.

An analysis of ABC's media coverage of the scandal showed how deeply the scandal had affected coverage of the administration: During the two peak news periods (the five days following the first news of the arms sale and the five days following Ed Meese's press conference), nearly 50% of all news stories contained stories about the scandal, and "in 30% of these stories, the reporter's closing lines . . . were clearly negative." Worse,

> Jeff Greenfield, media and political analyst for ABC News and frequent *Nightline* guest said that in the first ten days after the arms sale was revealed, conservative spokesmen he interviewed were unable to fashion a defense of the President. Some blamed the problems on Shultz and Regan, others reluctantly said that one could not say, "If only the Czar knew" forever. (Rodota 1987)

With this kind of media coverage, Reagan had little chance of controlling the agenda.

There were frequent references in the media to "Irangate," and comparisons were drawn between Nixon and Reagan. Congress also entered the fray, and investigative committees began organizing. Some Senators even went to Reagan with a suggestion that he call Congress into a special session to deal with the issue openly and expeditiously, a suggestion he rejected in early December (Press Secretary 1986c).

Soon afterward, however, White House aide Pat Buchanan was able to provide some reassurance, telling Reagan that "there may be signs of issue exhaustion" and encouraging him to reply to implied connections between Watergate and the "Irangate" scandal with the assertion, "The best one word tag for the actual situation is 'investigate'" (Buchanan 1986). He also supplied Reagan with numerous quotes from prominent Democrats (including Jimmy Carter, Pierre Salinger, and Andrew Young) on Iran's strategic importance.

As the controversy continued to escalate, so did the number of investigatory committees, commissions, and counsels. Reagan, in an effort to appear on the side of the angels, announced:

> There is an urgent need for full disclosure of all facts surrounding the Iranian controversy. I want to get this information out. . . . It is my desire to have the full story about Iran come out now—the alleged transfer of funds, the Swiss bank accounts, who was involved—everything. (Press Secretary 1986d)

He called on Congress to offer Poindexter and North "use immunity" toward that end (Press Secretary 1986d). On December 19, Reagan appointed an Independent Counsel. At the same time, the president's special review board, or the "Tower Commission," was also investigating, with the full cooperation of the White House. Reagan had even appointed Ambassador David Abshire as a Cabinet-level aide with responsibility for coordinating the Iran inquiry. The Tower Commission Report was issued on February 26 and contained a scathing critique of the Reagan administration and its managerial organization. As a response, Reagan's acerbic Chief of Staff, Don Regan, was fired the next day and replaced by Howard Baker.

The White House hoped to put the Iran-Contra affair behind them with the publication of the Tower Report, emphasizing the fact that the Report confirmed the president's contention that he had not known of the diversion, declining to comment on other specific items in the Report, underlining the finding that the President had not violated any laws, and arguing that "America went through a long summer of self-examination. But now we are through it. We are moving on" (Talking points 1987). This last point is particularly interesting for its claim that "America" had some self-examining to do, not merely the Reagan administration, implying that we were all equally culpable and were now equally forgiven.

In January 1987, both the House and the Senate appointed Select Committees. These Committees agreed to hold joint hearings, which began on May 5, and involved 41 days of questioning spread over a three-month period. The Committee heard 250 hours of testimony from 29 witnesses (Segev 1988). Their final report was issued on November 18, 1987, also condemned Reagan's policymaking and procedures.

Finally, the Independent Counsel issued the results of his investigation. On March 11, 1988, McFarlane pleaded guilty to four counts of withholding information from Congress; on March 16, indictments were returned against Oliver North, John Poindexter, Albert Hakim, and Richard Secord. All these indictments have since been overturned or withdrawn, but the damage to the Reagan administration was irrevocable.

Reagan's Strategy

Reagan's handling of the Iran-Contra scandal was based in his earlier rhetoric regarding Nicaragua, which entailed three strategies: denying the charges, linking Nicaragua to other issues, and retooling the image of the contras (Stuckey 1990). These efforts were only sporadically successful.

Consistent with his other Nicaragua-related rhetoric, Reagan's (1986a) first attempt to deal with the Iran-Contra allegations was to deny them by discrediting their source:

I know you've been reading, seeing, and hearing a lot of stories the past several days attributed to Danish sailors, unnamed observers at Italian ports and Spanish harbors, and especially government officials in my administration. Well, now you're going to hear the facts from a White House source, and you know my name.

Having established himself as the most—indeed, the only—credible source, Reagan (1986a) proceeded to present "the facts," which were that "we have had underway a secret diplomatic initiative to Iran," in order to "renew a relationship...bring an end to the . . . war between Iran and Iraq . . . to eliminate state-sponsored terrorism and subversion . . . and to effect the safe return of all hostages."

He also emphasized Iran's geographical importance and the need to protect national security. The secrecy, according to Reagan, was essential to protect lives: "This sensitive undertaking has entailed great risk for those involved. There is no question but that we could never have began or continued this dialogue had the initiative been disclosed earlier. Due to the publicity of the past week, the entire initiative is very much at risk today" (Reagan 1986a).

If this last point was intended to suppress investigation, the results were disappointing. The rhetorical strategy of this first speech failed utterly in protecting the president's credibility and competence. His refusal to admit mistakes brought his judgment and political savvy equally into question, and his continued emphasis on the position that no laws were broken and no secrecy intended increased the public perception of a cover-up.

Reagan continued to have difficulty locating an appropriate strategy to handle the Iran-Contra revelations in early 1987. In January of that year he attempted to displace Iran by altering the agenda to issues of unity and cooperation in the face of the Soviet Union and the importance of the defense budget. Reagan (1987a) wanted the entire Iran affair placed firmly in the past:

> But in debating the past, we must not deny ourselves the successes of the future. Let it never be said that this generation of Americans that we became so obsessed with failure that we refused to take risks that could further the cause of peace and freedom in the world.

This served as both a justification for the Iranian arms deal and a prod to stop focusing on it to the exclusion of the rest of the Reagan presidency. This was an attractive possibility, but it did not work. Presidents can offer an interpretation of an event or situation, but cannot guarantee that that interpretation will be a plausible or acceptable one. In this case, the environment was imposing too many constraints on

Reagan's choices to make the interpretation he offered in the State of the Union address viable.

Reagan's next strategy was to drop the subject altogether. He refused to comment while the various investigations continued and would take no questions regarding those investigations. Instead, he focused on other issues and made his argument indirectly: "What we accomplished these last 6 years wouldn't have been possible without a solid foundation, painstakingly laid" (Reagan 1987b). In other words, "I haven't done such a bad job as president, don't be so eager to condemn me now." And Reagan did retain some support, although there was much concern over "what the president knew and when he knew it."

Reagan was eventually assisted by this concern, for it became the focus of the attention paid to the Iran-Contra affair. When it became clear that Reagan would not be implicated in this scandal the way that Nixon had been implicated in Watergate, much of the furor evaporated, and the criticisms of Reagan's performance were diminished by the previous anticipation of greater involvement.

Still, the problems caused by the Iran-Contra affair continued well into the spring of 1987. Reagan made the first tentative steps toward a recovery in a March 4 "Address to the Nation," in which he finally implemented a workable strategy regarding the scandal. This strategy had three steps. The first and most important was the recognition that he had made mistakes that affected his relationship with and standing in the entire country: "The power of the presidency is often thought to reside in this Oval Office. Yet it doesn't rest here; it rests with you, the American people, and on your trust" (Reagan 1987c).

The second step was equally important. More than just affecting the emotional life of the nation, Reagan had denied that the public understanding of the Iranian scandal was the correct one. In this speech Reagan (1987c) admitted that the scenario was, in fact, an arms for hostages deal:

> A few months ago, I told the American people that I had not traded arms for hostages. My heart and my best intentions still tell me that's true, but the evidence tells me it's not . . . what began as a strategic opening to Iran deteriorated, in its implementation, into trading arms for hostages.

This was an important step, for it involved the recognition that his interpretation of events had lost out. Everyone now shared the same understanding of the situation.

The third step in the recovery of his national reputation was to correct the mistakes that had been made. His strategic response was both political and rhetorical. Reagan promised action in three areas: personnel, national security policy, "and the process for making sure the system works."

The strategy of this speech was an effective one because by agreeing to an interpretation of events that his audience shared, Reagan validated the fact that the public no longer trusted him. By admitting to mistakes and promising to correct them, Reagan provided an emotionally satisfying and an intellectually solid speech.

It was also strikingly similar to the strategy employed by Richard Nixon in his April 30, 1973 address, when he announced the resignations of Haldeman and Ehrlichman. This strategy worked for Reagan as it had not for Nixon for two reasons: ethos and context. The "old Reagan" was a more dependable and trustworthy character than was the "old Nixon." Reagan's ethos was that of a simple and sincere man; such a man could easily be led astray by his convictions. Nixon had no such reputation to fall back on.

Furthermore, Reagan operated in a political context that was, in significant part, shaped by Watergate and Nixon's subsequent resignation. In the absence of incontrovertible evidence that Reagan had been personally involved in the Iran-Contra affair as Nixon was in the Watergate cover-up, the White House could restrict the damage to the president.

Reagan's strategy was not immediately effective, however, for the admissions were a long time coming, and people needed time to absorb events. It also took time for the promised reforms to take effect. In addition, Reagan's real upsurge in the polls came only after the affair had dragged on throughout a summer of hearings, and a certain amount of damage had already been irrevocably done.

Reagan did not act as though he understood that the person of the president and the requirements of the presidential role are distinct, that there are some things even a president may not do with impunity. In one of his numerous defenses of Reagan's policy, Speakes made this revealing statement:

> He thinks in this case he got pro and con advice. He got go, no go advice. And as the President was elected to do, he made a decision. And, as he told you, it was a risk, and had it not been exposed and had it run its course, it stood an excellent chance of paying off and paying major dividends for U.S. policy. At that point, it—the president and his administration and the NSC—all those who participated in—would have come out as brilliant foreign policy strategists and heroes. But the exposure of this operation destroyed it and it was a risk we took and a risk that he says was worth taking. (1986d: 13)

This is the attitude of an administration—and of a president—who do not recognize the limits on their personal authority.

Although Reagan avoided impeachment and regained some of his damaged credibility, the Iran-Contra scandal brought a taint of dishonor and incompetence to the Reagan administration—a taint that may prove more important in the long than in the short run, as scholars evaluate the Reagan presidency.

Discussion

To some people, the most disturbing element of the Iran-Contra affair was the Reagan administration's belief that they alone were privileged to decide what was the moral choice, and the democratic process was subordinate to that moral good (Ledeen 1988). On the one hand, for people who believe that democracy is not an end but a process, not a goal but a procedure, Reagan's apparent willingness to allow ends to justify means was extremely disturbing because it contradicted what they expected from a president.

On the other hand, many people sympathized with that goal, and understood the administration's frustration in trying to accomplish it. As Don Regan (1988: 85), no fan of Oliver North's, said, "I offer excuses for Oliver North with great reluctance, but it is possible that he would have acted differently if he had not imagined, as he has testified he did, that it was his mission to relieve the President of burdens that could not be lifted by the usual methods of democratic government."

The question that remains, of course, is whether the president should be "relieved of the burdens" of "the usual methods of democratic government." Assuming that this is a government of laws and not of people, adherence to those laws ought to be a paramount obligation of public officials. The issue of who gets to decide national policy—the president, the Congress, or the citizenry—is not an issue confined to the recent past, nor is it an easy one to resolve. It is not likely to be resolved soon. Although personal views on the moral rightness of the arms diversion may vary, the Iran-Contra affair as a strategic problem differed from the BIR case and Watergate in one important respect: motivation.

Truman's aides and Richard Nixon were all viewed as abusing the power and privilege of government in order to advance personal aims and fulfill personal agendas. In the Iran-Contra affair, "the sale of weapons to Iran and the diversion of money to the contras were perceived as misguided abuses of process rather than arrogant abuses of power" (Cohen and Mitchell 1988: 50). That perception, combined with Congressional unwillingness to bring down another president, made all the difference.

Truman and his aides were perceived as using power for selfish aims; the political and institutional context in 1951 supported the president, and mitigated against the possibility of serious damage to the Truman presidency. Richard Nixon operated within that changed context, and it worked against him. Nixon's possibilities for action were curtailed by the political expectations of him and his presidency.

Ronald Reagan assumed office in the aftermath of the "imperiled" presidency. He was a president people hoped would succeed, and they gave him every opportunity to do so. Even his failures were overlooked, understood, or forgiven, for Reagan appeared to be fulfilling the expectations of the role to near perfection. But in the Iran-Contra affair, Reagan violated parameters for his role that he had set up himself—he negotiated with terrorists. In so doing, Reagan allowed the possibility that there were other areas of his presidency that were also inconsistent with his self-proclaimed expectations, a possibility that could have destroyed his ability to govern effectively.

CONCLUSIONS

Slippage is the difficulty faced when the personal character of the president is seen to conflict with the role requirements of the office. This sort of dissonance can occur in mild forms and have few if any consequences, as when a president takes an occasional false step. Scandals are a particular problem in this regard because they reveal an apparent pattern of behavior, a systematic violation of the presidential role. It is this sense of patterned inconsistency that make responding to scandals difficult for most presidents.

Presidential responses to scandal form a discernible pattern across situations and administrations. Presidents initially respond to all accusations with denial and express support for and faith in their staff. This is a frequently effective and low-risk response—if that support must later be withdrawn, the president at least preserves the image of a trusting executive duped by a deceitful aide.

After the original denial, presidents generally then refuse further comment, ostensibly either to preserve the sanctity of hearings or other investigations, or as a refusal to extend the prominence of their office to the accusations. This can limit the news play of the accusations and may indeed end the scandal. If this tactic fails, it is because more evidence has been uncovered, or simply that, despite presidential denials, enough of an image of wrong-doing has been created that speculation persists. In this case, presidents are forced to somehow respond.

This response is important, for it is at this point that a president can, through the appearance of openness and honesty, end the relevance of the charges, or, by choosing an inappropriate strategy, create the expectation for increased White House involvement. Presidents must, at this juncture, restore the consonance between their character and their role. This is the time for a president who wishes to lose as little time and political capital as possible to jettison aides and publicly disclose as much information as possible. Failure to do so will inevitably engender the impression of presidential complicity and adversely affect the president's credibility.

Presidential secrets have a nasty way of becoming public. If the president is to have any voice in how those secrets are to be interpreted, the sooner they are revealed, the better. For once a president loses credibility on an issue or set of issues, it can never be regained and may spread to the rest of the administration and policies.

Apart from this pattern, several other aspects of presidential scandals are illuminated by the examples presented in this chapter. There is no doubt, for instance, that the nature of presidential scandal has changed in modern times. The BIR scandal involved a relatively straight-forward case of influence-for-hire. Watergate and the Iran-Contra affair were much more complicated series of events. This increased complexity indicates both the growing complexity of the executive branch of government and the sensationalism that typifies the media presentations of that government.

Government scandals have grown more intricate because government itself is more intricate. Gone are the days when one person may unilaterally influence the outcome of a policy decision. Oliver North may have been a "loose cannon," but in these days of bureaucratic complexity, even loose cannons report to somebody. This aspect of the executive branch as an institution offers both advantages and potential difficulties for the president. The clearest limitation is that the president is held accountable for everything that occurs in the executive branch. This is true even if the president is not aware of the activities, or if the decisions were handled by a minor functionary. Those authorized to speak in the president's name do not answer for the policies thus enacted—the president does.

Even given this presumption, however, the layers of bureaucracy enfolding the president may provide protection as well as potential danger. If a highly placed advisor—a Don Regan, for instance—can be found responsible for a scandalous activity, and if the president's "plausible deniability" can be protected, then the president can be perceived as "too trusting," "duped," and thus avoid the stigma of scandalous duplicity. Generally, being perceived as stupid (if the perception is confined to relatively few instances) is preferable to being perceived as venal.

The increased complexity of presidential scandal is also reflective of media and societal norms. The BIR scandal would be considered pedestrian in today's political context. To qualify as an administration-threatening event these days, a scandal must involve considerably more than several greedy aides, but must entail dramatic wrong-doing at the highest levels.

Additionally, all these scandals played out within different political and institutional contexts. None of these presidents operated within a strong institutional environment. As president, all were in a position of initial strength vis-à-vis Congress and the Courts. Yet, in these days of media-influenced public politics, all were in a position of initial weakness vis-à-vis the mass media. Neither Truman nor Nixon, products of an earlier political culture, knew how to manage the media, although as skillful politicians, they both understood the importance of its management. Reagan, on the other hand, had a communicative style that, when meshed with White House control of the media, made for very effective persuasion.

The interaction between the scandalous behavior and ethos, or public character of the president, is a key factor determining the outcome of the various scandals. As Orrin Klapp (1964) reminds us, every image has its strengths and weaknesses. When a president—or a member of the president's staff—does something potentially scandalous, two things matter most: how this action fits with the president's perceived ethos, and how close the guilty party is to the president. The further from the president's inner circle the actor is, the more inconsistent the action can be, for with distance comes ease of disassociation. If the actor is the president or a close advisor to the president, it is significantly harder for the president to disassociate himself.

If a president must identify with the scandalous behavior, the extent of damage is related to how the action fits with what we already "know" about that president. This is what made the Iran-Contra affair so problematic for Reagan. He was thought of as a foreign policy "expert" of sorts, a man who would "stand tall" and eschew the easy route of compromise and conciliation. Reagan was not a man who would "trade arms for hostages"; he was a man who wanted opponents to "make his day." The Iran-Contra scandal, in violating that image, left Reagan two choices: He could appear culpable, a president who knowingly lied to the American people and our allies for a greater moral good, or he could appear simple, detached, and ill advised. Given the Reagan ethos of genial good will, the latter was the only choice he could have realistically made.

In Nixon's case, Watergate fit with what many people "knew" about Nixon; indeed, it confirmed many people's worst fears. Here,

Nixon had a problem with his original ethos: People expected him to act dishonorably and were not surprised when he fulfilled their expectations. Nixon's trouble was less a lack of coherence between his actions and his ethos, as a lack of fit between his actions and the political/institutional culture in which they were embedded. Once in trouble, Nixon had no image of honorable political behavior to provide a counterargument to charges of corruption. He also had no institutional support other than his position as president. Once he had undermined that position by acting unpresidentially (revealed by the tapes of him swearing and discussing blackmail in the Oval Office), there was no hope for his political survival.

Harry Truman's situation was similar to Nixon's in that the scandal surrounding the BIR was exactly the kind of thing one could expect of Truman; he was dogged by charges of shoddy political dealings throughout his career and was notable for the loyalty he displayed to his aides and associates. The essential difference between Nixon and Truman was the institutional context in which they operated. Truman's position was more ambiguous. He was a Democrat with a Democratic Congress and a New Deal agenda. Yet, he was not FDR, and much of the antagonism New Deal policies attracted rebounded on Truman, as they could not on the more charismatic Roosevelt. The BIR scandal contributed to "K1C2" or "Korea, Communism and Corruption," and helped put Eisenhower and the Republicans in the White House.

Each president had a specific image. They could be expected to excel at certain matters, be less competent at others, and ignore still others. As each president had strengths, so each had weaknesses. Scandals are damaging to a president to the extent that they feed into those weaknesses in ways that undermine the image that helped elect that president. Every image entails transgressions that may not be committed. The crux of avoiding disastrous scandals is for a president to understand the nature and limitations imposed by their choice of image and abide by those limitations.

2

Singularity: Failed Appointments

Presidential standing in both Congress and the mass public is most affected by issues and events that are highly salient for those groups, such as elections, scandals, and the day-to-day conduct of the president's involvement in the legislative process. These issues tend to focus attention on the person of the president and thus matter greatly in terms of the president's ethos. When a president is elected, a presidential administration is also elected (Hart 1987). The conduct of that administration affects the public interpretation of the presidential office and the character of the individual president. A poorly handled nomination is not likely to destroy or even seriously weaken a president, but it can affect the margins of the presidential ethos, and failed nominations are worthy of consideration.

The problem of singularity is the problem of a president's inability to recognize the plural nature of the presidency and failure to understand that a nominee reflects the presidential character in ways that must be consistent with the expectations of the presidential role. The most important aspect of that role in terms of the appointment process is the representative nature of the chief executive. The president is the embodiment of the nation; presidential nominees—especially high-profile presidential nominees—are the further embodiment of the nation. Presidents who fail to recognize this are presidents who are headed for trouble in Congress and with the public.

The power to nominate governmental officials is one of the most important of the constitutionally guaranteed presidential prerogatives. As with all important presidential powers extended via the Constitution, the president's power of appointment is limited by the participation of Congress. The president may nominate, but the Senate has the privilege of confirming or rejecting the nomination. Generally, the nomination and confirmation process works smoothly. When presidents remember to seek the advice of the Senate, senatorial consent is generally given.

This is especially true for executive branch appointments. Unless there is clear evidence of a nominee's unsuitability, the Senate tends to act on the assumption that presidents have the right to choose their own advisors and assistants. Even if individual Senators disapprove of a president's choice, they are more likely to indicate their reservations for the record than to block the appointment.

The same cannot be said for presidential nominations to the federal judiciary. Although relatively uninvolved in appointments to the lower courts, Senators take much more interest in Supreme Court nominations, which are seen as more lasting and less confined to the president's exclusive bailiwick than are executive branch or lower court nominations. Senatorial hearings on judicial nominations are generally longer, more public, cover more ground, and are potentially more damaging to a president's standing than are those on executive branch nominees.

The appointments process is fairly routinized and follows a pattern of consultation, hearings, and decision. The consultation occurs within the executive branch, with relevant congressional committees and subcommittees and specifically concerned individual Senators. For Supreme Court nominees, it is the Attorney General's task to propose a slate of candidates for the position. Presidents vary in the degree to which they rely on the Attorney General or become personally involved in the process. Hearings begin in the relevant committee, which then makes a recommendation to the full Senate. Appointment is confirmed with a simple majority of participating Senators.

This routine, simple as it is, presents a danger to the president in its very simplicity. It is easy to take the process for granted and fail to give it the attention it merits. When this happens, presidents suffer doubly: first for being remiss, and second for sustaining a public rebuke.

The appointments process tends to flow more smoothly for presidents who have a partisan majority in the Senate (Cameron, Cover, and Segal 1990). Partisan loyalty tends to override political differences on appointments. For that reason, Republicans have had more difficulty in modern times than have Democrats. It is important to note that this has had more to do with the political and institutional context in which modern presidents operate than with the political skill or acumen of the presidents themselves. Although the three cases presented here all concern Republican chief executives, the problems that they faced are not necessarily confined to Republicans. The same context of divided government and increased politicalization of the appointments process creates similar problems for Democratic presidents, as Bill Clinton is learning.

Richard Nixon became the first modern president to have two nominees to the Supreme Court rejected sequentially. (Whig John Tyler holds the record for rejection. He had five nominees rejected sequentially by the Democratic Senate.) The nomination of G. Harrold Carswell remains an example of how not to approach the appointments process. Ronald Reagan, who early in his administration had remarkable success imposing his will on a reluctant Congress, engaged in a lengthy and acrimonious debate with the Senate before Robert Bork, Reagan's Supreme Court nominee, was rejected. This debate hurt both Reagan and the reputation of the Court.

In George Bush's failure to win confirmation of John Tower as Secretary of Defense, we have a rare example of a failed executive branch nomination. This failure was doubly surprising because Tower had been a Senator himself, and the Senate very rarely denies one of its own.

These cases illuminate the potential problems when presidents fall victim to the error of singularity. Presidents are restricted in their selection of personnel by the Constitution, which decrees that they must obtain senatorial approval of their nominees. They are tempted by the routinized nature of the process to take success for granted and by the privilege of their own institutional position to resent senatorial "interference." It is, after all, the president's function to provide national representation, the president's privilege to determine how he will define his character in terms of the presidential role. This, as we shall see, is a potentially dangerous combination of temptations.

RICHARD M. NIXON AND THE CARSWELL NOMINATION

The Political and Institutional Context

The U.S. Supreme Court is important both politically and symbolically. This was particularly evident in the political context of the late 1960s. By the time Nixon took office, the Vietnam War, the assassinations of the Kennedys, of Martin Luther King, Jr., of Malcolm X, the student protestors, civil rights movement, and race riots had created seemingly irreconcilable schisms within the nation. "The people longed for a little peace of mind. The climate of expectations called for reassurance" (Barber 1977: 419).

Reassurance was precisely what Richard Nixon (1969a) promised in 1968. He asked that the nation "lower our voices" and learn to listen to one another. Promising reassurance was easier than providing it however. In 1969, Richard Nixon became the first first term president in 120 years to have both houses of Congress in the hands of the opposition party. The Democratic majority was both strong (242-190 in the House, 57-43 in the Senate) and committed to opposing Nixon. The partisan opposition to Nixon was exacerbated by antagonism to him, his tactics, and his policy preferences and by his less-than-generous response to that antagonism.

These difficulties were particularly important within the prevailing political context. The Vietnam War and social unrest combined to create a breakdown of the national consensus on the efficacy of New Deal programs and of the importance of the Cold War as the motivation behind American foreign policy (Hoff-Wilson 1988). Americans could not seem to agree on even broad policy goals. The challenge facing the political leadership was to create and direct a national consensus in the face of widespread and often violent confrontation.

Nixon inherited a wartime presidency complete with the enhanced extralegal powers that entailed. Yet Lyndon Johnson had just been driven from office as a result of dissatisfaction with that war, and Nixon faced a Congress and a media that were hostile to presidential power and suspicious of Richard Nixon. Nixon could not rely on a mobilized mass public to support him; although the public was clearly mobilized, they were also clearly divided. He could not expect to enact his policy proposals through Congress because a majority of legislators considered Nixon a threat to the programs they had founded their careers on.

Increasingly, Nixon turned to administrative solutions to his political problems. Instead of fighting Congress, Nixon circumvented it and favored executive action via administrative channels over political action via the legislative process (Hess 1976; Nathan 1975; Rose 1978). First, Nixon circumvented members of Congress. As time went on, however, he also became disenchanted with the bureaucracy and increasingly moved administrative functions into the White House. Nixon became entrenched and ever more isolated.

This did not stop him from attempting to orchestrate public opinion concerning himself or his policies however (see Chapter 1). This tendency toward image making succeeded more in creating an image of Nixon-as-cynical-manipulator than in changing minds about the character of the president. Nixon tried so hard to be "presidential" that he subsumed his character into the role; a more balanced approach, allowing him to be the man that he was, and still accommodate that to the requirements of the role, would probably have been more effective than all the endeavors of his "anecdotalists."

As the president moved from Congress to the bureaucracy, political activists moved from Congress to the Courts. Southern legislators were so effective at blocking liberal legislative proposals that remedies—especially civil rights remedies—were increasingly sought in the courts. Because of the Supreme Court's symbolic importance, regional and political balance has always been an important aspect of the Court's membership. As the Court became the focal point for controversy over social change, that balance became a volatile issue.

Ever since the inception of the New Deal, the national government had taken on more and more of the nation's social agenda. By the early days of the Nixon administration, that social agenda was under debate, and the controversy was clearly the responsibility of the federal government. Given the context of the late 1960s, that meant that social issues were the responsibility first of the president and second of the Supreme Court. Nixon's nominations to the Court were thus caught in the controversy that surrounded the intersection of the executive and the judicial.

The Carswell Nomination

The history of Richard Nixon's difficulties with his Supreme Court nominees actually began in the later days of the Johnson administration. On June 13, 1968, nearly three months after Johnson's decision not to seek another term as president, Supreme Court Chief Justice Earl Warren resigned. On June 26, Johnson nominated his close friend, Abe Fortas, as Chief Justice. Fortas had been an Associate Justice since 1965, and Johnson assumed his elevation would be fairly routine.

Several months after the nomination, however, *Life* magazine charged that Fortas had accepted improper fees and had intervened with a federal regulatory agency on a client's behalf. More evidence of impropriety was reportedly discovered by the Justice Department. Faced with the choice of having the unsavory details made public or withdrawing his nomination, Fortas withdrew on October 2, 1968.

It was impossible for Johnson to nominate another Justice so close to the presidential election. Following his election to the presidency, Richard Nixon nominated, and the Senate approved (by a vote of 74-3), Warren Burger. Burger was sworn in on June 23, 1969.

The month before, Abe Fortas, responding to further attacks, resigned from the Court. There was no evidence that Fortas was guilty of anything other than incredibly poor judgment, but the prestige of the Court was such that poor judgment was reason enough for his resignation.

The opportunity to nominate another justice so early in his administration could have been a valuable one for Nixon, for he could have used the nominations to

> reinstill the sense of majesty, probity, and dignity that Americans have felt about their High Court, which is now suffering after the Fortas affair [and to] stress the President's concern that the Court interpret the law rather than make the law. . . . This is the stuff of high drama and history in the making, and requires no showmanship or pyrotechnics. (Safire 1969)

Nixon had his own reasons for selecting his nominees to the Court: "Filling those seats with conservatives, especially if one were a Southerner, would keep [his] campaign pledge, appear to balance the Court ideologically, and perhaps add more Southerners to his constituency" (Vatz and Windt 1987: 240). There is evidence that the administration devoted considerable time and energy to this latter goal and was indeed committed to a "Southern strategy" (Wasden 1969). As Pat Buchanan (1969) wrote:

> The Republican Party is the party of the future in the South—not because of the race issue—but because on foreign policy, economic policy, and governmental policy, our views are far closer to those of the New South than those of the ultra-liberal Northern Democrats now in ascendancy of their party. . . . The Republican party is a national party—it is the only party that is strong and vibrant in every section of the country—and we intend to keep it that way.

In keeping with this strategy, Nixon decided to go with Attorney General John Mitchell's suggestion of Judge Clement F. Haynsworth of the 4th Circuit Court of Appeals, a native of South Carolina and an alumnus of Harvard Law School.

Nixon nominated Haynsworth without first checking with either the Senate or the American Bar Association. Both of these were powerful potential sources of support (or opposition), and by refusing to consult with them, Nixon denied himself their support while opening himself up to their opposition. The Senate Judiciary Committee split on their vote, a signal that the nomination was in trouble. Nixon refused to withdraw Haynsworth's name, despite requests from his allies in the Senate that he do so (Brooke 1969; Smith 1969).

It can be argued that the Senate opposed Haynsworth on political grounds, that they were unwilling to grant conservatives more seats on the Court. "But Haynsworth had just enough vulnerability as a Supreme Court nominee to enable the Senators to rationalize their opposition on more than political or ideological grounds" (Kutler 1991: 145). The Senators, especially Birch Bayh (D-IN), leader of the opposition, had questions concerning Haynsworth's personal ethics and the propriety of his decisions concerning labor and civil rights issues. In the highly charged partisan atmosphere that followed Fortas's withdrawal from the Court, the charges garnered much attention, especially those concerning any potential conflict of interest.

Nixon, never shy about making his feelings known in such matters, went on the offensive. He felt that in the prevailing political climate, Senators sought not only evidence of impropriety, but even the appearance of impropriety would be sufficient cause to defeat an otherwise qualified nominee (Nixon 1978). He went further and accused the Senate of "character assassination." His speechwriters prepared "briefing book," on Haynsworth that included charges to be leveled against his critics:

> Judge Haynsworth has done nothing illegal, nothing unethical, nothing wrong. . . . He is the victim of an irresponsible and reprehensible attack. His good name as a judge and as a man have been impaired by the scattershot allegations of a small clique of politically motivated men—men who know that you can put a cloud over a man by simply making enough charges against him. I intend to do what I can to show the judge as the man he is, and to insure that the nation and the Court benefit from the service he has to offer this country. (Mollenhoff and Buchanan 1969)

In addition, Nixon attempted to control network news coverage of the nomination battle by demanding "equal time" for Haynsworth's supporters and by attempting to discredit Birch Bayh (D-IN), Haynsworth's most vocal opponent in the Senate (Brown 1970a, 1970b; Cole 1969).

Such gentle prodding did not help Nixon's case. On November 21, 1969, 17 Republicans joined 38 Democrats and defeated the Haynsworth nomination 55-45. It was the first rejection of a Supreme Court nominee since 1930. Worse, it happened only one year after Nixon's election and thus made public the fragility of Nixon's power base. It also indicated the power of his opposition.

Knowing that "to oppose the president on two successive Supreme Court nominations is difficult for a Democrat and close to political treason for a Republican" (Vatz and Windt 1987: 246), Nixon believed that he had should face little difficulty in securing his next nomination. But the rejection of Haynsworth left Nixon enraged. He nominated G. Harrold Carswell, a former U. S. Attorney and Judge of the 5th Circuit Court of Appeals. If the Carswell nomination was intended to secure the appointment of a Southerner to the Court, it was poorly handled. If it was intended, as some scholars believe, to illustrate Nixon's contempt for the Senate (Kutler 1991: 146) or to "teach the Senate a lesson" (Abraham 1985: 16), it was somewhat more effective. Whatever Nixon's motives, the Carswell nomination was damaging to Nixon insofar as it became immediately controversial and widely reported in the media as endangered.

The most damaging revelation was a quote from a speech Carswell gave to the American Legion on August 2, 1948, in which he said, "I yield to no man as a fellow candidate or as a fellow citizen in the firm, vigorous belief in the principles of White Supremacy, and I shall always be so governed" (Harris 1971: 15-16). Although he repudiated the statement, which was, after all, 20 years old, there was more evidence that he was less than balanced on racial issues (Kutler 1991).

Despite the furor over the nomination, Attorney General John Mitchell was reluctant to get involved in the confirmation process except as the formal process dictated, as he was "worried that he would be undercutting the Judiciary Committee's prerogatives by preempting the Committee's disclosure of Carswell's positions in open hearings" (Krogh 1970).

During the subsequent hearings, Carswell was denounced as a racist, a sexist, as antilabor, and as incompetent. The charge of incompetence was to prove the most difficult, for "the candidate was patently inferior, simply on the basis of fundamental juridical and legal qualifications. If Judge Haynsworth had merited a 'B,' Judge Carswell scarcely merited a 'D' on the scale of relevant ability" (Abraham 1985: 16). Despite reservations, the Senate Judiciary Committee voted 13-4 in favor of the Carswell appointment.

Senator Roman Hruska (R-NE), the president's floor manager for the nomination, decided to refute the incompetence charge. When he could not do so on the evidence (Carswell had the dubious honor of being one of the top 10 federal judges in terms of decisions reversed, a standard measure of judicial competence), Hruska decided on what can only be called an unfortunate rhetorical strategy. In defense of the nominee, Hruska said, "Even if he is mediocre there are a lot of mediocre judges and people and lawyers. They are entitled to a little representation, aren't they, and a little chance? We can't have all Brandeises, Cardozos, and Frankfurters, and stuff like that there" (Abraham 1985: 17).

If nothing else, Hruska's comments provide evidence that presidents can be as badly damaged by their allies as by their opponents. Hruska got some support in his defense of inferiority from Russell Long (D-LA) who said, "Would it not appear that it might be well to take a B student or a C student who was able to think straight, compared to one of those A students who are capable of the kind of thinking that winds up getting us a 100-percent increase in crime in this country?" (Abraham 1985: 17).

The White House dedicated considerable time and effort in attempting to confirm Carswell. Nixon put heavy pressure on Republicans in the Senate, offering both carrots and sticks (Kutler, 1991: 147), as well as launching more aggressive measures: White House memos show Haldeman demanding action on the "President's request for a report on the number of Supreme Court Justices who own stock in corporations" in an endeavor to remove any taint of impropriety through comparison to sitting Justices (Staff Secretary 1969), and seeking ways to discredit those who were opposed to the nomination (Brown 1970a), as well as sitting Justices, such as Hugo Black (Young 1971). Nonetheless, only 45 senators supported the president, and the Carswell nomination died an ignominious death on April 8, 1970.

Nixon, predictably enough, did not take the defeat well. "His reaction was swift and vitriolic. Conveniently ignoring the basic issues for his candidates' defeat, he blamed it instead on sectional prejudice, abject politics, and philosophical negations" (Abraham 1985: 17). Nixon claimed publicly that because the Senate would never accept a strict constructionist from the South, he would have to abandon his quest for a regionally and philosophically balanced Court. He followed this public statement with a petulant letter to Senator William Saxbe (R-OH; authored by Charles Colson, whom Watergate would later make famous), complaining that the Senate denied him his presidential prerogatives. This only added to the interbranch tension.

Having been defeated, the administration attempted to turn the defeat into a campaign issue in hopes of attaining a Republican Senate after the 1970 election. White House aides contacted "most loyal Republican and selected Democratic Senators...with a hard suggestion to speak out publicly in favor of the President's next nominee to the Court." Lyn Nofziger wrote that at least 17 separate speeches for delivery by key Senators, and both Bill Brock and George Bush, were instructed to "get statements out" and "keep the issue alive" (Haldeman 1970).

On April 14, 1970, Nixon nominated Judge Harry Blackmun, Judge of the 8th Circuit Court of Appeals, a native of Minnesota, and a close friend and ally of Chief Justice Warren Burger. Blackmun was confirmed by unanimous vote on May 12, 1970. Nixon finally had a nominee confirmed. The year-long confirmation process had damaged Nixon's public stature, that of the Supreme Court, and by revealing new lows in interbranch animosity, all but destroyed Nixon's already poor relationship with Congress.

Nixon's Strategy

Nixon wanted to appoint a conservative to the Court. He also wanted to increase his electoral appeal in the South without appearing too heavy-handed or too blatantly opportunistic. As a nominee, Haynsworth was suited to both of these goals. What happened to Haynsworth should have alerted Nixon, if not his staff, that if they wanted a conservative nominee confirmed, they would have to choose one whose judicial competence was beyond reproach.

Nixon ignored the obvious lesson of the Haynsworth experience. He decided that the Senate was ideologically opposed to his goal of an philosophically balanced Court, and that the best approach was to directly confront the Senate's bias. That may have been an effective strategy if the Senate had been overt in claiming geography or ideology as the rationale for Haynsworth's rejection. But the Senate was not overt about that; opposing Senators redefined the issues as competence and the nominee's financial and other improprieties as the justification for his rejection. Thus, the Senate could claim to be making an *unbiased* judgment based on judicial competence, whereas the president argued that they were making political arguments based on bias. To win this argument over the meaning of the Haynsworth nomination, Nixon needed to "prove" the competence of his nominee. This he did not even attempt to do.

Instead, he first indicated his support for Haynsworth in characteristically autobiographical terms:

> When a man has been through the fire, when he has had his entire life and his entire record exposed to the glare of investigation, which, of course, any man who is submitted for confirmation to the Senate should expect to have; and in addition to that, when he has had to go through what I believe to be a vicious character assassination, if after all that he stands up and comes through as a man of integrity, a man of honesty, and a man of qualifications, then that even more indicates that he deserves the support of the President of the United States who nominated him in the first place and also the votes of the Senators who will be voting on his nomination. (Nixon 1969b)

Nixon then cited his own expertise on investigatory matters, saying that, "I should say that I have some experience in investigations myself, and I have studied this case completely in every respect." The Hiss case was never far from Nixon's immediate frame of reference, and Nixon tended to refer to that investigation as evidence for his own competence to judge a variety of matters (O'Neill 1986).

When Nixon began to defend Haynsworth, he started with the charges that, in the context of Fortas's problems, he considered most damaging: conflict of interest. Using legalistic arguments, Nixon stated that Haynsworth's actions followed the requirements of the law as well as accepted judicial practice. He did not address the most important concern, which was the appearance of impropriety and how it affected the stature of the Court. That he failed to see the issue in these terms contributed to Nixon's problem with trustworthiness. His behavior throughout the nomination battle appeared to confirm his critics' worst fears about his personal character and, consequently, his fitness to be president, in this case translated as having his nominee accepted by the Senate without question.

Note that Nixon conflated his experience with that of his nominees and appeared to recognize both the plurality of the presidency and the implications of his nominations for his own ability to play out the presidential role. In fact, Nixon failed to recognize those implications until his nominees were attacked and rejected; then they fit into the Nixonian autobiographical mode, and he defended them in the same terms he consistently used to defend himself—as martyrs to a partisan cause. Had Nixon recognized that his nominees brought with them baggage that would weigh down his own image, he might have looked for—and found—conservative Southern judges whose competence and probity were beyond question.

The Supreme Court has only its legitimacy to protect it. The Court's decisions must be seen as legitimate if they are to be followed. The members of the Court, therefore, are expected to fulfill both representational functions as they are designated by the president (in terms of religion, race, gender, and geographical location) and to be competent as constitutional scholars. When Nixon addressed the strict legality of the accusations against Haynsworth, he ignored these symbolic requirements, and, in ignoring them, essentially lost the nomination.

Nixon's biggest mistake after Haynsworth's defeat, of course, was in letting his temper get in the way of his political judgment. By responding to the Haynsworth defeat by proposing someone as vulnerable as Carswell, Nixon provided evidence for the Senate's argument that Nixon's nominees were lacking competence and thus undermined the president's strategic position by making Nixon appear to be acting both crassly and politically, fulfilling his "Southern strategy" at the expense of the quality of the Supreme Court.

The first and most damaging charge against Carswell was that of racism and his position on white supremacy. Although that is a controversial position at any point in modern times, in 1970, it was particularly volatile. The civil rights movement was at its peak; race riots were tearing cities apart; Martin Luther King, Jr., Robert Kennedy, and Malcolm X had all been assassinated. In the intensity of that political context, no national politician could support an avowed racist for the Court and hope to survive politically. Worse, Richard Nixon already had trouble on issues of civil rights and race generally. As with Haynsworth on ethical matters, the nomination of Carswell served to crystallize elements of Nixon's ethos that did not improve either his credibility or his stature.

Nixon's tie to Carswell was heightened by his dismissive response to the white supremacy speech: "I am not concerned about what Judge Carswell said 22 years ago when he was a candidate for a State legislature. I am very much concerned about his record for 18 years" (Nixon 1970a). However unwittingly, in stating that it was Carswell's record that mattered, Nixon was leading with his nominee's chin. The evidence did not support Nixon's claim that "looking at a man's record over the past, any individual may find instances where he has made statements in which his position has changed." The evidence in Carswell's case was that his views had not substantially changed. Nixon's claim that they had helped to focus attention on those views.

More important even than the racism charges was Nixon's characteristic but misguided reliance on the theme of presidential prerogative as a defense of his nominee. Although it is certainly arguable that the competence issue was, to some degree, camouflage for the Senate's more ideological agenda (Nixon 1978), it was a mistake to shift the focus off of competence and onto constitutionally prescribed prerogatives. Nixon could have defended Carswell's record; he could have invoked the relatively impressive list of Carswell's supporters (Kutler 1991). Instead, he chose to challenge the Senate on a theoretical issue, which, even had he been correct, would not necessarily have won confirmation for his nominee. Nixon was thinking of himself in the singular, not in the plural. He focused on what was due him as president, not what the institution and executive branch symbolized as due to others.

Had Nixon left the Senate alone after his public chastisement, it is possible that the breach between the executive and the legislature would have healed in time. But Nixon being Nixon, he could not leave well enough alone. Nixon had a penchant for expressing things in moral terms and for attempting to delegitimate his opposition (Windt 1990). In a letter to William Saxbe (R-OH), released to the press on April 1, Nixon (1970b) wrote:

> What is centrally at issue . . . is the constitutional responsibility of the President to appoint members of the Court—and whether this responsibility can be frustrated by those who wish to substitute their

own philosophy or their own subjective judgement for that of the one person entrusted by the constitution with the power of appointment. The question arises whether I, as President of the United States, shall be accorded the same right of choice in naming Supreme Court Justices which has been freely accorded to my predecessors of both parties.

In framing the issue this way, Nixon made constitutionally proscribed powers the issue. Senators would defend theirs against what was perceived as presidential encroachment. Appointment is *not* a presidential prerogative; presidents nominate, but the Senate confirms that nomination. Nixon, "with vintage self-pity" (Kutler 1991: 148), accused the Senate of violating the proscribed limitations of their power and made it an institutional battle rather than a personal one. When presidents challenge the Congress as an institution, even individual members who would have been likely supporters of the president will defend their institution. It is never wise for presidents to frame the issue in this way, for Senators will be very unlikely to support the diminution of their own institution.

Nixon thus helped to seal his nominee's fate. Even after Carswell's rejection, Nixon refused to accept any responsibility for the failed nomination. Instead, he (1970c) said, "After the Senate's action yesterday, I have reluctantly concluded that it is not possible to get confirmation for a judge on the Supreme Court of any man who believes in the strict construction of the Constitution, as I do, if he happens to come from the South." This was clearly an effort to salvage what he could of his "Southern strategy" and blame the Democrats for refusing to confirm a Southern nominee. In case anyone might have missed the point, he (1970c, 1970d) reiterated it again and again: "The next nominee must come from outside the South. . . . [I] asked the Attorney General to submit names to me from outside the South. . . . I believe that a judge from the North who has such views will be confirmed by the Senate...I chose them because they were both men of the South...I understand the bitter feeling of millions of Americans who live in the South.

There is little evidence that this attempt to inflame Southerners was effective. There is a great deal of evidence that Nixon's approach to the Carswell nomination created a rift between the White House and the Senate that created additional difficulties for the president; difficulties that could have eased if not avoided by a different strategy.

Discussion

The problem with assessing Nixon's approach to the appointments process is that all his responses were so clearly characteristic ones: the attempt to delegitimate his opposition, the tendency to personalize issues, the emphasis on autobiography, the dichotomous choices, all of these tendencies are reflections of Nixon's communicative style (Stuckey 1991; Windt 1990). Thus, to alter Nixon's strategy in this instance is tantamount to creating (yet another) "New Nixon."

Still, the Carswell nomination stands as an example of how not to approach the Senate during the confirmation process. Nixon's initial appointment of G. Clement Haynsworth was both reasonable and reasonably well orchestrated by the White House. The chief error was in the administration's failure to understand that Haynsworth—and Nixon himself—were vulnerable on civil rights and in not preparing a defense of that vulnerability. The Carswell nomination, however, is much less easily defended. Carswell was not an experienced judge, nor was he demonstrably a particularly good one. This fed into the problem, for Carswell's lack of qualification provided evidence that Nixon was, in fact, acting improperly given the expectations for the role, in seeking a justice who would conform to an ideology rather than respect the Constitution.

A bigger and more lasting mistake was Nixon's attempt to "transform [a] shared constitutional power into, as he instructed Saxbe, the exclusive 'constitutional responsibility of the president' with Congress assigned the duty of endorsing the presidential choice" (Schlesinger 1973: 245). As with overreaching, presidents are advised to keep their arrogance, if not within bounds, then at least to themselves. Once Nixon made the issue one of constitutional powers between branches, he practically ensured his nominees' defeat. He also hurt himself because he lent credibility to the belief that he would act intemperately, if not imperially.

Presidents need a certain amount of good will and the cooperation it engenders in order to function in the office. They sacrifice that good will only to their cost. Nixon preferred to circumvent Congress whenever possible. When he had to face them, he did not take care to approach them as equally responsible and responsive professionals. Strategically, this was a mistake that all but guaranteed loss of good will and lack of interbranch cooperation. It was particularly lamentable in that the defeats came so early in Nixon's administration, thus helping to create an image of himself that would affect the remainder of his time in office.

RONALD REAGAN AND THE BORK NOMINATION

The Political and Institutional Context

Ronald Reagan assumed office in 1980 with the promise to "Bring America Back," to restore the United States to a position of military and economic dominance abroad and to the values of "family, work, neighborhood, peace, and freedom" at home. He brought with him a number of experienced and talented people, dedicated to the ideas of what would become known as "the Reagan Revolution," conservatives with a clear social and economic agenda (Noonan 1990; Stockman 1986). Although there exists considerable doubt as to what, if anything, the "Reagan Revolution" accomplished (Jones 1988; Kymlicka and Matthews 1988; Schwab 1991), there is little controversy over what Reagan stood for on the symbolic level (Muir 1988: 262).

Nothing was more important to the communication of Reagan's symbolic message than the mass media. Reagan understood the importance of mass media communication. He understood how television works, how to use it to his advantage, and how to structure his own appeals to best communicate through television, the dominant medium (Denton 1989).

Reagan—and his staff—understood that much of politics is theater, and they designed a presidency capable of taking full advantage of that understanding (Speakes 1988). This involved both relations with the media and appeals designed for the public. In dealing with the media, Reagan's people understood that the national media corps, despite its reputation for aggression, is in reality, "fundamentally passive" (Bonafede 1987; Hertsgaard 1989; Karp 1985; Tebbel and Watts 1985). This appearance of control over the media broke down as the Iran-contra revelations (see Chapter 1) became public. "The result was White House confusion. The President's staff became part of a growing communication problem. The media and the public pressed for details and the communication control that had marked his administration was not there" (Griscom 1989: 340). As a result, the media portrayed the president as inattentive, detached, and tentative. Reagan's competence was frequently called into question.

Because Reagan came to Washington with a clear and frequently enunciated ideological agenda, he aroused both strong support and intense opposition. The support stayed with him during most of the Iran-Contra affair; the opposition became even more vehemently opposed, seeing in the allegations proof of all that they had feared about a Reagan presidency. To make matters worse for the Reagan White

House, as of 1986, the Democrats regained control of the Senate, and Reagan's proposals, especially regarding appointments, were guaranteed close scrutiny. This was particularly true for Robert Bork, who as a result of his role in the "Saturday Night Massacre" (see Chapter 1) was guaranteed special attention from Senate Democrats.

This scrutiny was intensified with the approaching election. Reagan was in his second term and could not run again. His Vice President, George Bush, was perceived as vulnerable. The Democrats saw their best opportunity to regain the White House in years and had no intention of missing a chance to attack the Republican's main strength, Ronald Reagan.

In the midst of all this, Justice Lewis Powell resigned from the Supreme Court, giving Reagan his third opportunity to appoint a Supreme Court Justice. Powell was no ordinary justice; he had been the crucial swing vote on the Court, the pivotal figure maintaining a delicate ideological balance. The thought of as publicly committed an ideologue as Ronald Reagan replacing Powell with a justice of his own choosing made liberal blood run cold, especially as ideology was not considered an appropriate criterion for rejecting a candidate for the Court (Bronner 1989; Vatz and Windt 1987).

Liberals had good reason to fear another Reagan appointment. In Justices Sandra Day O'Connor and Antonin Scalia, Reagan had already replaced two liberal justices with committed conservatives. In elevating William H. Rehnquist to the Chief Justiceship, Reagan had placed control of the Court in the hands of a conservative. In his lower court appointments, Reagan had placed an unprecedented emphasis on ideology as a criterion for appointment. In fact, "Behind the campaign rhetoric and political symbolism, Reagan's administration had a more coherent and ambitious agenda for legal reform and judicial selection than any previous administration. Indeed, judges were viewed as instruments of presidential power and a way to ensure the President's legacy" (O'Brien 1988: 60).

Yet conservatives had good reason to fear that the Court, which they felt had long—and unfairly—been the province of liberals, would not become the province of conservatives without a fight. The Senate was controlled by the Democrats, which meant that the Judiciary Committee was chaired by a Democrat, in this case Joseph Biden (DE), who took over the Committee when the ranking Democrat, Edward Kennedy (MA), decided to chair Labor and Human Resources instead. During the years when Republicans controlled the Senate, Strom Thurmond (SC) chaired the Committee, giving the White House a valuable ally. It was not surprising that during Thurmond's tenure as chair the Judiciary Committee ratified nominees in record numbers and in record time.

The Rehnquist elevation from Associate Justice to Chief Justice was the most controversial of Reagan's appointments during that period. Despite Thurmond's leadership and the Republican control of the Senate, the opposition to Rehnquist managed to find 33 Senators to vote against the nomination—the largest number ever to oppose a sitting justice.

Thurmond was replaced as chair of the Judiciary Committee by Biden following the 1986 election. The calculus from the Republican point of view was complicated by the fact of Biden's presidential ambitions. He was running for president, and the public hearings on the next nominee to the Court were likely to provide a forum for Biden to assert himself as a viable contender for the Democratic nomination. Politics are never far from the nomination process. In this case, however, they were unusually apparent.

The Bork Nomination

On June 26, 1987, Associate Justice Lewis F. Powell stepped down as a member of the Court. Powell had been the pivotal vote on a divided Court 75% of the time in his last two years as a Justice (O'Brien 1988). On July 1, to no one's surprise, President Reagan nominated Judge Robert H. Bork of the U.S. Court of Appeals for Washington, DC as Powell's replacement. Bork had been a law professor and a judge and was widely considered to be competent, if not highly qualified, for a position on the Supreme Court. When announcing the nomination, Reagan (1987a) said, "Judge Bork is recognized as a premiere constitutional authority. His outstanding intellect and unrivaled scholarly credentials are reflected in his thoughtful examination of the broad legal issues of our times." It appeared to those both inside and outside of government that Bork would be confirmed in a walkover. Apparently no one predicted that it was precisely those qualifications that Reagan praised most highly that would cause the greatest difficulty for Bork.

The Reagan administration needed a victory. The Iran-Contra allegations were becoming more and more of a political problem for Reagan as the Senate hearings continued. Reagan's personal management style, his choice of aides, and the legality of his dealings were all under intense scrutiny. A quick confirmation in the same Senate that was holding hearings on the Iran-Contra affair seemed both possible and a viable means of reasserting badly damaged presidential strength.

It was not to turn out that way however. As soon as the Bork nomination became public, Senator Edward Kennedy immediately took to the Senate floor and denounced the nomination and Bork, saying:

Robert Bork's America is a land in which women would be forced into back alley abortions, blacks would sit at segregated lunch counters, rogue police could break down citizen's doors in midnight raids, schoolchildren could not be taught about evolution, writers and artists would be censored at the whim of the government, and the doors of the Federal courts would be shut on the fingers of millions of citizens for whom the judiciary is often the only protector of the individual rights that are the heart of our democracy. (McGuigan and Weyrich 1990: 14)

This was an unprecedented attack on a judicial nominee. Ideology is a difficult basis for rejecting any presidential nominee, especially a judicial one (Vatz and Windt 1987). To make ideology so clearly the issue so early in the confirmation process was so unusual as to have Bork's supporters feel that it was a serious error on Kennedy's part. They neglected to remember how astute a politician Kennedy is; if he took such a risk at this stage of his career, it was a calculated risk.

The risk paid off. More than 83 organizations followed Kennedy's denunciations with objections of their own, generating a campaign atmosphere around the hearings (O'Brien 1988). Group after group registered their dissatisfaction with the ideas, politics, and person of the nominee. Eventually, more than 300 national organizations joined in the loosely organized "Block Bork" coalition (Pertschuk and Schaetzel 1989). These organizations included the American Civil Liberties Union, which had never taken a position on a nominee to the Supreme Court before, and the AFL-CIO, which had not opposed a nominee since G. Harrold Carswell was defeated in 1970.

Reagan's staff could not, however, devote their full time and attention to Bork's troubles. On July 8, 1987, Marine Lieutenant Colonel Oliver North testified before the Senate concerning the Iran-Contra allegations. His testimony was a masterful performance and a lesson to the senators involved in how not to handle a hostile witness. North took the initiative away from the investigators and gave one ringing and patriotic speech after another.

Although North certainly helped to defuse the negative publicity created by the hearings, he indirectly hurt Bork's efforts. Bork was well known as a debater and as a persuasive and effective speaker. The Reagan people simply assumed that anything North could do, Bork could do better. They believed that Bork's superior intellectual and communicative ability would practically guarantee him the nomination. They thus made two mistakes; they did not adequately prepare their nominee, and they raised expectations regarding his probable performance.

Things did not look good for Bork on the public relations front either. An *Atlanta Constitution* poll of 12 Southern states showed 51%

opposed Bork; a *Washington Post*/ABC News poll showed that nationally 52% were opposed. All through the summer, while the president rest-
ed at his California ranch and his staff relaxed, secure in the knowledge
that the Bork appointment was all but assured, the opposition worked,
planned, and organized. They launched a public campaign against the
Bork nomination, sure that it was the "Book of Bork" that would lead to
the defeat of Bork: that his views, if widely known, would be widely
deplored (Pertschuk and Schaetzel 1989).

A week before the hearings were scheduled to begin, the vote of
the Select Committee on the Federal Judiciary, the body of the American
Bar Association charged with determining the fitness of presidential
nominees, was leaked to the media. Ten committee members voted Bork
"well qualified," four voted him "not qualified," and one voted "not
opposed." For the first time in 16 years, the Committee split its vote on a
Supreme Court nominee; for the first time in the 35-year history of the
ratings, a member voted "not qualified" (Bronner 1989: 205). The ratings
had the effect of undermining the basis for the Reagan administration's
defense of Bork: The Senate had to ignore his ideology because he was
so well qualified. If the extent of his qualifications could be opened to
doubt, then it was more legitimate to oppose his ideology.

The Bork hearings opened with unprecedented input from politicians, lobbyists, and even other justices. Gerald Ford introduced Bork to the
Committee. It was a good opening gambit, and one that one have been
more effective if Ford had not made it clear that he knew little of Bork's
record as a jurist (Pertschuk and Schaetzel 1989). Former Chief Justice
Warren Burger testified, as did sitting Associate Justices Stevens and White.

The most important testimony, however, came from Bork himself. Having been billed as the best show since Oliver North, Bork's
demeanor and performance were disappointing. He was given several
opportunities to sound the ringing phrases that would prove he was not
a strict constructionist monster, and that his America would not fit the
description offered by Senator Kennedy. He refused to take these opportunities and responded to questions with a dry legalistic approach that
seemed to confirm accusations that he lacked genuine human feeling.

A good example of this seeming lack of humanity occurred
when he was asked why he wanted to be on the Supreme Court, and he
replied that it would be "an intellectual feast." Although many justices
(including Powell) had referred at one time or another to the intellectual
stimulation of the Court, none of them had to contend with Bork's problem concerning ethos. With Bork already under fire, the remark
appeared as if he were unconcerned with the human consequences of
the Supreme Court's decisions. Bork thus unwittingly played directly
into the hands of those who wished to discredit him (Bronner 1989).

As the hearings continued, Biden found his presidential ambitions frustrated. First charges of plagiarism rocked his campaign, then accusations concerning his exaggeration and embellishment of his past record caused him to withdraw from the presidential race. Although this had the advantage of giving the Committee a full-time, focused Chair, it also created problems, for the ranking members on the Democratic side were Biden and Kennedy, neither of whom could claim an ethos of public morality or personal probity.

Reagan (1987b) finally spoke out forcefully and publicly on July 29, asking the audience of law enforcement officials to lobby for Bork, comparing the judge to Lewis Powell. It was, however, very little, very late. The Bork camp and many conservatives felt that the president and the White House were more interested in their broad agenda, and were consequently not doing enough to help Bork (McGuigan and Weyrich 1990).

On October 6, 1987, the Senate Judiciary committee voted 9-5 against the Bork nomination. In keeping with tradition, Committee Chair Biden asked the president if he wished to withdraw the nomination. Reagan refused. On October 21, the floor fight began. It was vituperative, nasty, and bitter. On October 23, 1987, Robert H. Bork's nomination as Associate Justice of the United States Supreme Court was defeated by a vote of 58-42, the largest margin ever. He became the 27th nominee to be defeated in the Senate.

A few weeks later, Douglas Ginsburg, faced with the certainty of becoming the 28th, withdrew his name from consideration after it was revealed that he had smoked marijuana occasionally in college and while a law professor. On November 1, Reagan tried for the third time to fill Powell's seat, this time nominating Anthony M. Kennedy. Kennedy was confirmed with a unanimous vote on February 3, 1988.

Bork's nomination and subsequent rejection reflected and created as much bad feeling and bitterness as any nomination ever has. How a White House so skilled in the use of communication and media politics could have let things get so far beyond their grasp in such a short period of time is discussed next.

Reagan's Strategy

Throughout the entire confirmation process, the White House kept the Justice Department at a distance, neglecting their advice and dominating the strategy and planning sessions. This hurt Bork because the denizens of the White House had an ideological and political agenda that extended beyond the Bork nomination and included the ideological goals of the entire Reagan administration. Although it was important to Bork and to his supporters that Bork be confirmed, it was important to the Reagan administration that a judge of a certain judicial philosophy be confirmed. This difference in viewpoints led the White House to make certain strategic choices that differed from those preferred by the Justice Department. The failure of the nomination thus led Bork's supporters to bitterness not only at their liberal opponents, but also at their conservative allies.

The White House thought that the Bork nomination would follow the pattern laid out by the fight to elevate Rehnquist from Associate to Chief Justice, that is, that it would be a struggle over the moderate northern Republicans and Southern Democrats. Reagan therefore concocted appeals to the center and played down Bork's association with the Right. This strategy accomplished two things. First, it confused potential supporters, for if Bork was a moderate, why was the conservative Reagan supporting him? Second, it left Bork and the administration open to charges of duplicity, for all of the available evidence—and there was a lot of available evidence—indicated that Bork was *not* a moderate, but was in fact a strong conservative. By attempting to position Bork as a moderate, the administration thus led credence to the opposition's argument that Bork could not be trusted.

The Reagan administration made another huge error in failing to understand that the battle ground had changed from previous nominations. As one analyst noted:

> The administration expected a difficult confirmation battle. It thought, however, that the fight would occur *inside* the hearing room, as it had with Rehnquist. All the while, it was priming its candidate on his role in Watergate and on technical legal issues. The country beyond Washington was virtually ignored until too late. While liberals had discovered an issue to embody their anger and frustration of seven years and were mobilizing their troops, the administration was in a state of confusion. (Bronner 1989: 187)

It is not that Reagan's staff failed to understand the nature of the problem. They knew that Bork was likely to be a very controversial nominee, and that there would be enormous opposition to him. They did not, however, anticipate the form that the opposition would take. Although believing that "the Bork nomination has taken on the aspects of a political campaign" (Ball 1987), the Reagan strategists thought that they could blame this "politicalization of the process" on the Democratic opposition to Bork, and thus win on both the nomination and the broader issue of how nominations should be handled.

Consequently, the Reagan strategy included what was by then a standard appeal to place "the public interest" above the special interests," who were threatening the republic through special pleading. A memo detailing "talking points" for the president's conversation with Warren Burger on Burger's testimony includes the following suggestion:

> I believe that your presence at the hearings will contribute toward a better understanding of what the Bork confirmation is all about. The question is whether the special interests will be able to defeat a highly qualified judge simply because he is not a sure vote for their cause—or whether the Senate will confirm to the Supreme Court one of the most outstanding nominees of our time. (Culvahouse and Griscom 1987)

But the "special interests" did not behave the way the White House predicted, thus undermining this appeal. Instead of mass protests, placard waving, and disruptions that could easily be turned to the nominee's advantage, the liberal opposition was well organized, well orchestrated, and responsible. They did not hit the streets; they did not engage in heavy-handed lobbying. The opposition to Bork thus grasped and kept the moderate position. When the Reagan White House began to call them shrill, it appeared like a political tactic on the administration's part, for they were not acting shrill. The Reagan position became the one that appeared overtly and unfortunately "political," whereas the opposition to Bork waged a campaign based on information and let Bork's record speak for itself.

That record was voluminous. "Bork's paper trail included his seventy-nine law review articles, newspaper and magazine articles since 1954, a book on anti-trust law, prior congressional testimony, eighty-four speeches in the past decade, and 150 court decisions" (Pertschuk and Schaetzel 1989: 63). The opponents of the Bork nomination compiled, analyzed, and disseminated this material.

Despite the growing public attention and concern focused on the nomination, the White House refused to consider the nomination in serious trouble and act accordingly. To be sure, the administration had its hands full with the Iran-Contra hearings and the subsequent Tower Commission Report, but they failed to use fully their most potent weapon, Ronald Reagan. Reagan certainly made his share of telephone calls to members of the Judiciary Committee and the Senate in general (Telephone Records 1987), but he did little to influence the nomination in the public arena.

Reagan finally became involved on July 29, when he spoke to a group of law enforcement officials. He defended Bork, his record, and his politics:

he has been widely acclaimed for his intellectual power and his fairness. No man in America, and few in history, have been as qualified to sit on the Supreme Court as Robert Bork. . . . If you want someone with Justice Powell's detachment and statesmanship you can't do better than Judge Bork. (Reagan 1987b)

This, however, was a case of preaching to the already converted, and it did little to help Bork. It may in fact have hurt him, for liberals were enraged by what they considered Reagan's duplicitous packaging of Bork as a Powell moderate.

Once Reagan was involved, he did step in with very standard rhetoric. As with much of his early presidential rhetoric (Stuckey 1990), Reagan attempted to label opponents as special interests, shift attention from Bork's judicial philosophy to the campaign to defeat him, and charge them with using illegitimate tactics. "His nomination is being opposed by some because he practices judicial restraint. Now, that means he won't put their opinions ahead of the law; he won't put his own opinions ahead of the law. And that's the way it should be" (Reagan 1987c). This appeared more than a little disingenuous when later, in Los Angeles, Reagan (1987d) praised Bork for his advocacy of a specific constitutional agenda:

It's time we reassert the fundamental principle of the purpose of criminal justice is to find the truth, not coddle criminals. The constitutional rights of the accused must be protected but so must the rights of our law-abiding citizens. During his distinguished career in law and public service, Robert Bork has demonstrated a genuine concern for the right of our citizens to live in safe communities and a clear understanding of the problems facing today's law enforcement professions.

Reagan then virtually ignored the Bork nomination for about a month, not speaking publicly again until September 25. This lack of attention hurt the nomination effort, for while the administration was silent, the opposition was very vocal, and their charges were heard without any real response. By the time Reagan began publicly condemning the liberal opposition, Bork had completed his testimony, and the damage had been done. All Reagan (1987e) could do was attempt to limit the damage:

Before the hearings began, there was a lot of talk by certain interest groups to the effect that Judge Bork was a political ideologue. On TV's across the Nation, those who tuned into the hearings saw something very different indeed. They saw a judge who impressively argued against ideology—and that is, against the current fashion in some legal circles that says a judge should bend the law to suit his own political agenda.

This may have been effective at undermining the legitimacy of the opposition to Bork, but this speech came too late. After Bork testified, it was less his ideology than his compassion that were at issue. By defending him against charges that were less relevant than they had been, Reagan was more effective at promoting a rationale for a certain judicial philosophy than he was at defending the nomination of Judge Bork.

Reagan himself appears to have realized that Bork could not be saved. On September 30, he (1987f) applauded the "noteworthy people who are coming forward" in support of Bork, but by then it was manifestly unlikely that their support could do any good.

An October 1 issue of the *Atlanta Constitution* carried results of a Roper poll revealing that 51% of Southerners, the group most likely to support Bork, opposed the Bork nomination, whereas a mere 31% were in favor of the nomination. The article concluded, "The results of the poll reflect a growing negative feeling toward Bork throughout the country. . . . Support for the nomination is borderline, even in the most conservative part of the country. . . . Of the 3,311 people who described themselves as politically conservative, 44% opposed his appointment" (Thompson 1987).

Reagan (1987g, 1987h) was reduced to deploring the nomination process as a "disgraceful situation. . . . I think that the process of confirming a Supreme Court Justice has been reduced to a political, partisan struggle." Deplorable, maybe; partisan, certainly. But the Bork nomination was not lost because Reagan faced liberal opposition in the Senate. He had faced such opposition before and had attained much of what he wanted. It was not lost because a group of unprincipled liberals saw that the president had been weakened by the Iran-Contra affair and, smelling blood, they moved in for the kill. The Bork nomination was lost because the Reagan White House believed that they could choose the forum for discussion, that the relevant forum would be the hearing rooms, and they were wrong.

Certainly, it was not unreasonable to assume that the nomination battle would occur in the hearings. That had been true for Rehnquist, and it had been true for other nominations. But that was before Lewis Powell retired from the Court. With Powell's departure, the stakes became frighteningly clear. Liberals seemed to wake up and realize that all of their gains could be lost.

The irony, of course, is that Justice Anthony Kennedy is, in all likelihood, every bit as conservative as Robert Bork. In that sense, when Reagan lost the Bork nomination, he lost a potential jurist who was likely to be a strong and influential intellectual force on the Court. But he did not lose the ideological battle. By the end of the Reagan administration, the balance of the Court was undeniably moving toward the conservative end of the spectrum. But Reagan did lose a long and protracted battle, and he lost it in a very public way. Substantively, Reagan may have come out ahead. Symbolically, he suffered a clear defeat.

Discussion

The Bork nomination hurt Reagan and his relationship with the Senate, for it created an enormous amount of ill will. Accusations of political misbehavior and underhandedness proliferated, and, as Reagan (1987b) himself said, trust between the branches suffered. Worse, from the president's point of view, however, is that Reagan's relationship within his own administration was hurt by the Bork nomination process. "The defeat was a major setback for the Justice Department and the administration. Bork, Meese, and others in the department were bitter, and blamed White House staff for not pushing hard enough for confirmation" (O'Brien 1988: 94). This blame led to a rift within the administration that Reagan could ill afford and helped to weaken the Reagan-Bush administration perilously close to the presidential election.

In his actions during the Bork nomination, Reagan confirmed many of his opponents' worst fears about the ideological implications of his administration. Despite all of the progress Republicans had made in distancing themselves from the more painful reminders of the Nixon years, when Reagan nominated Bork to the Court, he also appeared to many of his opponents to implicitly endorse the violations of law that had characterized the Nixon administration.

In addition, Reagan chose to believe that a judge with academic qualifications was sufficient; the content and tone of the publications themselves was not deemed worthy of attention. Furthermore, Reagan thought he could discredit the opposition without addressing the substance of their concerns, another act of apparent arrogance that further inflamed the opposition to Bork.

All these errors are attributable to one error: singularity. Reagan did not realize that he and Bork would be considered as extensions of one another. Reagan's opponents would blame Bork for Reagan's actions, and vice versa. In failing to protect Bork, Reagan's staff also failed to protect the president.

The Bork nomination is an even greater dilemma for later presidents than it was for Reagan however. The problems that Richard Nixon had with his nominees to the Court were generalizable only to Richard Nixon. The problems generated by the Bork nomination, on the other hand, affected the nomination process itself. Not only is a nominee's ideology now a fit subject for senatorial inquiry, but it is now acceptable to wage a nomination battle as if it were a political campaign rather than part of the governing process.

It is not coincidental that battle metaphors and the language of war have run throughout this section; such metaphors are suited to campaigns, if not to governance (Windt 1986). Nominations will now bear more resemblance to political campaigns, with the image presentation, orchestration of consent, and other tactics associated with "going public" (Kernell 1986), than they will resemble previous confirmation processes. The Tower nomination is a superb example of this result and its consequences for the president.

GEORGE BUSH AND THE TOWER NOMINATION

The Political and Institutional Context

When George Herbert Walker Bush assumed office in 1989, he was the first sitting vice president to succeed to the presidency since Martin van Buren in 1837. Despite this triumph, 1988 was not a particularly good year for Republicans. They lost seats in Congress: Democrats gained majorities of 10 seats in the Senate and 85 seats in the House. George Bush faced a Congress that was antagonistic to presidential power and the Republican agenda. His potential problems with Congress were deepened by the widespread Democratic resentment against the negativity of Bush's presidential campaign and the "perception that Bush's campaign played dirty pool" (Rockman 1991: 9). Willie Horton may have helped Bush win the 1988 election, but the ads featuring him made the president few friends among Democrats on the Hill. His lack of coattails within Republican ranks added to the weakness of his position (Bass 1992).

Bush's problems with Congress were exacerbated by his lack of any real mandate. The one clear theme of the 1988 presidential election was that it was an election that really had no theme (Blumenthal 1990; Rockman 1991). The election was characterized by a lack of attention to policy initiatives, little discussion of issues, and a great deal of posturing on both sides. George Bush's "mandate," such as it was, appeared to be "to continue the Reagan agenda in a more tempered way" (Rockman 1991: 3), to make the Reagan revolution "kinder and gentler."

In a very real sense, then, the Bush agenda was identical to the Reagan legacy (Berman and Jentleson 1991). Reagan left Bush a legacy of political achievement and popular success particularly difficult to match for several reasons. Politically, Reagan bequeathed Bush an ideological commitment to a reduced federal role in the affairs of the nation. Financially, Reagan left a deficit that limits government spending. Popularly, Reagan's style of rhetoric and communication, perhaps the harbinger of a new relationship between leaders and followers in the United States, challenges any successor. Bush's difficulties as Reagan's successor have led to a troubled relationship with moderates and liberals for not being "kinder and gentler" enough (Jones 1992), and with the right wing of the Republican party for not being ideological enough (Moen and Palmer 1992).

Bush's response to this legacy during the transition was to lower the presidential profile and to emphasize the virtues of "prudence." At the close of his inaugural address, Bush (1989a) said:

> Some see leadership as high drama and the sound of trumpets calling, and sometimes it is that. But I see history as a book with many pages, and each day we fill a page with hopefulness and meaning. The new breeze blows, a page turns, the story unfolds.

This type of rhetoric affected expectations of the president. In lowering his profile in general, Bush gave himself room to maneuver. He offered a standard of judgment that was not connected to Ronald Reagan, thus attempting to establish himself as "his own man" from the beginning. Because expectations concerning Bush were low, he benefitted from doing almost anything right (Edwards 1991).

Bush (1989a) also used the inaugural to establish what would be the theme of his early administration, the importance of being prudent:

> A profound cycle of turmoil and great change is sweeping the world from Poland to the Pacific. It is sometimes inspiring, as here in Warsaw, and sometimes it is agonizing, as in China today. But the magnitude of change we sense around the world compels us to look within ourselves and to God to forge a rare alloy of courage and restraint. The future beckons with both hope and uncertainty.

Partly this prudence was a response to the very real constraints placed on the government by the realities of the world situation and the budget deficit. Bush could not necessarily control—and was not even be able to influence—the changes occurring in much of the world. Instead of "talking tough," he talked prudently. Partly it was due to the fact that although Bush had some public support, his style was conciliatory, not confrontational (Kenski 1992). Facing a recalcitrant Congress and lacking a solid mandate, Bush did not want to raise the level of conflict.

Despite his extensive governmental resume, his eight years as vice president, and the recent election, George Bush in early 1989 was largely an unknown quantity. It was not clear what his agenda was or how he planned to pursue it. Pundits and politicians thus watched his initial Cabinet-level appointments very carefully, for it was felt that the clue to Bush's character and plans would be first revealed in his appointments (Duffy 1988).

The Tower Nomination

If George Bush's character was revealed by his nomination of John Tower as Secretary of Defense, the president would stand exposed as both impulsive and stubborn. The aftermath of the nomination also revealed him as a president who valued political capital over personal frustration. Of the three presidents discussed in this chapter, Bush is the only one who did not allow a failed appointment to significantly worsen his relations with Congress. Politically vulnerable, Bush realized how important his stance on bipartisanship was to his success as president. Although the nomination process itself hurt Bush, the damage was not allowed to create further problems for the new president.

On December 16, 1988, after his election to the presidency but before his inauguration, President-elect George Bush held a press conference at which he announced his new Cabinet. Former Texas Senator John Tower was Bush's choice for Secretary of Defense. This announcement was not met with universal approbation, although few people were surprised. Bush was known to prefer old friends and allies, and Tower had a considerable history with Bush.

Tower's doubters had positions both inside and outside of the Bush administration. Bush's old friend and Secretary of the Treasury-designate Nicholas Brady had opposed the nomination, as had Bush's vice presidential Chief of Staff Craig Fuller and pollster Robert Teeter (Woodward 1991). No one, however, could come up with a consensus alternative, and the nomination was duly announced.

The decision on Tower was an impulsive one, based on Bush's loyalty to their past association and Tower's past support. There had long been whispers and rumors concerning Tower's personal life, but when the preliminary FBI report discounted many of these allegations, Bush decided to go ahead with the nomination without waiting for the completed FBI report. It was a decision he would regret.

By early February, Washington was full of rumors, allegations, and charges concerning Tower's alleged womanizing and heavy drinking. The nomination, consequently, was in deep trouble (Biskupic 1989). Despite Gary Hart's experience, the womanizing charge was the one least likely to prove serious enough to endanger Tower's appointment. The alleged abuse of alcohol, on the other hand, if it could be substantiated, would mean disaster. To have a person in charge of the Pentagon who may or may not be sober was, at the very least, undesirable.

Once allegations concerning a political candidate or a political nominee become public, they either die down very quickly, or they are continually augmented by news of further charges, new indiscretions, or more information on old accusations (Pfau and Kenski 1990; Sabato 1991). In Tower's case, the allegations did not die down quickly. On February 7, C. Boyden Gray, Bush's White House counsel, and the man in charge of the White House side of the Tower confirmation hearings, heard about a new allegation linking Tower to corruption concerning defense contracts. As a result, Tower considered withdrawing his name from consideration. At Bush's request, Tower decided to "hang in" (Woodward 1991).

On February 8, Georgia Senator and Chair of the Senate Armed Services Committee Sam Nunn, previously uncommitted regarding the Tower nomination, was asked about the alcohol issue. He replied:

> It's a matter of a person in the chain of command that has control over the arsenal of the United States of America, and it's a very serious position as Secretary of Defense. The Secretary of Defense has to, in my view, have clarity of thought at all times. There's no such thing as an eight-hour day in that job. The young men and young women who defend our nation have to have people all the way up the chain of command that have entirely clear thought at all times. (Woodward 1991: 58)

If this was the job description, the information available to the public made it ominously clear that John Tower was not qualified for the position. It thus came as no surprise that on February 23, Nunn's committee voted 11-9 to recommend that the full Senate reject John Tower as Secretary of Defense.

At this point, one would expect the White House lobbying effort to intensify, as the nomination appeared headed for trouble in the full Senate. At the very least, one might expect that the president would look for another nominee, if he were not interested in salvaging Tower. Instead, Bush left for a tour of Asia, leaving Tower to fend for himself in the Senate.

On March 9, the Senate rejected John Tower by a vote of 53-47. The rejection of Tower was the first time any president in history lost an initial Cabinet appointment (Sinclair 1991). Bush was angry, he was upset, but he nonetheless avoided making a bad matter worse. He deplored the rejection of his nominee, but recognized that the Pentagon desperately needed someone in charge, and that he could ill afford another long, contentious confirmation battle. In addition, he may have realized fairly early on that the Tower nomination was doomed, and thus allowed the process to continue so as to appease the Republican Right while risking little of his own political capital.

On March 10, Bush announced the nomination of widely respected Representative Richard Cheney (R-WY) as Secretary of Defense. On March 14, the Senate Armed Services Committee voted 20-0 in support of Cheney's nomination. Cheney was confirmed by the full Senate on March 17 by a vote of 92-0.

Congress, however, could not let it rest there. Even though the initial furor over the Tower nomination died relatively quickly, in the wake of the Cheney confirmation and the NATO summit, both houses of Congress seemed determined to tear themselves to shreds as they hurled ethics violations at each other from across the partisan aisle. Bush remained relatively aloof, but partisan feeling ran high, and on domestic issues, this increased partisanship did not bode well for the new president.

Bush did many controversial and several unhelpful things concerning the Tower nomination. Tower's rejection and Bush's incapacity to avoid it hurt Bush (DeFrank 1989; Fly, Gleckman, Harbrecht, and Griffiths 1989; Klein 1989). The allegations and the persistent ethics questions wounded Congress as well as the president, for it began to appear that everyone in Washington lived in a glass house yet was determined to continue throwing stones. Congressional Republicans began to hurl ethics in Democratic faces, House Speaker Jim Wright resigned amid accusations concerning his finances, and the score appeared even.

Relations between the White House and Congressional Democrats seemed headed for certain disaster. There is little evidence that the two sides ever warmed up to one another, although once the arena switched from domestic to foreign affairs, the president enjoyed more support than was otherwise the case. But the Tower nomination and the ethics battle that followed it left a bad taste in many Senators' mouths, and it was particularly unfortunate from Bush's point of view that it came so early in his administration.

Bush's Strategy

The Tower hearings put the Bush administration in a particularly difficult position, for the president had talked long and loudly about the need to restore ethics to the national government. Once a key member of

Bush's administration was accused of ethical problems, the charges of hypocrisy were not far behind. At a news conference in early February, for instance, Bush was asked about the disparity between his speeches on ethics and the actions "involving members of the administration, or members-to-be of the administration." Bush (1989b) responded:

> I learned long ago in public life not to make judgments based on allegations. But having said that, I want to have my administration aspire to the highest possible ethical standards. . . . But I do think...that its fair that we not reach judgment on Senate hearings before the Senate hearings are concluded because it's very hard to filter out fact from fiction, spurious allegation from fact.

When pushed further about reports of new problems, including Tower's alleged loss of control over "highly classified security documents and computer disks," Bush simply denied knowledge of the new charges and refused to comment on "every rumor and innuendo." This was an attempt to undermine the legitimacy of the charges, which Bush claimed he had never heard of despite having access to legitimate sources (the FBI reports). If the accusations could be dismissed as "rumor and innuendo" instead of credible charges made by reasonable people, then Bush could have both his nominee and the high moral ground on the ethics issue.

Bush did stick by his nominee, even if he and his staff did little in the way of lobbying individual Senators on Tower's behalf. On February 8, Bush (1989c) said:

> I have seen nothing, not one substantive fact, that makes me change my mind about John Tower's ability to be Secretary of Defense, and be a very good one. And so, I have to ask you, because there's always some other allegation. And to my knowledge, each one of them has been reviewed and shot down in flames. So, what's fair? What is fair in the American process? That's the question I would rhetorically ask in defense of my nominee.

Bush here responded to the nomination process as it has been politically charged in the aftermath of the Bork nomination. Presidents—especially Republican presidents—can hope to get some serious rhetorical mileage out of impeaching the process if their nominees are damaged by that process. It is very easy for them to accuse the Senate of acting "politically" and thus unfairly toward nominees who have a different philosophy than the majority of the Democratically controlled Senate.

Bush (1989c) then asked for "prompt fulfillment of the responsibilities of the Senate committee, prompt action by the United States

Senate, and then a broad appeal for fair-play." The implication here was that the Senate committee was somehow acting improperly, irresponsibly, by refusing to take prompt action. Bush did not go so far as to indict the investigatory process, but he did express concern that the public airing of unconfirmed and unproven allegations could—and had—damaged the reputation of the nominee.

Bush's efforts to discredit the process was hampered by the national reputation and probity of Sam Nunn (D-GA), chair of the Senate Armed Services Committee and the man in charge of the Tower hearings. Whereas during the Bork nomination the Democrats were disadvantaged by the presence of Ted Kennedy and the accusations against Joe Biden, the Republicans had a different communicative problem with Nunn. The evidence is that the White House underestimated Nunn (Smith 1992), and that this helped cost them the nomination. Nunn was scrupulously fair and made sure that the process could not be seriously damaged. In fact, Nunn's conduct of the hearings restored some integrity to a process that had been undermined during the Reagan appointments confrontations.

Throughout the hearing process, Bush volunteered little or nothing on behalf of his nominee. All the president's remarks on Tower, in support of Tower, came in the form of answers to questions posed at news conferences. This, of course, does not mean that Bush and his staff were not active behind the scenes, although there is little evidence that they were. But even so, the important decision for the Tower nomination, as for most nominations in the post-Bork era, was going to be made in public, and publicly Bush was supportive of but removed from his nominee. Bush (1989d) persisted in claiming that his nominee was receiving "unfair treatment," and that the facts did not bear out the allegations. But his support was, given the intensity of the concern about Tower's nomination, tepid at best.

Worse, from Tower's perspective, Bush decided to leave the country in late February and visit Japan, the Republic of Korea, and China. Although the president was in Asia, the confirmation hearings continued. The Democrats were there, Tower was there, but the president, Tower's main hope now that the nomination was a matter of public contention, was absent.

This absence seemed to indicate that the president had better things to do than get his Secretary of Defense-designate confirmed. For a president to leave the country so soon after his inauguration is very unusual. For him to leave it in the middle of a political controversy that affects his administration is even more rare. For him to do so and not pay a political price is beyond the bounds of imagination. Bush appeared unconcerned about the fate of his nominee. He was content with gesturing toward the process as the culprit, without being personally invested in the outcome.

　　This brought up several misgivings that were already current concerning Bush and his devotion to principle (Malecha and Reagan 1992). He had assumed Reagan's ideological mantle, but whereas everyone knew what Reagan stood for, and what he stood against, it was difficult to know that about George Bush. Bush did not seem terribly committed to anything, although he did appear willing to make the requisite gestures. His treatment of John Tower seemed to confirm the image of Bush as a man with no real commitment.

　　To the extent that Bush did indicate commitment, it was to the principle of fair play and to the spirit of bipartisanship. There was no screaming and threatening after Tower's rejection as there had been after the Senate rejected Haynsworth or Bork. Instead, Bush (1989e) commended Tower for his "dignity and lack of rancor" rather than for his importance as a symbol of the cause. George Bush is no ideologue, and in the Tower rejection, Bush revealed himself as a man able to cut his losses and move on. Because of that, he had a Secretary of Defense within a week and managed to avoid an outbreak of hostilities between the White House and the Senate.

Discussion

Bush was very lucky in the timing of the Tower rejection. Immediately after the vote, Bush went to the NATO summit, and foreign policy consensus dominated the news, so that Bush was not punished publicly for his failures regarding the Tower nomination. In the eyes of potential supporters and allies on the Hill, however, Bush's initial support for Tower, his failure to follow through and give his nominee the attention he deserved, did nothing to encourage support or respect for George Bush. Most members of Congress are professionals. They want to be treated professionally and be surrounded by other professionals.

　　Although it was certainly a point in his favor that Bush did not try to inflame people on Tower's behalf, the Senate did have cause to wonder about Bush's level of commitment. With Reagan, if one were to fight him, one had to fight. He would compromise, he would deal, he would accommodate. But it was up to the opposition to create the need for accommodation. With George Bush, there appeared to be no line he would not cross, no issue that he would really stand for. This was an ominous signal to send a Congress controlled by the opposite party; during Bush's attempts at budget making and other domestic issues, it hurt him time and again.

Bush and Tower were, for a time, synonymous. What could be said about one, reflected on the other. That Bush would propose an old friend, regardless of qualifications, and then provide him with such weak support, spoke volumes about Bush's character and its fitness for the role of president. He seemed to waver, to lack commitment, to be unsure of his ground, to be more political than principled. In all these areas, Bush had to work hard to overcome the initial impression created in part by the Tower nomination.

CONCLUSIONS

Presidents can be wounded at the margins of their images by a failure to understand either the mechanics or the implications of the appointments process, for failing to understand that they and their nominees are for a time, at least, considered extensions of the presidential character. This is particularly important at the beginning of a presidential term, for the nominations process is the first real look the nation gets at how the president will define himself as president, how he sees himself carrying out the institutional role.

Mechanically, presidents are notoriously defensive about their powers and prerogatives. They sometimes fail to remember that Senators are equally defensive of *their* powers and prerogatives. Worse, they fail to remember that it is appropriate that Senators defend their constitutional privileges. Presidents who have difficulty with the appointments process are presidents who assume too much. They take the process as a matter of right and prerogative rather than as a matter of compromise and communication between branches. When handled well, appointments can build bridges between the branches, bridges that the president may one day find very useful. When handled poorly, however, communicative chasms remain or are enlarged.

The implications of the process are as important as the mechanical details. The public perception of a nominee's character affects the perception of the president's character. Presidents are at least partially understood by the company they keep; their nominees to high governmental office are important members of that company. The presidency is a plural office; presidents who behave as if their actions are the only ones that can affect the perception of their character and fitness for the presidential role are presidents who will commit the error of singularity. They are also presidents who are likely to face a public rebuke for that error.

Handling the process well has become increasingly difficult as the appointments process has become ever more the province of governmental "outsiders," who see in appointments threats and opportunities for their own agendas. The Tower nomination battle may well have been made possible by the increasing focus on the private lives and personal predilections of government officials. The Bork nomination heralded an era of politicized confirmation hearings, in which a nominee's ideology and personal life can be expected to encounter close and attentive scrutiny. Although this can make a nominee's life very difficult for a time, and although everyone deplores this trend (while continuing to participate in it when it suits them), it is not clear that standards of ethics are to be universally deplored.

What is clear is that the nomination process has changed. George Bush, a Washington insider with enormous governmental experience, was not prepared for this change. He seemed to believe that the traditions he was accustomed to would continue forever. He was wrong. The confirmation process, for better or worse, is now one that more closely resembles campaigning than it does the processes of governance. Like most of the routines that involve the White House, media attention and the techniques of "going public" are increasingly important. Confirmation is no longer an event that concerns only government insiders who control the process. It involves the public, and it thus involves public politics. Presidents who ignore or fail to understand this do so at their peril.

3

Mismanagement: Failed Congressional Relations

Presidents define themselves and are defined not only in relation to the mass public, but also in relation to the other institutions of the national government. These two relationships are not distinct, but are mutually reinforcing. How presidents strategically approach their relationships with Congress can have tremendous impact on how they are perceived both in Congress and among the broader electorate.

The presidential role vis-à-vis Congress is particularly complicated. Public expectations of the president as a legislative agent increased under Franklin D. Roosevelt and have remained high. Yet whereas the president is, on the one hand, expected to exercise leadership in the legislative arena, on the other hand, the president is given neither constitutional nor legal authority to act unilaterally (Bond and Fleisher 1990). Presidents, as Richard Neustadt (1990) wrote, cannot command. They can only persuade. Presidents do have formidable advantages and tools to assist them in their persuasive task, but they also have impressive constraints. This is not the proper forum for a complete discussion of these advantages and constraints, but a brief summary of the pertinent institutional and political factors influencing presidential relations with Congress that will provide a useful context for a discussion of failed presidential strategies in Congress.

One of the most important constraints relevant to presidents regarding their relationship with Congress is the nature of the federal system. Whether it is a system of separated powers or separate institutions that share power (Neustadt 1990), the members of the legislative branch have developed different goals, different priorities, and different perspectives from those of the executive branch (Edwards 1980; Fisher 1987; Polsby 1976).

This is partly due to the different time frames associated with the branches. Presidents are elected to four-year terms and have (at most) eight years in office. Senators serve six-year terms and Representatives two years at a time. This structural design was intended to accommodate the potentially conflicting needs of stability and responsiveness, but the differing temporal orientations caused by the varying electoral cycles increase the strategic pressure on the president.

Another important source of conflict between the branches is the diffuse nature of congressional power. Only rarely can 535 people, split into two different Houses, each with its own organizational peculiarities, speak with a united voice. Each House is fragmented. Worse, from the president's perspective, they are fragmented in different ways, increasing the complexity of the coalition-building task (Edwards 1980; Seligman and Covington 1989).

Additionally, Congress serves local constituencies, whereas the president's constituency is national (Edwards 1980). This means that the members of the two branches have different sets of priorities, which can create many strategic problems. The most important issues from most Representative's point of view will be what affects their constituents (Fenno 1978). Those are not likely to be the same issues affecting the president (Buchanan 1991).

Finally, presidential strategic difficulties with Congress are exacerbated by the partisan structure of the federal government (Schlesinger 1973). In 1960, Richard Neustadt noted that, "what the Constitution separates our political parties do not combine" (29). Although some research indicates that the fact of divided government may not be as inimical as conventional wisdom suggests (Mayhew 1991), with the White House generally in Republican hands and the Congress usually controlled by Democrats, there is little reason for the branches to cooperate. In a context of particularly difficult national problems, there are, in fact, sound political reasons for not cooperating—it is easier to shift blame if collaboration is avoided.

George Edwards (1980) found that "the president is in a weak position with regards to Congress. His burdens are great and his assets are few" (205). But the president is not completely powerless. Relations between presidents and Congress are not always characterized by conflict and animosity, nor do they always devolve into acrimonious stalemate. Presidents and members of Congress need one another, for neither can get anything accomplished without the other (Neustadt 1990).

Additionally, despite the fact of divided government, many individual members of Congress share the president's ideological and programmatic goals.

There is also persuasive evidence that members of Congress may cooperate with the president for purely instrumental reasons. Opposing a president, particularly a popular president, can cost a Senator or Representative his or her reelection. Few are willing to risk that unless it is a matter of principle vitally important to them (Mayhew 1974).

Presidential relations with Congress are a complex and intricate web composed of many strands of connecting and conflicting interests. An enormous body of political science literature is devoted to this topic (Bowles 1987; Edwards 1985; King 1983; Pritchard 1983; Rivers and Rose 1985; Rohde and Simon 1985), and a detailed discussion of it is beyond the scope of this book. By focusing on three cases when presidential strategies regarding Congress failed, we hope to increase our understanding of the relationship between the branches and how it affects and is affected by presidential character as it adapts to the complexities of the presidential role in legislation.

FRANKLIN D. ROOSEVELT'S ATTEMPTED CONGRESSIONAL PURGE

The Political and Institutional Context

In 1936, Franklin D. Roosevelt (FDR) was elected to the second of what would be a record four terms. He was elected by the largest plurality of votes in any presidential election, losing only two states (Vermont and Maine) and obtaining an electoral college majority of 523 to 8. Whereas his popular support was high, the same could not be said for his relations with Congress (Pechatnov 1987) or with the media (Winfield 1990). As a consequence, FDR came to rely heavily on his relationship with the electorate to motivate and threaten the other branches of government. But, as FDR was to learn, public politics can be a dangerous weapon.

Early in his second term, Roosevelt attempted what has become known as "the court-packing plan," in which he attempted to circumvent the "nine old men" on the U.S. Supreme Court and "save" liberal New Deal policies. It was a dismal failure, both instrumentally in allowing FDR to appoint more justices to the Court and strategically in Roosevelt's long-term relationship with Congress (see Chapter 4). By furnishing Congress with the opportunity to firmly and publicly rebuke—and thus weaken—him vis-à-vis Congress (Savage 1991), the court-packing failure also provided "moral justification for Roosevelt's enemies in both parties, but particularly his own, to oppose the entire New Deal program in 1937" (Wolfskill and Hudson 1969: 269). Thus, by overreaching the boundaries of his political authority regarding the Court, FDR sabotaged himself in Congress, one of the two important communicative forums of his presidency.

Roosevelt in 1937 had other troubles as well, some not entirely of his own devising. The Great Depression that began in the late 1920s lingered into the 1930s, despite the Roosevelt administration's frenetic policymaking. The national economy, which had been growing steadily albeit slowly, suffered a sharp setback in 1937. The "Roosevelt recession" was interpreted by some as a clear repudiation of Roosevelt's economic policies (Wolfskill and Hudson 1969).

A rash of strikes beginning in 1936 compounded concern over the economy. The United Auto Workers sit-down strike at a General Motors plant in 1936 was particularly worrisome, as was the threatened strike of the steel industry in 1937. Both areas were the symbolic core of American industrial strength, and the threat to paralyze those industries was a very powerful one, made more so by the fact that they occurred without official union sanction—sometimes without even official union knowledge. Roosevelt, who was in principle a supporter of organized labor, was no fan of John L. Lewis or of the "unauthorized" strikes (Zinn 1980).

The labor strife had particular importance for Roosevelt, for he was trying to build a national political party (Pechatnov 1987). Despite his class-based rhetoric, Roosevelt knew that to build a national constituency he needed support from both business and labor. Operating in an environment that increasingly emphasized the differences between the two groups, Roosevelt found himself in a correspondingly constrained position. An astute politician, he was tempted to stick to the middle ground and thus hoped to lose as little moderate and conservative support as possible. This moderate position cost him support among both pro-business and pro-labor factions however. It finally became completely untenable in April 1938 when Robert LaFollette of Wisconsin announced the formation of a third party, the "National Progressives of America." This party, led as it was by the most famous "progressive" force in the country, posed a serious threat to Roosevelt, who was now accused by the Right of creating the recession through his antibusiness policies and by the Left for not taking decisive enough action against business and lacking real sympathy for labor.

The new party also posed a very real threat to the Democrats as a national party in the 1938 congressional elections, for they could syphon off enough support in key areas to allow Republican victories and seriously undermine the Democratic majorities in Congress. As Roosevelt's perspective was a persistently national one, this was a dangerous time for him and for his party, and he knew it.

At the same time, events in Europe demanded increasing amounts of the president's attention. The compromise and conciliation of Munich gave way as German troops marched into the Sudentenland and Austria. The beginnings of World War II helped to convince Roosevelt that only a united nation could survive. Nationalism and the importance of collective action on a national scale became crucial themes in his rhetoric (Stuckey 1991).

This belief in the importance of nationalism made opposition to his policies in the media and judicial and legislative intransigence all the more frustrating for Roosevelt. Believing as he did that he spoke for the entire nation, and with the recent election results providing strong evidence of his popularity, it was easy for FDR to conclude that he was right and that those opposing him were not only wrong, but posed a danger to democracy. Such faulty logic seems to be an occupational hazard of American presidents (Buchanan 1978). In Roosevelt's case, this logic led him first to challenge the Supreme Court and then to challenge Congress.

There is evidence that when presidents act to increase their institutional prerogatives at the expense of the other branches, they are often successful (Rockman 1984). They tend to be most successful in times of national crisis (Windt 1987). In the absence of such crises, the members of the other branches are likely to defend their institutional duties and constitutional responsibilities.

It is a sign of Roosevelt's political acumen that he sought to place the congressional purge in the language of crisis. Yet he did not fully adapt the strategy surrounding the purge to the requirements of the genre. Roosevelt failed to convince either of his two audiences that a crisis was imminent. He thus opened himself up to charges of rash, unconstitutional, and even dictatorial behavior; charges that, given events in Europe, had a particularly strong resonance and that helped to weaken the public perception of his character as well suited for the presidential role. That a politician and a communicator as astute as Franklin Roosevelt could have gotten himself into a position whereby his critics could, not only with impunity, but also with apparently sound reasoning, liken him to Hitler, provides powerful evidence for the importance of a solid political and communicative strategy.

The 1938 Congressional Purge

FDR in his second term was interested both in establishing the New Deal as a permanent part of the national government (Wann 1987) and in establishing the Democratic party as the national vehicle of the New Deal. He had both programmatic and political goals, and because of the 1936 election results, he believed that the vast majority of the electorate agreed with those goals. He was frustrated in the accomplishment of those goals by an anti-New Deal congressional coalition. By the middle of his second term, Roosevelt was irritated with members of Congress in general and conservative Democrats in Congress in particular.

Roosevelt's complaint was clear and appeared on the surface, quite reasonable. He felt that many of the Democrats who opposed him in 1937-1938 had been elected, or in some cases reelected, in 1936 on the strength of his coattails and out of generalized support for the New Deal. For these people to then turn their backs on the New Deal was, to FDR, both insolent and antidemocratic (Ryan 1988).

With partisan majorities in both Houses of Congress, FDR sent to them a reform agenda in early 1937. It was quickly and decisively rejected. Two pieces of legislation were of particular interest to the president: the Governmental Reorganization Bill and the Wages and Hours Act. The first formally provided the president with an official White House staff. The second offered some minimum wage protection for hourly workers and was strongly opposed by business interests. In the South, where union organization was limited and "open shops" dominated, the Act was an anathema. Rage at this opposition helped to propel FDR into active participation in the 1938 congressional purge.

The purge proper began with the Florida senatorial primary. Roosevelt put his considerable charm and influence to work on liberal Claude Pepper's behalf. Pepper's somewhat surprising primary victory convinced Roosevelt that intervention in the primaries was a viable means of eliminating his conservative enemies (Berman 1987).

Once the decision to inaugurate the purge was made, the actual announcement had to be made. On June 24, FDR broadcast a Fireside Chat. In it, he sharply criticized conservative Democrats and announced that he would become personally involved in the upcoming congressional elections. This Fireside Chat was particularly important, for this was Roosevelt's opportunity to definitively set the agenda and influence the interpretive context for his involvement in the primaries.

These days, the presidency has become so politicized an institution that we expect presidents to be involved in political campaigns at all levels of government. Indeed, presidents who fail to perform this celebratory and legitimating function for the electorate and their partisan colleagues will have violated the expectations of the office. In the 1930s, however, the presidency was not nearly so politicized nor personalized an office. Presidents were expected to remain above politics; violating that expectation was politically dangerous.

Even today, presidents tend to avoid embroiling themselves in primary battles. Presidential involvement in an intraparty fight must be justified. Furthermore, such involvement must be justified in clear and principled terms. This, as Halford Ryan (1988) noted, is precisely what Roosevelt failed to do. As a result, Roosevelt was excoriated by the media following the June 24th Fireside Chat.

Media criticism notwithstanding, Roosevelt went ahead with the purge. The first real struggle involved the question of wording: "Purge" came from the newspapers, with its imputations of Hitler and Stalin, which incensed Roosevelt. Essentially, once the dispute over the label was over, and Roosevelt's plan was clearly and consistently called a "purge," the outcome was all but inevitable. Given events in Europe and charges of incipient dictatorship at home, few Americans were likely to support a "purge." Roosevelt failed to recognize the dangers for his publicly perceived character as he became associated with a "purge," and he continued to act as if his definition of events was the only relevant definition, thus contributing to the negative perception of his character.

That negative perception was particularly important among those Americans residing in the South. Although congressional elections tend to be about local rather than national issues (Fenno 1978; Mayhew 1974; O'Neill 1987), what is true for the nation as a whole is doubly true for the South. Predominantly rural, lacking strong networks related to industrialization, much of the South was outside of the national economy. Culturally, the South was also outside of the northern mainstream. As a region, the South could be expected to vote Democratic. It could also be expected to vote for conservative candidates. Finally, the South could be expected to resist the imposition of federal will on local affairs.

All these expectations were fulfilled, with disastrous results for Roosevelt. Only one targeted incumbent was defeated. Republicans did better nationally than at any time since the early 1920s, winning 81 new seats in the House. Republicans also picked up 8 seats in the Senate and 13 new governorships (Winfield 1990). Worse, by enacting the attempted purge, FDR had seemingly confirmed conservatives' fears about an incipient dictatorship. By focusing on Congress, FDR allowed his opposition to unite self-interest with institutional interest, and they were doubly motivated to fend off what they regarded as Roosevelt's unwarranted attack on them and their institution. An examination of FDR's strategy surrounding the purge can help determine how FDR lost control of the definitional process and allowed the interpretation of his character to shift from one of strong leadership to one of incipient dictatorship.

Roosevelt's Strategy

The most important thing to remember about Roosevelt's strategy during the 1938 attempted purge is that, in a very real sense, there *was* no strategy worthy of the name. Mismanagement begins with the neglect of the basics of persuasion. Roosevelt failed to target all the conservative Democrats, and he failed to use consistent tactics across campaigns (Ryan 1988). By refusing to approach the purge strategically, Roosevelt allowed his opponents to control the agenda. Furthermore, because he was trying to move the nation from locally to nationally dominated politics, Roosevelt's failure to understand and act on the influence of localism in congressional elections provided the appearance of inconsistency, which was very confusing to the electorate and to his potential supporters in Congress. Worse, the appearance of inconsistency contributed to the image of Roosevelt as acting personally rather than presidentially, an image that in turn made the accusations of dictatorial behavior more credible.

Roosevelt sent mixed signals regarding his attitude toward Congress. He began the June 24th Fireside Chat, for instance, by recounting "the most important . . . achievements of the recent legislative session" (Roosevelt 1938a). It was not a short list. This was the start of the consistency problem, for if there were so many achievements, why was FDR upset? Roosevelt left no doubt that he was upset, for he referred to his congressional opposition as "Copperheads," saying that, "you will remember that it was the Copperheads who, in the days of the War Between the States, tried to make Lincoln and his Congress give up the fight, let the nation remain split in two." In addition to the inflammatory nature of this attack, it was an appeal hardly likely to win Roosevelt's support in the South. Nevertheless, Roosevelt (1938b) thus likened himself to Lincoln, his task to the Civil War, a parallel that he continued throughout the purge. He also clearly indicated that any divisiveness was attributable to his opposition, not to Roosevelt himself. Although this tactic worked well for Roosevelt when he made class-based appeals, as in his famous "money-changers" speech, it was Southerners who were not likely to respond to an appeal based on accepting the blame for national divisiveness, either in the 1860s or in the 1930s.

Roosevelt (1938a) then moved to the specifics of his talk, and outlined his task as he understood it: "It is because you are not satisfied, and I am not satisfied, with the progress we have made in finally solving our business and agricultural and social problems. . . . In simple frankness and in simple honesty, I need all the help I can get." The "help" Roosevelt sought was in "matters of principle in all parties. . . . It is my hope that anybody affiliated with any party will vote in the primaries, and that every such voter will consider the fundamental principles for which his party is on record."

He then outlined the difference between those partisan principles, "the liberal school of thought recognizes that the new conditions throughout the world call for new remedies," and asserted, "as President of the United States, I am not asking the voters of the country to vote for Democrats . . . nor am I, as President, taking part in Democratic primaries. As the head of the Democratic Party, however . . . I feel that I have every right" to speak when it involves "principles or . . . a clear misuse of my own name." Roosevelt attempted to inoculate the audience against associating the purge with "any single issue," but his whole stance as party leader rather than as president was patently absurd. That absurdity and obvious disingenuousness provided grounds for suspicion rather than proof against such suspicion.

More grounds for suspicion concerning Roosevelt's motives became apparent. On a trip through the South in July 1938, Roosevelt clearly assumed that his personal ties to Georgia would resonate with a Southern audience, that as "one of them" his motivations would be assumed benign—especially because his "interest" was accompanied by hefty amounts of federal largesse. Despite the assertion that "this interest is far more than a sentimental attachment born of considerable residence in your section and of close personal friendship with many of your people" (Roosevelt 1938c), this assertion of common identity was not sufficient, particularly when the opposition was a "real" local.

Not only did FDR lose on the localism issue; localism became a powerful weapon against the president. Southerners' fears of "Carpetbaggers" more than matched the national fear of "Copperheads." Roosevelt, despite—perhaps because of—his economic incentives, was resented as a nationalistic force operating in what should have been a strictly local election. Given Roosevelt's rhetoric, this interpretation is certainly easy to understand. In Oklahoma City, for example, he said, "I have to think along national lines and, in the last analysis, you do too. It is essential, of course, that if the national policies of the National Administration are to be carried forward, there must be a general agreement on those policies among those who are responsible for the legislation that makes them possible" (Roosevelt 1938d). Similar appeals filled his speeches throughout July and August (Roosevelt 1938e, 1938f). It is not a natural logical leap for Southerners to assume that their local or regional interest is identical to that of the nation as defined by a Northern politician.

In Georgia, Roosevelt (1938f) further confused the issues by asserting that even though Senator George was not part of "the liberal school of thought," the president and the senator would "always be good personal friends." This was clearly an attempt to counter charges of personal vindictiveness, and it clearly did not work. George likened

Roosevelt's actions to Sherman's "March on Georgia," thus casting the friendship in serious doubt, and providing a powerful campaign appeal (Savage 1991). George won both the primary and the ensuing general election.

Ryan (1988) presented an astute analysis of why Roosevelt's strategy concerning the 1938 congressional purge failed, and listed five reasons for the failure. In the first place, although FDR *claimed* that the nation was facing a serious and urgent threat, nothing in the rest of his speeches or in the overall national environment supported this claim. Second, Roosevelt allowed "charges of vindictiveness" to overshadow the issue of principle. That is, nearly all of the targets of the purge had sided against Roosevelt in the battle over the Supreme Court. By attempting to have his opposition removed, Roosevelt appeared to be playing the pettiest of politics. The presidential role demands dispassionate behavior on the part of the president. When presidents take politics personally, they undermine their own strongest advantage—the nonpolitical role of president.

This appearance was, for Ryan, supported by the third reason for the purge's strategic failure, which is that Roosevelt attacked the *character* of his opponents' rather than their policies. Although Roosevelt clearly felt personally as well as politically abused by the conservative Democrats, he indulged himself and allowed expression of those personal feelings to dominate discussions that he claimed were properly devoted to policy. This created both confusion and suspicion, undermining the thrust of the argument Roosevelt was trying to make.

Ryan's fourth point is that FDR assumed that he was "not only the *vox populi* but also the voice of the Democratic party" (137). Presidents tend to assume that they are the most legitimate—and sometimes that they are the only legitimate—voice in the country or in their party. FDR was sharply reproved by both Congress and the American electorate for falling prey to this belief.

Finally, Ryan believes that FDR miscalculated, and that he believed that "his personal popularity transcended the separation of powers doctrine" (137). For Roosevelt, the results of the 1936 election gave him a "mandate," clear public sanction of his politics and his policies.

Ryan's list emphasizes the importance of Roosevelt's public character. Roosevelt acted as if his image of himself was both widely shared and immutable, when in fact it was neither. He failed to understand that a president's public character is fluid, subject to change as the context changes, as presidents and their allies and opponents act. It was not sufficient for Roosevelt to assume that either his intentions or his character were beyond question.

Discussion

The president sits alone as the guardian of the "national interest." Only the president sees the issues from a national perspective. But like all perspectives, this one has blind spots. One of those blind spots was clearly evident in Roosevelt's attempted congressional purge. The purge succeeded in defeating a grand total of one targeted incumbent, Representative John J. O'Connor of New York. His defeat, although a major victory for the president (O'Connor had been Chair of the very powerful House Rules Committee, a major obstacle for New Deal legislation), probably had less to do with support for Roosevelt personally or the New Deal programmatically and more to do "with efficient exploitation of local political factors" (Savage 1991: 152).

Presidents who see the national implications of issues and elections are potentially blind to the power of local political factors. Presidents see themselves as the center of the known universe. The impulse to evaluate all matters in terms of the narrow vision imposed by their complicated political calculus is all but irresistible (Kernell 1986; Lowi 1985; Tulis 1987).

This is a particularly important problem insofar as Congress is concerned, for members of Congress can often feel institutionally, personally, or politically bound to confront the president. Presidents who assume that all such confrontations are the product of willful malice are presidents who are bound to create a poor relationship with Congress. Presidents have a tendency, evident in this single case, to assume that communication on Pennsylvania Avenue only needs to run in one direction—that anything else is a favor, a product of *noblesse oblige* on the part of the president. This is, to say the least, a poor understanding of congressional-presidential relations.

Roosevelt's interference in local affairs—particularly in the South—was badly conceived and widely resented (Price and Boskin 1966). Although "Roosevelt's failure to defeat the southern conservative incumbents did not represent a rejection of the New Deal and Roosevelt's party leadership" (Savage 1991: 154), it did him little good with either of the electorate or the other main forum for presidential persuasion, Congress.

However the voters saw the 1938 purge campaign, members of Congress saw it as a definite and offensive encroachment by the chief executive on their prerogatives and power. At least one analyst believes that the purge helped to strengthen the conservative coalition of Republicans and Southern Democrats that would last for another 30 years (Milkes 1984), although this is a matter of some controversy (Savage 1991).

Whatever the long-term effects of the failed purge, in the short term, it helped to foster an environment of mistrust and acrimony between the president and Congress. The environment in which communication occurs is a key determinant of the tone and style of the communication (Nimmo and Swanson 1990). Presidents are usually keenly aware of this, and they work very hard to structure political situations to their advantage. But sometimes, the very act of attempting to control the situation can be a powerful message—and one that is likely to be powerfully resisted by Congress. Members of Congress have loyalties to their careers, their constituents, their colleagues, and their institutions as well as to their presidents. This is not something that any president is well served by forgetting. These complicated loyalties are facts, supported and encouraged by the formal structure and informal practices of the federal government.

There are more ways of forgetting how complex and demanding a place Congress is than by simply and boldly challenging members to a power struggle. As the next case study indicates, poor relationships between presidents and Congress are not always the result of presidents who are confused about their place in the federal system. Sometimes, as in Gerald Ford's case, presidents are confused about Congress' appropriate role and organizational requirements as well.

GERALD R. FORD'S WIN CAMPAIGN

The Political and Institutional Context

For Gerald Ford to ignore the institutional requirements of Congress was particularly surprising, because he had been a member of the House and part of the House leadership for years before his unusual ascension to the presidency. The circumstances surrounding that ascension are a major part of the political context for the WIN campaign.

When Vice President Spiro T. Agnew resigned after pleading no contest to charges of tax fraud in his home state of Maryland, President Richard Nixon needed to replace him. Moreover, he needed to replace him with someone who could bolster the administration's badly damaged reputation. He picked Gerald R. Ford (R-MI). Ford's nomination was announced on October 12, 1973, six days into the Yom Kippur War.

Nixon, attempting to cope with the crisis created by the war while fending off assaults on his power and his presidency, gave Ford little of his time and less of his attention (White 1975). As Nixon's presidency increasingly degenerated into a battle for his political survival, fewer and fewer non-Watergate-related matters received presidential concern. Ford's staff, like most of the nation, realized that Nixon's days in office were numbered. Ford (1979) himself, anxious to avoid any appearance of impropriety, remained distant and aloof from the consequent political maneuvering.

When Ford became president, therefore, there had been very little planning or preparation for the transition (Pfiffner 1988). As a new president, Ford had not been sanctioned by the electorate; he could not therefore claim any sort of "mandate" to justify and legitimate his policy preferences (Porter 1988). Ford, as Richard Neustadt (1990) noted, was in a particularly difficult position:

> Succeeding a disgraced man, but not himself legitimated by a popular election, Ford needed to assure the continuity of the office by his demonstrated *difference* from his predecessor. This called . . . for unquestionable decency. That he managed to convey for just a month, then blurred it when he pardoned Nixon, who had not yet been indicted. (259; emphasis in original; see also Porter 1988).

Watergate and the subsequent Nixon pardon combined to leave Ford, a man previously remarkable for his reputation for probity, tarnished. Given the hostile mood of Congress and the national fear of a strong executive abusing power, in some senses, the smartest thing Ford could have done was nothing. Yet he was president; the impetus of the office is toward presidential action.

Action, however, was difficult. Despite Ford's willingness to pursue open and candid relations with Congress, his use of the phone and stress on personal contact with members (Wayne 1978), Congress was in no mood to reciprocate. Partially, this had to do with the legacy of the Nixon administration and Nixon's extraordinarily hostile dealings with denizens of the Hill (Reeves 1976). Partially, it had to do with the fact of a Democratic Congress feeling its power (DiClerico 1990). And partially, it had to do with the difference in priorities and preferences between the Republicans in the White House and the Democrats in Congress.

Whatever the reason, Ford's relations with Congress remained amiable on the surface, but there was little bipartisan action. The two branches did more checking and balancing than cooperating during the mid-1970s, and "Ford used the veto as an offensive weapon—a first strike capability against Democratic legislation" (Berman 1987: 295; see also Wayne 1978). He vetoed 66 bills during his short term in office. Congress responded to this unusual use of the veto with an equally unusual high percentage of vetoes overridden, overriding 12 of the 66 vetoes, including the Budget and Impoundment Control Act and the War Powers Resolution, both of which were designed to redress the balance of power between Congress and the president and provide Congress with an institutionalized rather than informal consultative role.

Ford had other problems besides his relations with Congress however. As part of the trend begun at least as early as Franklin Roosevelt's administration, the national media were an increasingly important audience for national leaders. In Ford's case, this created many problems, for the media felt newly powerful and powerfully legitimated as a result of their role in exposing the improprieties and illegalities of the Nixon White House. Ford had to be very conscious of his image, and he had to consciously design that image essentially from scratch, for in the arena of national politics he was a virtual unknown. This consciousness extended to the staging of presidential news conferences and other symbolic and ceremonial aspects of the office (Ford 1979).

Ford's attempt to design an image that was open, accessible, and yet also presidential was not an unmitigated success. In fact, it could hardly be termed a success at all:

> One Ford insider remembers an article that was published at that time (I think in *The New Republic*) called "The Flowering of Contempt" about how, as a result of Watergate and Vietnam, we had grown contemptuous of our leaders, and were therefore contemptuous in the way we covered them in the media. Ford was the first victim of that attitude. (Nessen 1988: 187)

In addition to overt hostility from the media, Ford also had to deal with his image as an incompetent, clumsy stumbler. This image began after he fell from an airplane ramp in Salzburg, Austria, and became an ongoing image problem for the Ford presidency. In part, this may be due to a suspicion among the press that Ford was not up to the job. They then looked for ways to convey that suspicion to the television audience. In part, it was due to the Ford administration's inability to focus his administration in an intelligible way.

Ford's problems with a recalcitrant Congress and an uncooperative media were reflected and exacerbated by his dealings with the administrative bureaucracy. Ever since the governmental reorganization bill passed during FDR's second term, the administrative bureaucracy surrounding the White House had been increasing steadily. President Nixon, frustrated with what he perceived as a politically motivated and entrenched opposition in the bureaucracy, attempted to circumvent it and created a "counterbureaucracy" via the White House staff (Nathan

1982). Ford thus not only had to contend with opposition from the administrative departments, a problem that faced all modern Republican presidents, but also with the remaining Nixon staffers in the White House, a problem unique to Ford.

In the administrative departments, the growth and burgeoning dominance of interest groups were becoming serious barriers to action by executive fiat (Lowi 1979). These groups became entrenched within the bureaucracy and the subcommittee structure within Congress and powerful political forces, no less powerful because they operated outside the corridors of electoral politics. Neither Ford nor his staff were prepared for or ultimately able to contend with these interests, which, circumvented by Nixon, assisted Congress in its bid to regain some discretion over policymaking from the executive.

Ford's staff, like that of other vice presidents who assumed office without benefit of an intervening election, was an uncomfortable combination of the ex-president's staff and his own personal staff. In Ford's case, his personal staff had little time to adapt to the massive changes associated with moving from the congressional level to the new and expanded duties of the vice presidency. Before they had even been able to accommodate themselves to their new offices, they became the presidential staff and could be, as one Ford watcher remarked, "most charitably described as being in over their collective heads" (Reeves 1976: 24).

Most presidents prefer to surround themselves with people they trust. This generally means that they surround themselves with people they have known a long time, people who have experienced both the highs and lows of electoral politics with them. It does not tend to mean that presidents are served by those most able to dispense advice, most competent in an issue area, most dispassionate about the president's proposed course of action. Presidents prefer those loyal to them personally rather than those loyal to the presidency as an institution (Pfiffner 1988).

In Ford's case, this meant that he had two White House staffs: those who were members of the Nixon administration and who still hoped to accomplish some of the goals associated with that administration; and his own staff, inexperienced in executive politics and ignorant of the national implications of the staff decisions. The two staffs did not exactly mesh well (Hartmann 1980), increasing the political pressure on Ford without increasing his ability to respond to that pressure.

Ford assumed the presidency under a particularly difficult set of circumstances. Nixon had just left the office in disgrace, Congress was more dominant than they had been since Roosevelt, and the partisan division between the presidency and Congress exacerbated the tension. Although willing to be open and accommodating, Ford also attempted to assert his leadership over Congress, which increased the tension between the branches. In addition, the Nixon holdovers on his staff and his pardon of the ex-president undermined Ford's image as a man of decency and honor and increased speculation that he had attained the vice presidency as the result of a "deal" with Nixon.

As a result, Ford never seemed to find his stride as president, but lurched and stumbled from one situation to another, promising continuity and difference, accommodation and leadership, openness and action. He thus created strategic difficulties by failing to structure expectations in an intelligible and predictable way. This failing is readily apparent in the 1974 "Whip Inflation Now" (WIN) public campaign.

The WIN Campaign

As Gerald Ford took office, the national economy was suffering from slow growth and high inflation. In 1974, "prices and wages were increasing at an annual rate of nearly 17 percent, far too high to produce stable growth" (Denton and Woodward 1990: 4). The traditional Republican answer to the problem of inflation was to control prices and wages. Ford liked neither of these options, thus alienating potential Republican supporters in Congress.

Early in his presidency, and as a result of congressional insistence, Ford convened an "economic summit" to discuss the problem of the economy and solicit advice. Participants included members of the bureaucracy, Congress, and the public. Ford himself attended most of the official sessions.

In his first news conference as president, and in his first speech before a joint session of Congress, Ford highlighted the economy as the dominant area requiring presidential attention. In part, this may have been an attempt to refocus the national image of the presidency away from Richard Nixon and onto Gerald Ford. Nixon had been primarily concerned with foreign policy; he and Secretary of State Henry Kissinger had allowed foreign policy to dominate the Nixon presidency until Watergate. Nixon's focus on foreign policy was so absolute, in fact, that some Nixon supporters claimed that it was his attention to foreign matters that allowed Nixon to lose his sense of perspective on domestic issues, thus allowing his aides to perpetrate Watergate.

Whatever the truth behind Watergate, by turning his attention to the national economy, Ford emphasized an area that had received little of Nixon's notice, and he could thus begin his administration with an area relatively free from Nixon's taint. It was also an area badly in need of attention. In the early 1970s, the first signs of transition from an industrial economy to a service economy were being felt if not understood; slow growth and unemployment were matters of concern. For Ford, economic growth and unemployment were problems, but the root problem was inflation. If inflation could be controlled, economic growth would be encouraged, and new jobs would inevitably be created.

Ford took office in August and immediately announced his intention to curb inflation. But announcing intentions and creating policies are two different things. Although he got a decent amount of advice from the economic summit, much of that advice conflicted. More importantly, Ford realized that he needed more than a policy, he also needed a way to sell that policy to Congress and the public.

For Ford, the policy amounted to a program of volunteer national action, much like the National Recovery Administration (NRA) under Roosevelt. He wanted a symbol, like the NRA's blue eagle, to mobilize and advertise his anti-inflation program. Ford apparently had forgotten that the NRA was not an unmitigated success, and that the contrived nature of the program contributed to its controversial nature. Thus, when a member of his staff announced a plan to design and promote a symbolic campaign, Ford (1979) found the idea "intriguing."

The rationale behind the WIN campaign was that "the best way to implement a voluntary citizen's program to combat inflation . . . was to have a campaign with a symbol" (Ford 1979: 194). That symbol was a button marked "WIN," which was intended to facilitate public information and education as well as public motivation. The WIN symbol would be awarded to those who had engaged in public service by prominently displaying forms of belt tightening and encouraging less spending. The Ford White House went overboard on the "campaign" aspect of the WIN program, suggesting things like a presidential presentation of a WIN flag to "a company or group that goes beyond the call of duty in the WIN field" (Korologos 1974) and prompting one aide to write the President of ASCAP requesting that an Irving Berlin-style songwriter produce a WIN song:

> The purpose of a song would be to help create and sustain a battle psychology and a patriotic spirit of fighting a common foe. . . . Melodies like "Bridge on the River Kwai," or "Over There" come to mind as spirited marching types that could fill the role. or, a catchy tune like "Tie a Yellow Ribbon," is also a possibility. . . . Would it be possible to have arrangements for country and rock? These two areas are so popular now. (Freeburg 1974a)

That no one at the White House boggled at the notion of a rock version of "Bridge on the River Kwai" was an indication of how effective they were to be at selling WIN to the nation. Other examples abound. They include an ad campaign using race car drivers to promote gas conservation (Petty 1974) and a request that the Penn State Nittany lions wear

WIN buttons while on the sidelines of the Cotton Bowl (*New York Times* 1975).

The WIN campaign was announced on October 8, in a televised address before a joint session of Congress. The address was scheduled for 4:00 p.m. eastern time, timing that was hardly likely to produce a national audience. The speech itself was less a format for the announcement of WIN than it was a recitation of the evils of inflation and a laundry list for proposed legislation. Ford chose to present a public campaign in a legislative format and legislation within the context of a public campaign. The result was that neither audience seemed to have a clear idea of what was expected of them; consequently, neither audience responded to Ford's appeal.

Ford did not give up however. On October 15, he went to Kansas City, MO, and delivered another nationally televised address, although the networks did not consider the speech "newsworthy," and the White House was forced to formally request television time (Nessen 1974). Again, Ford stressed the need for voluntary and national action to combat inflation. But inflation is just not one of the issues people tend to be willing to mobilize around. Given a war, an international enemy, or a clearly definable crisis at home, mobilization of the public is at least potentially feasible. But it is difficult to portray an element as impersonal as inflation as an enemy that justifies a national call to arms. In the aftermath of Vietnam, such a call was not likely to be welcomed under any circumstances. The Ford administration, however, thought otherwise:

> The problem that exists is complex. Through a series of emotional disasters from the assassination of John Kennedy to the resignation of Richard Nixon, the American people have become cynical and skeptical. The nation is fragmented and tired. In inflation, there is a common enemy. (Freeburg 1974b)

Ford and his WIN campaign received little support in the national media, who preferred disease metaphors to war imagery (Baroody 1975; Stelzner 1987). Had Ford decided to adapt to the media-proffered interpretation and call for mobilization against a national epidemic, his campaign might possibly have enjoyed at least a little more success. Instead, Ford chose to continue with the war metaphor that was challenged or ignored by the media.

Ford's timing for the WIN campaign was disastrous. He announced a war on inflation just as the national economy slid into a recession, further complicating the economic picture and creating widespread public concern over unemployment (Davis 1987). This meant that Ford had to work doubly hard to focus national attention on inflation as a cause of concern. By ignoring what the media and the electorate saw as the dominant concern, Ford allowed himself to be perceived as out of touch.

Nevertheless, Ford kept insisting that he was a national leader and then defining that leadership in terms of public behavior. These two elements are inconsistent for they place the proof of presidential leadership in the public's behavior—proof that lies outside of presidential control. This can be particularly problematic in an era when the public is already disaffected with their leadership and already saturated with messages from the Capital, as was the case in 1974. After Watergate and Vietnam, many Americans wanted a respite from national politics. To call for massive public mobilization at such a time was to beg for rejection.

Rejection is exactly what Ford and the WIN campaign received. As a result of the WIN campaign, "Ford's reputation slumped, his prestige was already falling, and the media bore down on him" (Neustadt 1990: 259). The failed campaign thus increased Ford's difficulties with Congress and the electorate. It did so because he risked so much of his personal reputation on it and then failed to attain anything significant. How that came about is the subject of the next section.

Ford's Strategy

Presidents are credited—and blamed—for events that occur during their tenure in office, whether they created the circumstances or not. Part of Ford's difficulty with the WIN campaign was bad timing. Ford announced a war on inflation just as the country slid into a recession. But most of Ford's problems were self-inflicted. Ford entered the presidency with extraordinary flexibility regarding his public character. A relative unknown nationally, he could essentially create himself publicly. But this was also an important liability. His first actions in office, before he learned the job, became magnified. His pardon of Richard Nixon and his inability to function smoothly and effectively from the beginning created a negative impression of him personally and of his presidency politically. Lacking a well-known political past and an image of strength and ability with Congress, that initial impression was difficult to overcome.

Three days into his presidency, Ford addressed a joint session of Congress. In his speech, he highlighted the issues that he thought would dominate his presidency. By discussing them in such a way, at such a time, he gave those issues dominance and priority that they might not otherwise have had. After asking for "unity in diversity," and pledging to keep his "door open to Congress," he stated that even though "the state of the union is excellent . . . the state of our economy is not so good" (Ford 1974a).

Despite the depressing message of his speech, Ford attempted to get his relationship with Congress off to a good start, saying, "Mr. Speaker, I am a little late getting around to it, but confession is good for the soul. I have sometimes voted to spend more taxpayer's money for worthy Federal projects in Grand Rapids, Michigan, while I vigorously opposed wasteful spending boondoggles in Oklahoma." Here, he reminded members of Congress that he had been one of them, that he understood their perspectives and their motivations. He sought common ground with the Democratically controlled Congress: "You and I have always stood together against unwarranted cuts in national defense. This is no time to change that nonpartisan policy."

His commonality with the audience established, Ford moved back to the real topic of the speech, the economy. He called inflation his "first priority" and thus accepted the responsibility for reducing it: "To restore economic confidence, the Government in Washington must provide some leadership. It does no good to blame the public for spending too much when the Government is spending too much." Note that last sentence, for it is a lesson that Ford was to forget later, as much of his rhetoric on WIN would, in fact, appear to blame the public.

On August 28, Ford (1974b) held his first news conference as president. Ford's first problem was the agenda, as the press were interested in Watergate, and Ford was confused and unable to contain the topic. Inflation also figured prominently, as Ford called it "public enemy number one." When asked if he had any plans to control inflation, however, Ford said only that the government would be spending less. He added, "We are collecting other ideas from labor, from management, from agriculture, from a wide variety of the segments of our population to see if they have any better ideas for us to win the battle against inflation." This statement did two things: It undermined the image of Ford's leadership while reinforcing the notion of an open and collegial presidency, and it began Ford's use of the war metaphor for the inflation campaign.

In terms of his leadership, Ford concentrated heavily on the notion of separation between himself and Nixon. He was going to be a different sort of president, an open, honest, and cooperative president. His early use of staging and symbolism contributed to this effort (Stuckey 1991). The problem with this image is that it is difficult to portray oneself as the strong and decisive leader when concentrating on being open, accessible, and collegial. The more one listens to others and profits from their advice, the less one can claim individual credit for accomplishments. And in the contemporary presidency, individual credit is important.

Second, Ford introduced the war metaphor regarding inflation. In an insightful analysis, Hermann Stelzner (1987) argued that the war metaphor failed because in the aftermath of Vietnam, the nation was not likely to respond to more war rhetoric, and because even within the rhetorical framework constructed by the war metaphor, Ford stressed volunteerism rather than government action. Finally, "though inflation was the clearly designated enemy, Ford could not portray the severity of the crisis and did not propose short term, precise, realistic incentives for engaging the enemy" (Stelzner 1987: 300). If Ford's description of the problem was accurate, his proposed solutions were clearly inadequate to the task. Ford thus invited the country to participate in a war without the proper tools to win it. In the context provided by the intense conflict over the Vietnam War and the reasons for the American defeat there, this was hardly an invitation that was likely to be joyously accepted.

The problems with the war metaphor were cogently spelled out by one White House aide:

> This is not the day after Pearl Harbor. There is no Axis whose target coordinates are known. There are no beaches to hit or ships to sink or ports to capture by which we may know, week by week, whether we are winning or losing. This is the day after Hugh Hefner and instant credit and barbecue grills and two cars in every garage and other great acquisitive expectations. And, simultaneously, it is also the day after OPEC and the Third World and global interdependence and, yes, the balance of terror. Given these realities can WIN really win? Can WIN even help? Maybe. (Hartmann 1974: 1)

The memo went on to indicate that the president needed to choose and then follow a clear and concentrated strategy if the WIN program was to have any hope of survival: "Frankly, it is not enough to merely offer advice, encourage local initiative, and then hope that grass roots support will emerge and translate your entreaties into prompt, effective action" (Hartmann 1974: 3). At first, it appeared that Ford took this advice to heart.

Ford used his early appearances as president to define the national agenda, placing inflation and the economy at the top of the national priority list. This could have been a valuable use of presidential priming; a few hints here, a few hints there, a sense that an issue area is important, culminating in a legislative program that would solve the problem as the president has defined it. Priming can be a powerful tool of presidential persuasion, for it is how presidents can get their definition of a problem—and thus their solution to that problem—accepted by Congress and the public. Ford's problem was not with the priming; it was in the follow through. After placing inflation at the top of the agenda, he then proposed no real solution to it as a national problem.

On October 8, Ford (1974c) again addressed a (nationally televised) joint session of Congress, wearing a WIN button on his lapel. He began his speech with a direct quote from Franklin Roosevelt, saying: "The people of the United States have not failed. . . . They want direct, vigorous action, and they have asked for discipline and direction under our leadership." He noted that the current "economic difficulties" were not as severe as the Depression, but added that "the message from the American people is exactly the same. . . . Our constituents want leadership, our constituents want action." Here, by citing FDR, Ford depended on symbolic parallelism to launch WIN, which was supposed to bring Roosevelt's NRA and its blue eagle to mind. The parallelism was either too subtle or too poorly presented, for the connection was never made in either the media's or the public's mind (Hartmann 1980).

Ford then did an interesting thing, one unusual for president. He said (1974c), "All of us have heard much talk on this very floor about Congress recovering its rightful share of national leadership. I now intend to offer you that chance." Ford was offering also a clear recognition that with Vietnam and Watergate, presidential power and prerogatives were under attack. Congress was willing and (given the number of his vetoes that would be overridden) apparently able to recapture some of the power that they had been busily ceding to the president since the days of Franklin Roosevelt.

Ford's early quote from Roosevelt thus provided a nice symmetry, because he was relying on an implicit use of symbols associated with Roosevelt to "offer" Congress "a chance" to regain some of the power they had lost under Roosevelt's leadership. That power was clearly now the president's to "offer" back to Congress. This "chance" for Congress to recover national leadership was a product of a crisis, which for Ford meant: "We must whip inflation right now." He also said (1974c): "None of the remedies proposed, great or small, compulsory or voluntary, stands a chance unless they are combined in a considered package, in a concerted effort, in a grand design." After this build-up, the audience was prepared for a listing of this grand design, perhaps along the line of early New Deal legislation, and, indeed, after a slightly puzzling reference to the need for international cooperation (something Congress could hardly be expected to enact as legislation), Ford detailed 10 "areas for joint action." The problem was that in all these areas, despite his request for congressional leadership, he presented little that could take the form of legislation, which is, after all, the sort of action one would expect Congress to take.

Most importantly, Ford refused to even consider the traditional Republican weapons against inflation—wage and price controls (Stelzner 1987)—thus violating the expectations and traditions of his own party in Congress (Rozell 1990: 419). He could thus clearly delineate an enemy—inflation. But he could not pinpoint a cause for the problem, so no obvious solution presented itself.

In the absence of a structural cause (wages and prices), Ford was left with human agency: consumer spending. He thus did what he claimed in his first speech before Congress he would not do: blame the public for spending. Now that he had found a cause, the solution was readily apparent. The American public had to stop spending and save energy:

> Here is what we must do, what each and every one of you can do: To help increase food and lower prices, grow more and waste less; to help save scarce fuel in the energy crisis, drive less, heat less; Every housewife knows almost exactly how much she spent for food last week. If you cannot spare a penny from your food budget—and I know there are many—surely you can cut the food you waste by five percent. . . . I think there is one final thing that all Americans can do, rich or poor, and that is share with others. We can share burdens as we can share blessings. . . . I ask you to share everything you can and a little bit more. And it will strengthen our spirits as well as our economy. (1974c)

This section of the speech served reasonably well as a call for national unity. But as a call for direct action against "public enemy number one," it was laughable. Ford (1974d) seemed to assume that the American public was constituted as a massive volunteer army, waiting only the president's command to begin marching down the road of self-sacrifice, for he continued to stress volunteerism as the way to lower inflation. This is a poor comprehension of presidential persuasion. Not only did Ford fail to provide inspirational rhetoric to galvanize the public, but he failed to recognize that such rhetoric was even necessary. Sacrifice is notoriously difficult to inspire and is possible only in the presence of clear necessity, which is why presidents seeking sacrifices often point to or rhetorically create the presence of crisis (Windt and Ingold 1987).

Large-scale crises must be met with large-scale action. Yet, even though Ford called inflation a large-scale crisis, as Robert E. Denton and Gary Woodward (1990: 5) point out, "No recommendation was too small for a presidential endorsement." In his Kansas City address on the subject of inflation, for example, Ford's attempts at personalizing energy concerns merely trivialized them:

> From Hillsboro, Oregon, the Stevens family writes they are fixing up their bikes to do the family errands. . . . Bob Cantrell, a 14-year-old in Pasadena California, gave up his stereo to save energy. . . . Kathy Daly, a student at Sacred Heart High School in Weymouth, Massachusetts, has one formula for shopping wisely and saving

energy. Kathy suggests buying warmer clothes this winter. . . .
Sylvia Porter tells me that $10 worth of seeds on a 25'-by-30' plot
will grow $290 worth of vegetables. (Ford 1974e)

This attempt to personalize economic matters fell far short
because Ford failed to provide a central theme through which the commonality could become clear. Instead he provided little examples and
sounded more like a column for "Hints from Heloise" than presidential
speech. The dissonance thus created did neither Ford nor his recommendations any good.

Ford's problems with the WIN campaign were at least partially
attributable to his definition of the problem. He sought legislative remedies for what he saw as a problem of consumer behavior. As a result, he
looked incompetent and uncertain of his leadership task. Neither of
these appearances were good for his relationship with either Congress
or the American electorate.

Discussion

Ford made several important mistakes with the WIN campaign: He
placed the power of his office and staked his political prestige on a "policy" that he could neither enact nor completely control; he did not provide appropriate follow through to make sure that what he could control was done effectively (Hartmann 1980: 299-300); he used a war
metaphor inappropriately and ineffectively (Stelzner 1987); and he
talked in terms of crisis while offering small-scale solutions (Denton and
Woodward 1990: 5). Finally, Ford sought to use Congress as a forum for
public persuasion, a use to which Congress is poorly suited.

If public persuasion is the goal, then presidents do better when
Congress forms part of the background for the persuasive act as the
main forum—as when Ronald Reagan spoke *in* Congress but *to* the public on the subject of tax reform. Ford spoke *in* Congress and *to* Congress,
but expected the television audience to react as participants rather than
viewers.

By giving inflation the stature of "public enemy number one,"
and announcing the WIN campaign as he did, Ford risked a considerable amount of his political prestige on the outcome of the fight against
inflation. As a result of his unconventional ascension to the presidency
and the lack of a national political mandate or constituency, Ford did not
have all that much prestige to risk. If Neustadt is right, and the presidency is an office characterized by weakness rather than strength, presidents should try to cultivate their sources of power and not risk that
power unnecessarily. Ford's experience with WIN certainly provides

solid evidence for Neustadt's argument. In first risking and then not following through on that risk to ensure success, Ford lost not only the fight against inflation, but undermined his future presidency and relations with Congress as well.

Members of Congress had little incentive to cooperate with Ford before the disastrous WIN campaign. After WIN, they had even less reason. WIN made Ford look both feckless and incompetent at a time when he could afford neither. His attempt to make the presidency open and accessible, while important in the aftermath of Vietnam and Watergate, did little to bolster his image as a strong leader.

Members of Congress need strong leaders in the White House, for the president is a valuable foil for them, either as an ally or as an opponent. A president who refuses to play either the hero or the villain frustrates Congress, for that president deprives individual members of a way to define themselves. The president is the best-known member of the federal government. When presidents are clear about who they are and what they want, it is easier for members of Congress to define themselves in relation to the president. Ford could, at least potentially, have used his stance on the economy as a way to define himself in the national mind. He failed, and in failing, created a definition of himself as an incompetent. That image was readily transmitted through the media as this most athletic of presidents was constantly seen stumbling, tripping, and falling.

Administratively, Ford could have done more in advocating and pursuing anti-inflationary policies and in communicating those policies—and their success, whether real or contrived—to Congress and the public. But neither he nor his staff seemed able to do so. Thus, they took the risk, and instead of working to see that they did not lose as a result, they apparently chose to treat it as a gamble whose outcome was beyond their control.

In Roosevelt's case, I argued that presidents attempt to control too much, and that can lead to communicative and political disaster. Presidents can, however, control some events and some perceptions of those events. Failure to attempt and accomplish such control can lead to communicative and political failure. The difficulty is for presidents to heed their environments rather than their preferences and determine what they can and cannot control.

Ford's choice of the war metaphor was badly conceived and poorly implemented. Given the political context in which his administration was embedded, Ford would have done better to use a metaphor that had fewer associations with the recent—and divided—past. Vietnam was not a war of national unity, but it was the country's most recent war. The use of the war metaphor thus conjured up images of a divided rather than a united nation. It was a poor choice for a president seeking united action.

By using the war metaphor, Ford attempted to give inflation in the stature of a national crisis. As with the war metaphor generally, given the political context, the appeal to yet another crisis was not likely to arouse the electorate. In a nation that had withstood the war in Vietnam, the national protests against the war, the civil rights movement, the assassinations of the Kennedys, Malcolm X, and Martin Luther King, Jr., the generalized unrest of the 1960s, and then Watergate, the notion that inflation was a crisis on a comparable scale served only to persuade them that Ford lacked perspective. This is not an image likely to contribute to presidential influence with either Congress or the electorate.

Finally, Ford used Congress as a forum for trying to influence public behavior. He announced WIN and the call for massive national volunteerism in a speech before a joint session of Congress, a forum in which he would normally be expected to call for congressional action. In that speech, he did call for such action, but in such a way as to obscure the relationship between national legislation and national volunteerism. Lacking a clear analysis and description of the enemy, no one was sure how to go about combatting that enemy.

Ford thus sabotaged himself with both Congress and the American electorate through his inept handling of the WIN campaign. Admittedly, as president, Ford was in a particularly difficult position. He lacked a mandate, he lacked a constituency, and he lacked a clear agenda. Given his unusual path to the presidency, he can perhaps be excused for failing to handle certain aspects of the office as well as his supporters might have wished. It is interesting that his successor in the office, a man who had actively sought the presidency for several years before attaining the office, could, with so much time to prepare and plan and a normal period of transition, make so many of the same mistakes. Yet, as the case of Carter's energy plan indicates, that is exactly what happened.

JIMMY CARTER'S ENERGY PLAN

The Political and Institutional Context

Conventional wisdom has it that without Richard Nixon, there would have been no Jimmy Carter, because Nixon, the consummate insider, left a cynical distrust for insiders behind as he left office. This distrust flared into anger as another insider, Gerald Ford, pardoned Nixon. The combination of an "insider's" war in Vietnam and an "insider's" scandal in Watergate opened national politics to the appeal of "outsiders."

Carter's character as an outsider was crucial to his election in 1976. He ran on a moralistic platform of ensuring "a government as good as the American people" and promised "never to lie, never mislead" the American people. He acted as if his character was both the necessary and the sufficient condition for a successful presidency, as if the requirements of the presidential role could be met by electing the appropriate character to the presidency.

Compounding the problem was Carter's status as an outsider to Washington. Carter understood little about the politics of federal policy-making. From his first days in office, he showed little sensitivity toward Congress, believing that he could simply bulldoze through them as he had in Georgia as Governor (DiClerico 1990). He was wrong. The Georgia legislature is a comparatively small body. The national Congress is not. And the national Congress Jimmy Carter was faced with was fragmented, characterized by increasingly weak party discipline and diffuse loci of power and increasingly susceptible to the influence of special interests and group pressures.

Ironically, the same fragmentation among the Democrats and the rising influence of television that had made Carter's rise to the presidency possible made it more difficult for him to govern as president. There was a history of contention between Congress and the president, and little or no shared programs that served to unite the Democrats as a party (Jordan 1981).

Carter compounded his own weakness in understanding the institutional organization of Congress by appointing an equally naive Congressional liaison. The liaison office is an important element in congressional-executive relations, for it is the office that is responsible for the care and nurturing of executive coalitions in Congress. Not only did Carter's liaison staff fail to understand their responsibility, but this failure was actively supported by the president. The liaison office was further hampered by its internal organization. Instead of organizing along regional lines in recognition of the informal networks and coalitions that govern Congress, Carter's liaison office was organized along issue lines (E. Davis 1979; J. Davis 1987).

This already poor strategic arrangement was buttressed on the other end of Pennsylvania Avenue, where the Democratically controlled Congress, thirsty for a Democratic president who could end years of congressional frustration with uncooperative executives, had expectations that far exceeded the president's capacity to fulfill (Wayne 1978). These Democratic members of Congress wanted patronage, and they wanted presidential support for projects in their districts, their "fair share" of federal largesse. No president could have given every member what they wanted. Carter did not even try. He "often projected the attitude of being morally superior to Congress" (Berman 1987: 316) and made no secret of his distaste for politics. He refused to trade in patronage or favors. Consequently, even when his liaison office remembered to call members of Congress and ask for their support, they had nothing to offer in return (Wayne 1978). This was hardly an ideal bargaining position, and it was created by Carter's steadfast and stubborn refusal to see politics as bargaining, to adapt when the requirements of his role conflicted with the preferences of his character.

Indeed, Carter not only refused to extend his support to Democrats seeking patronage and projects for their districts, he actively targeted such projects for elimination. Early in his administration, Carter attempted a "gratuitous assault" on water projects in Western states (Neustadt 1990). Western support had been instrumental in Carter's election, and this move made it clear that Carter had little or no understanding of his implicit obligation to the region. Individual members of Congress would be only to happy too reciprocate that lack of support.

Additionally, Carter offended some members and enraged others by getting them to support him on a controversial $50 tax rebate for every American as a means of bolstering the national economy. Many members were reluctant, but as loyal Democrats, they sided with the president. Carter then dropped the plan and did so without prior notification or consultation with his supporters. They were thus left bereft of presidential support and took a public relations beating that did not endear the president to them (Berman 1987).

Consequently, Carter's early days in office earned him a reputation for ineptness, a reputation that was consistently and vociferously reported in the media, who referred to his "inordinate attention to detail," who, because he was "anything but a master strategist, [was] dealing with a Congress that . . . [had] grown suspicious" (Neustadt 1990: 233). The media attention did Carter little good either with Congress or with the electorate. Having attention focused on his mistakes so early in his administration made the learning process all presidents experience particularly painful for Carter.

Once members of Congress are given reason to doubt a president's competence, they have more to lose than to gain by supporting that president. There are few incentives save altruism for members to help educate a president. Although executives who are well versed in Washington mores are easier to work with, and thus there is some small incentive to educate a president, for the most part, members of Congress stand or fall on their own merits; the less competent a president is, the less that president can hurt—or help—an individual member.

Carter, who as an outsider had few allies on the Hill, found that as his reputation as an effective manager declined, so did the legislative support available to him. As a man who found the informal aspects of politics repugnant, he did not appear to know how to parlay personal contacts into political support, how to use the elements of character to support his presidential role. Consequently, he could not communicate with Congress in a language its members understood. As a large, fragmented, and diffuse body, Congress has few institutional mechanisms of providing for collective action. One of the ways that such action is created is by an informal system of deference, bargaining, and exchange. Presidents who wish to be effective participants in the legislative process must be able to understand this informal system and bring to it their own unique arsenal of bargaining chips and compromises.

Carter scorned such behavior as cheap, showing a lack of understanding for the requirements of the presidential role. He "knew" what was best; so knowing, for him to compromise would have meant that he had to compromise on moral principle. Now, in any bargaining situation, everyone has a point beyond which they will not go, a principle that they will not compromise. Carter's problem was that he did not end at that position, he began there. Members of Congress were thus treated not as equal partners with equally legitimate perspectives and equally legitimate needs and preferences, but as illegitimate and obstructionist parasites on the federal system. This treatment was not the best way to ensure congressional good will or cooperation, as the case of the energy plan illustrates.

The Events Surrounding the Energy Plan

The events surrounding the passage of the energy plan are soon told. Less than a month after his inauguration, Carter gave his first speech to the nation on energy. Dressed in a cardigan sweater and speaking from the White House library, he used this speech to prepare the audience for the comprehensive energy plan that he pledged to send to Congress within his first 100 days in office.

On April 18, he followed through on this preparation. In another televised address, Carter called the energy crisis the "moral equivalent of war" and "the greatest challenge our country will face in our lifetime." As with Ford on inflation, and Roosevelt and the purge, Carter attempted crisis rhetoric to motivate the nation. However, he seemed to consider his job completed and declined to pursue the matter, either with Congress or the American public.

House Speaker Thomas P. (Tip) O'Neill (1987: 20)provided an illustrative story:

> After the speech I went up to congratulate him. "That was a fine address, Mr. President," I said. "Now here's a list of members you should call to keep the pressure on, because we'll need their votes."
>
> "No," he replied. "I described the problem to the American people in a rational way. I'm sure they'll realize that I'm right." . . . "Look," I said, trying to control my frustration. "This is politics we're talking about here, not physics. We need you to push this bill through."
>
> "It's *not* politics," he replied. "Not to me. It's simply the right thing, the rational thing. It's what needs to be done."

This story illustrates both Carter's attitude toward national politics and policymaking and the frustration that it engendered in his allies. Presidents have two main forums for presidential persuasion: Congress and the public. They are not distinct; communication in one forum can be parlayed into support in the other. Carter was not willing to exercise persuasive leadership in either forum and thus lost support in both.

Carter then sent to Congress a bill on energy. One member of his liaison office, Anne Wexler, who came to the Carter administration from a position as associate publisher of *Rolling Stone* and was responsible for public liaison, describes the energy bill as:

> a policy which was, in effect, conceived in secret, presented to the country as a fait accompli, without the consultation of interested parties, and handed to the Department of Energy for handling the legislation and implementation. The whole package sank like a stone out of sight. . . . The energy bill was one example of "how not to do it" right from start to finish. (Wexler 1981: 3)

The bill had 113 interlocking provisions. It dealt with such diverse areas as taxes on gasoline, taxes on inefficient cars, a wide variety of conservation measures, provisions for federal regulation of interstate natural gas, inducements of industry to use more coal, and tax credits for solar development (Hargrove 1988). Carter insisted that the plan be considered as one package. He considered the energy problem one that was best dealt with comprehensively, for all its seemingly diverse aspects are, in fact, interrelated, and to deal with any one aspect in isolation was, practically speaking, untenable.

Although this approach was both realistic and rational in terms of coping with the actual energy-related problems facing the nation, in terms of political strategy it was a miscalculation. Given the power of interest groups and their lobbyists regarding Congress, the task of passing legislation aimed at any one of those groups requires the marshalling of a coalition of at least some of the other groups. The broader the legislation, the more groups are likely to perceive themselves as negatively affected, and the harder it will be to muster a coalition. This is one of the reasons that policymaking in the United States tends to be of the incremental rather than the innovative kind (Polsby 1984).

Carter's presentation of the energy plan flew in the face of accepted procedure and process and immediately placed potential supporters on the defensive. Routinized communication has the advantage of providing a predictable environment. Stable expectations mean that everyone knows the steps of the dance, anticipates the next move, and avoids stepping on anyone else's toes. Carter set a new dance to the old music and confused and frustrated everyone involved.

Tip O'Neill did what he could to protect the president and the president's program. In response to the president's demand that the energy program be considered together, O'Neill set up an Ad Hoc Select Committee on Energy. That committee was charged with coordinating the activities of the 5 committees and 17 subcommittees that had some part of the responsibility for the energy plan. As a result of O'Neill's effort, the energy plan passed the House.

Carter had no such administrative and organizational support in the Senate, however, in which "rivalry among committees and open conflict between producing and consuming states delayed passage because of controversy over natural gas deregulation, which Carter opposed" (Hargrove 1988: 243). Carter could have gotten the plan approved in the Senate had he been willing to compromise on the issue of natural gas deregulation. Initially, he resisted such a compromise, but finally gave in and accepted the strategy designed by James Schlesinger and Frank Moore(1978) for presidential action for influencing Congress on the compromise. The plan passed during the second legislative session, after a "much longer, tougher, fight than he had envisioned" (Hargrove 1988: 243; see also Jones, 1988).

A more astute politician would have seen that tough and bitter fight coming and would have prepared for it. Carter chose to consult his preferences rather than his environment and ended by losing prestige and support in both Congress and the electorate (Watson 1979). Indeed, the Carter people never seemed quite able to recollect which audience they were playing to:

> The proposed strategy, a Panama-Canal-type "public selling" effort, is too unfocused and not timely. Our primary problem at this juncture is not the public-at-large but with certain key members of the United States Senate. The best way to deal with that problem is not with public relations, but with some hard, careful politicking. . . . In sum, we respectfully suggest that a more *flexible, low profile, highly targeted* approach would give us our best shot at getting an energy bill that we can live with this session. (Watson and Frank 1977; emphasis in original)

Carter did not lack for good advice; this memo clearly spells out the requirements of the presidential role, knowing when to "go public" and when to engage in private bargaining out of the public eye. Carter simply choose to ignore that advice. The price may have been passage of his energy plan.

Carter's Strategy

Jimmy Carter was an outsider to Washington politics with extraordinary legislative ambitions. Like many people with a limited understanding of political realities within "the Beltway," Carter assumed that what the president proposed, Congress would more or less automatically enact. He did not anticipate the level of animosity and opposition he would encounter by virtue of this assumption. He also appeared to minimize the extent and power of the groups that would oppose his proposed legislation (Briefing Material 1978). Worse, he did not, at least in this instance, grasp the necessity of fulfilling the expectations held by Congress and the public for the president's behavior.

As an outsider, Carter came to Washington without a clear sense of what was possible politically. As a result, he displayed "an uncanny knack of attaching himself to every controversial issue and, in so doing, raised the cost of losing" (Berman 1987: 315-316). Carter assumed that persuasion played only a minimal role in federal policymaking. He disdained "politics" and preferred to see himself as above the "dirty" aspects of government, such as trading favors. This led him to irritate both specific members of Congress and the body as a whole (O'Neill 1987). In the case of the energy legislation, Carter's refusal to design legislation with an eye toward its political passage rather than its rational and logical composition led to a humiliating defeat and the undermining of his image as a competent manager.

Carter's first mistake with the energy plan was to draft the legislation without consultation with the congressional leadership. Carter was the first Democratic president in eight years. Worse, many members of Congress had been elected as part of the post-Watergate "throw the rascals out" 1976 election and had never worked with a president of their own party. Many Democratic members ran ahead of Carter in their districts and felt little obligation to him personally or to the office institutionally (Johnson 1980; O'Neill 1987). Cooperation and conciliation were vitally important to a president facing a Congress jealous of its prerogatives and power. Carter, instead of offering that cooperation and conciliation, chose to ignore Congress completely, even when consultation would have cost him relatively little and might actually have improved both the composition of the legislation as well its chances for passage (Mullen 1982).

In addition, Carter further slighted and confused Congress by introducing the energy legislation along with a plethora of bills on a variety of unrelated topics (Light 1982; Ornstein 1981). Congress was thus given no sense of direction or priorities. Even assuming that individual members were unconditionally willing to cooperate with the president, in a world of limited political capital it was not likely that they could give him everything he asked for; some rank order, some sense of the relative importance of legislation was necessary. Carter gave his supporters in Congress no help in this regard and insisted that everything was equally important. This may have been an accurate statement of the president's beliefs, but it was a poor stance from a pragmatic point of view (Neustadt 1990: 255). As Chief of Staff Hamilton Jordan (1981:19) would later remark, "Privately and internally, the priorities of the administration were really fairly obvious, but we did a poor job of defining them and presenting them to the American people and to the political community."

Carter (1977a) began to focus attention on energy shortly after his election, calling a Cabinet meeting to respond to the problems created by the energy crisis less than two weeks after his inauguration. As in Ford's case, this could have been an effective tactic, beginning the process of presidential priming, preparing the public for action on a specific area of interest to the president. But any impact this might have had was lessened by the barrage of symbolic statements by the president on specific areas. He spoke to members of each of the executive departments within the next few weeks and gave each the same level of symbolic presidential support. As Anne Wexler (1981: 59) said, "Well, the problem was that he concentrated on so many items that it became a jumble in the public's mind. As a result, they didn't think he did anything. This impression was really the issue and it continued to be right through the campaign."

On February 2, Carter gave his first televised address and devoted it to the topic of energy. In it, he promised cooperation and consultation with both Congress and the electorate, in keeping with the promises he made during the recent presidential campaign. But this cooperation was not going to be at the expense of leadership:

> Some of our obvious goals can be achieved very quickly—for example through executive orders and decisions made directly by me. But in many other areas, we must move carefully, with full involvement by the Congress, allowing time for citizens to participate in careful study, in order to develop predictable, long-range programs that we can be sure are affordable and that we know will work. (Carter 1977b)

Carter thus promised that he was going to be not only inclusive, but cautious, that he would not rush headlong into national policymaking. The problem here is that the electorate had other things to do besides participating "in careful study." That is one of the reasons they elect leaders. To have elected someone who was not going to act, but who was going to demand participation, rang a disturbing note, even in the context of the "postimperial presidency."

Carter deepened that disturbing note by immediately calling for sacrifice: "Some of these efforts will also require dedication—perhaps even sacrifice—from you. But I don't believe that any of us are afraid to learn that our national goals require cooperation and effort." The problem here was that Carter had not yet elaborated on those goals. Before deriving consensus on the basis of shared principles and then using that consensus as a springboard to require action, Carter first demanded action (participation) and then sacrifice, and then alluded to a set of still mysterious national goals. Those not eager to sacrifice themselves were thus less inclined to agree with the necessity for such a sacrifice than had Carter structured the speech differently.

Without articulating any set of principles from which the national goals could be said to derive, Carter then announced that "one of our more urgent projects is to develop a national energy policy." Strangely, however, instead of relating this energy plan to contexts his audience could understand, Carter discussed energy in terms of national economic growth: taxes, jobs, and municipal services. He began by stating that a national energy policy was vital, then confused the issue and the audience by putting energy in the context of national economic recovery. The audience could not be certain if the energy policy was an end in itself, brought about by the international energy shortage, or if it was a means to an end, energy conservation being an important element in national economic recovery. The answer, of course, is that Carter saw energy as both a means and an end, but his communication on this point was not structured to invoke a national outpouring of support, much less massive and voluntary sacrifices.

Yet voluntary sacrifices were precisely what Carter (1977b) had in mind. At the close of the speech on energy policy (and inflation, and taxes, and jobs, and human rights, and so on) he said:

> I would like to tell you now about one of the things that I have already learned in my brief time in office. I have learned that there are many things that a President cannot do. There is no energy policy that we can develop that would do more than voluntary conservation. There is no economic policy that will do as much as shared faith in hard work, efficiency, and in the future of our system.

Although this is perfectly consistent with Carter's born-again approach to presidential persuasion (Hahn 1987), it did not resonate well with his secular audience. After less than a month on the job, Carter had already admitted to his limitations. This is not the stuff of presidential inspiration, even in the "political pulpit" (Hart 1977).

Once the energy plan was introduced, however clumsily, Carter compounded his problems with Congress by failing to follow up on it. As early as February 8, 1977, Carter was reputed to be having difficulty with Congress. Carter (1997c) admitted that "we have given them cause for some of the complaints, inadvertently. We have made some mistakes. . . . We have not been adequately careful in the initial days in dealing with the Congress." He announced that he was working on correcting those problems and would take better care with Congress in the future. This set up expectations that Carter had listened to, understood, and promised to heed congressional complaints with his performance. These expectations created all the more anger and frustration when they were not met by later actions of the Carter administration.

Carter did not really focus on the plan until it was in deep trouble in the Senate, and then he made the natural gas compromise legislation "a test of our nation's will" (Carter 1978), an argument that in the face of vocal opposition and lack of public support was very weak.

Carter attempted to pass an extraordinarily complicated piece of legislation in its entirety, which, given the fragmented nature of Congress, required careful tending and nurturing, not to mention explaining. Carter did not even attempt any of these tasks. The energy plan as originally composed "had over 113 interlocking provisions that the president demanded Congress consider as one package" (Hargrove 1988: 243). Congress is not well designed to approach either national problems or individual pieces of legislation holistically. Carter's failure to understand either the organizational requirements of Congress or the persuasive requirements of public politics ended by undermining him in both forums (Jones 1988).

Discussion

Carter appeared to believe as if the important aspect of the presidential role was the initiation of legislation; that all he had to do was propose the plan, and it would pass. He failed to take congressional and public expectations of his role into account and consequently violated those expectations, to the detriment of his policy and his administration as a whole.

Carter's decision to treat the energy plan as the only acceptable approach to the problems associated with the energy crisis was a clear mistake and cost him support in both main forums of presidential persuasion. A White House staffer said: "The energy bill was the single greatest political mistake we made in our first six months. When we couldn't pass it, people got the impression that the President couldn't manage the government. It came slowly, but we never recovered from that impression" (quoted in Berman 1987: 316).

Carter's staff realized, albeit too long after the fact, how costly the energy plan had been. Like Gerald Ford, Carter began by claiming the dire necessity of his plan, as "the moral equivalent of war." But then when faced with opposition in Congress and apathy in the public, he "retreated to a position which held that no real sacrifice was necessary" (Hahn 1987). As Theodore Windt (1987) noted, presidents in need of public support create crises as a means of bolstering potential support. When claiming a state of crisis, presidents must assert its existence as clearly, consistently, and persuasively as possible. It is not enough to simply declare a crisis and then expect a massive public mobilization to follow.

In addition, Carter attempted to assert control over policies and behavior that lay outside of his administrative purview. "His chief objectives . . . required implementation by executives outside the government, in places where the President's authority was weakest, where his constitutional and statutory powers were attenuated or did not apply" (Neustadt 1990: 238). He thus set a standard for judging his leadership that he could not meet because the behavior required was beyond his control.

In structuring the situation in this way, Carter thus permitted and encouraged the impression that the task of governance was also beyond his control. Essentially, his message was: "Look at the energy plan to see me in action as a leader. By its success you shall judge me." When the plan's passage took so long and was accompanied by acrimonious debate and lack of clear presidential leadership, that judgment was not one that Carter would have chosen for himself.

Policymaking in the American federal system is an enormously complicated and frustrating endeavor. There are far more obstacles to the passage of legislation than there are facilitators. Carter's case provides evidence that the presidency is still "no place for amateurs" (Neustadt 1960). Carter structured the strategy around the energy plan in an amateurish fashion, considering only his perspectives and his preferences, ignoring those related to Congress. As the other cases in this chapter combine to indicate, this is surely the shortest available route to strategic difficulties with Congress.

CONCLUSIONS

There are two main forums for presidential persuasive speech: Congress and the public. The cases analyzed in this chapter clearly indicate that these forums are not separate nor distinct, but overlapping. How presidents communicate with the public can affect their relations with Congress; how they communicate with Congress can affect their standing with the public. All the presidents discussed in this chapter forgot this at some point. Presidents tend to see themselves as the center of the national government. This is a perception widely shared among the electorate. It is not, however, a perception borne out by the political realities of the federal structure of government. Congress is not without power; a fact that presidents tend to remember only after they have been sharply rebuked by that body.

Roosevelt, who staked his personal prestige and political future on the outcome of New Deal legislation, took congressional repudiation of that legislation as a personal affront and a political challenge. His emotional involvement obscured his judgment, and his national perspective blinded him to local realities. Ford staked his political image as a strong and decisive leader by waging a "war" on inflation. His understanding of the problem led him to ignore the institutional requirements of Congress and of the nation as a whole. In his turn, Carter decided that he was the only one in the national government with a true perspective on the energy problem. His plan was therefore the best plan, and Carter needed to neither bargain with Congress nor persuade the American people. He was wrong on both counts.

Presidents need to pay attention to the organizational requirements of Congress. Large, comprehensive measures may well be the "best" way to solve national problems. But they are not the best way to approach Congress. Much of the literature on the presidency proceeds from the assumption that the office has become too central to the national government, too powerful to encourage or even permit democracy. In terms of presidential war making and foreign affairs generally, this is a persuasive argument, not easily refuted. But in terms of the presidential constituencies of Congress and the American electorate, presidents who believe that they can act unilaterally with impunity are presidents on the verge of being sharply rebuked.

Presidents, by the nature of their office, are inclined to view the world myopically. They consult their preferences and those who share their perspectives. This can lead them to ignore the wider environment in which they must operate. There is not one single perspective that dominates Washington; there is not one definitive political truth. Lacking any real access to what is, by definition, right, presidents must do what they think is probably best. But that "best" must include a variety of perspectives and must take the institutional requirements of both the presidency and the Congress into account.

Conventional wisdom seems to suggest that presidents lose power if they operate in a consultative rather than a commanding mode. The evidence presented in this chapter indicates that this is only true under certain, fairly unusual circumstances, such as when the majority opinion is for the policy already. Presidents must persuade members of Congress to their positions. One of the best ways to do this may well be by listening rather than by talking, consulting rather than commanding.

4

Over-Reaching:
Personal Failure

Presidents, acting from a wide variety of motives ranging from the altruistic to the venal, seek to expand the political and institutional limits of the office that they hold (Rockman 1984). Sometimes that endeavor highlights aspects of the presidential character that damage the president's public image, as in scandal. There are also cases, however, in which aspects of character previously interpreted as strengths can become problematic. Presidents, emphasizing strategies that have led to past success, can become prisoners of those strategies, and adopt them in inappropriate situations. This causes the strategic failure of overreaching.

Instrumentally, that failure is of greater or lesser importance depending on the centrality of the goal to the president's program. In terms of the president's public character, however, the damage can be severe. Aspects of that character previously understood as strengths can become reevaluated as weaknesses, undermining the entire presidential image and forcing the president to restructure or refocus that image if political recovery is to be possible. The cases presented here indicate how difficult such recovery can be: Although Franklin Roosevelt survived the Judicial Reform Bill fiasco and Harry Truman survived the attempted steel mill seizure, both were damaged by the changed perceptions of their conduct of the office. The Vietnam War, on the other hand, did not merely damage, but destroyed the Johnson presidency.

Although the three cases are very different from one another, they do have certain strategic elements in common. All three presidents argued for an expansion of presidential authority so that the public interest would be best served; none of these arguments were accepted. Instead, the presidents were all ultimately viewed by their constituents as acting inappropriately, pursuing a personal agenda rather than one supported by the public. In all cases, this perception damaged the president's public image. Presidents, although they are power seekers, must be perceived as minimizing personal attachment to power.

The presidency is a deeply personal office, yet it is one in which presidents must avoid conflating themselves and their goals with the institution. Operating in a constrained environment and with little time to accomplish their generally ambitious goals, presidents find themselves frequently frustrated (Buchanan 1978). If they have reason to believe that they have a chance to fulfill a promise, enact a program, or complete a project that is important to them, they will often attempt to do so. The strategic problem arises when, because of a misreading of context, poor timing, or willful self-delusion, presidents test the parameters of proscribed action and end by going "too far."

Context is an extraordinarily important factor in determining just how far is "too far." What one president may do with impunity, another president, embedded in a different context and possessor of a different public character, may not. Context affects the interpretation of the president's style and image, and the result is either an expansion of presidential power or, as in the cases studied here, rebuke and a subsequent contraction of that power.

In 1960, Richard Neustadt noted that the presidency is an office characterized by weakness. He was still of that opinion 30 years later (Neustadt 1990). Yet, although the power of the presidency is still limited and in many ways dependent on the skill and ability of the individual who is president, the expectations surrounding the president's performance have increased, probably beyond the bounds of human capability (Kernell 1986; Lowi 1985; Tulis 1987). In an effort to meet those expectations (or at least provide the appearance of meeting them), presidents sometimes exceed the limits of their skill and political mandate.

Neustadt (1990: 151) said that "the presidency is no place for amateurs." The cases presented here provide evidence that the presidency is also difficult for professionals. All the presidents studied in this chapter had considerable Washington and/or executive experience before becoming president. All had reputations as astute politicians who knew their business. Yet all made colossal and extremely damaging errors of overreaching. The following discussions illuminate the problem of overreaching as a pitfall of the politically experienced.

FRANKLIN D. ROOSEVELT
AND THE JUDICIAL REFORM BILL

The Political and Institutional Context

In 1932, the United States was in the middle of the worst economic crisis of the nation's history. The president, Herbert Hoover, had a traditional and minimalist conception of the office that led him to avoid executive involvement in resolving the problems of the economy and to resist what he considered "the weakening of the legislative arm [leading] to encroachment by the executive upon individual liberty" (Davis 1987: 21). He was consequently accused of lacking compassion for the thousands of unemployed and dispossessed. "Hoovervilles," or cities composed of people living in cardboard houses, became a symbol of Hoover's inaction. Franklin Roosevelt defeated Hoover in the 1932 election on a platform of presidential action aimed at resolving the economic crisis. In so doing, he took 42 of the 48 states and 472 of 531 electoral votes.

Roosevelt's first 100 days in office set a unique standard of legislative accomplishment (Leuchtenberg 1983). During those 100 days, Roosevelt proposed and Congress enacted a breathtaking number of new laws: The banks were closed, payments in gold were forbidden, exports were restricted, and relief programs were created.

Until Roosevelt assumed office, presidential activism had been the historical exception rather than the practical rule. His activism broke precedent and therefore needed to be continually justified. Consequently, Roosevelt was often on the defensive, answering accusations of dictatorial behavior, charges of violating the Constitution, and miscellaneous vilification of his character and policies. Nevertheless, because of his adroit use of personal diplomacy and the exercise of his considerable personal charm (Burns 1956; Hargrove 1974), Roosevelt remained effective throughout his first term.

That success was not without cost however. In getting his legislation passed, Roosevelt mobilized his opponents. Those opponents objected to Roosevelt's conduct of the office as unprincipled, to his policies as unwise, and to his presidency as undemocratic. There was little that they could do but wait so long as the New Deal remained popular and effective.

They waited a long time. Roosevelt ran for reelection in 1936 and decisively defeated his Republican opponent. Roosevelt saw the election as a mandate, a powerful vindication of the New Deal programmatically and of his leadership personally. His first term legislative success combined with the overwhelming margin of victory in 1936 boosted Roosevelt's self-confidence, never low, into the overconfident range.

From our historical vantage point, Roosevelt as president looms very large indeed. Given some of his successors in the office, he also looms fairly noncontroversially. It can be difficult to realize just how controversial Roosevelt was in his own time. Roosevelt's ideas on economic nationalism, and on nationalism in general, had fervent critics. Conservative charges that Roosevelt was asking for "dictatorial power" and was determined to lead the country toward totalitarianism were as much the product of legitimate and honest concern as of delegitimating demagoguery.

Given the national economic crisis, the criticism from the Left that Roosevelt had no real sympathy for the workers, that he was more interested in salvaging the capitalistic structure than in reorganizing it and supervising a national redistribution of wealth, had more than a kernel of truth as well. Roosevelt wanted a capitalist system that included a measure of fairness for workers and security for the underprivileged. For those who saw the system itself as corrupt and moribund, Roosevelt's New Deal did not go nearly far enough (Rowe 1978; Zinn 1980).

For Roosevelt, the "best" plan was the moderate course. He was an innovator, but he was no revolutionary. He strongly disagreed with those who believed that the federal government should play a limited role in national affairs, that the president's role was subordinate to that of Congress, and that the United States had no business involving itself in international affairs. Roosevelt was both a nationalist and an internationalist. He saw Washington, DC as the center of the nation, and he saw the United States as the center of all nations. He believed that the majority of the American electorate shared this vision. The results of the 1936 election supported him in this belief. However many citizens shared Roosevelt's vision, he still had to contend with a number of people, charged with enacting the policies supporting that vision, who did not.

Of those people, the U.S. Supreme Court Justices proved the most intractable from Roosevelt's point of view. During his first term, Roosevelt became the first president since James Madison (1809-1817) not to have the opportunity to appoint a Supreme Court justice. During the latter half of his first term, the Court became a major source of irritation for Roosevelt, as the "nine old men" on the Court declared one piece of New Deal legislation after another unconstitutional, emasculating the NRA, which Roosevelt saw as the heart of the New Deal.

Roosevelt's frustration was compounded by the knowledge that he was powerless against the Court. Supreme Court justices serve for "good behavior," which is tantamount to life. The Court is thus insulated against political pressure. Unable to alter the behavior of the Court, and unwilling to accept its rulings, Roosevelt began to believe that altering its composition was his best alternative. In Roosevelt's eyes, democracy meant responsiveness to the will of the people which translated to responsiveness to his will, as the representative of all the people. He was to discover that to many people these terms were not synonymous.

Roosevelt's Attempt to "Pack" the Court

It is difficult to determine just when Roosevelt decided on his plan to alter the composition of the U.S. Supreme Court. As early as May 27, 1935, FDR was publicly critical of the Court (Ryan 1988). It is clear that Roosevelt's frustration with the policies espoused by the Court and reflected in its rulings mounted throughout his first term.

On February 5, 1937, FDR called a special press conference, in which he announced his advocacy of the Judicial Reform Bill. The bill provided for the president to appoint a new Supreme Court justice for every one who failed to retire by the age of 70. The proposal was perfectly legal, as the U.S. Constitution does not state how many Justices will serve on the Court at any given time. There was even historical precedent for Roosevelt's position. Although FDR was the only executive to propose a systematic plan for increasing the number of seats on the Court, the number of Justices, fixed by statute, has varied. The Court started in 1789 with 5 Justices, and reached its zenith with 10 between 1863-1865. Roosevelt's bill indicated that the president would be allowed to appoint as many as 6 new Justices.

Congress, the media, and the American people reacted with shock and dismay. The proposal was publicly denounced as "court packing" and widely considered an illegitimate attempt to exert political control over the judiciary.

Uncharacteristically, Roosevelt had consulted neither members of Congress nor his own advisors before announcing the bill. The element of surprise worked against Roosevelt because he assumed support would be his by right, and Congress does not generally appreciate being viewed—or publicly treated—as a presidential rubber stamp.

Additionally, FDR's justification for the bill was clearly disingenuous, a fact that, combined with the secrecy that appeared to surround the preparation of the bill, contributed to the overall appearance of duplicity. Rather than basing his animosity toward the Court on its opposition to New Deal legislation, Roosevelt instead cited the Court's "inefficiency, congestion, and judicial delay—all due to the justices' advanced ages" (Winfield 1990: 133). This rationale was simply not credible. The Court's opposition to New Deal programs was widely known and widely discussed. For Roosevelt to ignore the Court's behavior while trying to alter its composition was interpretive arrogance and provided an example of Roosevelt's tendency to be "too clever by half" (Hargrove 1974).

Roosevelt compounded his initial presentational error by failing to follow up on his justification for the bill. Once he announced it, he appeared to drop all interest in it, apparently assuming that the Democratic majority in Congress would ensure the bill's passage. His efforts at mobilizing support for the bill in Congress were best described as "half-hearted, fumbling, and weak" (Winfield 1990: 134).

When it became obvious that he was losing the battle on the Hill, Roosevelt began to woo the public, speaking first at a March 4 Democratic Victory Dinner and five days later dedicating a Fireside Chat to the Judicial Reform Bill. It was too little, too late. Public and newspaper editorial opposition remained high. Worse, from the president's point of view, opposition exceeded the relatively narrow bounds of the proposed legislation and extended to the behavior of the president.

Roosevelt's position, already weak, was further undermined later that spring as the Supreme Court handed down a series of decisions favorable to the New Deal. The most important of these was the Wagner Act, which legalized collective bargaining. Roosevelt's opposition to the Court could thus be easily interpreted as a mean-spirited response to having his personal power limited instead of as a public-spirited attempt to restore beneficial legislation or improve the efficiency of the Court.

On May 18, 1937, the House Judiciary Committee was scheduled to vote on the bill. That same day, Justice William Van Devanter ensured the bill's defeat by announcing his retirement from the Court. Late that afternoon, Roosevelt tried to limit damage by holding a press conference and providing "alternative news," but to no avail. The Committee's repudiation of the president was clear and unambiguous.

The failure of the Judicial Reform Bill marked one of the few times that Roosevelt was clearly and consistently outmaneuvered by his opponents. It was also one of the few times that his own normally astute political instincts appeared to forsake him. By announcing a controversial policy in what looked like a dishonest manner and then failing to follow through and correct that appearance, Roosevelt set the stage for his own communicative failure and political defeat. A more detailed analysis of the communications strategy that contributed to that failure and defeat follows.

Roosevelt's Strategy

In his insightful book on Roosevelt, Halford Ryan (1988) details three reasons for the failure of the Judicial Reform Bill: the secrecy preceding the announcement, the death of Senator Joseph Robinson, and the nature of the bill itself, which sought to give the president political control over the Supreme Court. Given that Roosevelt's goal was to control the Court, and that he had little control over the timing of Robinson's death, it makes sense to focus on the first problem with Roosevelt's strategy—secrecy.

When presidents want to assist a piece of legislation through Congress with considerable public approval, they generally follow a fairly routinized procedure. First, they consult with their advisors and with key members of Congress. Second, they gradually increase the amount of public attention given to the issue area, announcing their concern, then announcing steps they plan to take in addressing that concern, and finally producing proposed legislation. This formula does not by any means ensure success, but, by using consultation and preparation, it does help to prevent certain failure. Although including others in the preliminary processes of designing legislation will not guarantee their cooperation, failure to include them will come close to guaranteeing their opposition.

This was Roosevelt's biggest mistake. He failed to consult with any of the key participants in the legislative process, and he took his party's support for granted. FDR apparently assumed that because the Democrats had amassed an impressive congressional majority in the 1936 election, the Democratic president had earned carte blanche as far as obtaining his will and aggrandizing his prerogatives. That the Judicial Reform Bill was intended to heighten Roosevelt's political power was never seriously doubted.

His second major strategic mistake was that he allowed the bill to be interpreted in personal rather than policy-driven terms by presenting the rationale for the bill in a painfully dishonest and noncredible fashion. First, he presented the proposed reorganization of the judiciary as part and parcel of the already proposed reorganization of the executive and as stemming from the same need for increased governmental efficiency and economy. He cited judicial delay as "the outstanding defect of our federal judicial system," a defect that, for Roosevelt (1937a), could only be remedied by "the appointment of a sufficient number of judges to handle the business of the federal courts."

Yet Roosevelt undermined his own argument by, second, outlining the requisite character of those judges: "These additional judges should be of a type and age which would warrant us in believing that they would vigorously attack their dockets, rather than permit their dockets to overwhelm them." Thus it is not the overwhelming workload, but the age and administrative style of the individual Justices that formed the basis of Roosevelt's objections. Once the focus turned to judicial style, Roosevelt's omission of the Justices' well-known opposition to the New Deal became strategically problematic.

Roosevelt had two concerns: the policies that he felt were threatened by the Court, and the organization of power within the federal government. These two concerns were reciprocal and reinforcing—by influencing the one, FDR could hope to affect the other as well.

Roosevelt believed in an active executive who operated within the framework of a strong national government, and he resisted what he considered unwarranted restrictions on either the power of the executive or that of the national government (Stuckey 1991). For Roosevelt, the niceties of constitutional interpretation were less important than the need to get certain programs enacted (Greenstein 1977; Lowi 1985). Yet, in the context of the early 1930s, this was a difficult argument to make explicitly. Both fascism and communism were threatening Europe; both favored ends over means, goals over procedures. It was strategically problematic for Roosevelt, already accused of appearing dictatorial, to make similar arguments (Hawley 1991). Thus, in making his argument against the Court, Roosevelt had to base his plan on democratic procedure rather than policy substance. He would have done better to unite the two, for stressing procedure alone lent his plan an air of subterfuge.

Roughly a week after the February 5 announcement, Roosevelt attempted to undo some of the damage caused by this appearance of subterfuge. At a February 12 press conference, he first tried to avoid the subject, then, in response to a question implying that the Judicial Reform Bill was the product of impulse, he insisted that "this particular message, which I think a week ago took most people by surprise, dates back over a year and a half" (Roosevelt 1937b). Thus, it was not the product of either irresponsible impulse or rage over recent Supreme Court decisions, but was the rational act of a president sincerely interested in promoting the public interest over the long term.

Roosevelt did not help his cause by failing to follow the initial announcement with a strategy designed to woo congressional and/or public favor. Instead, he chose to flout the need for such wooing and by his attitude reinforced the widespread impression of dictatorial behavior. His first speech on the Court battle occurred during the Democratic Victory Dinner, given in Washington, DC on March 4, 1937. In this speech, he appeared as the President-Of-All-The-People and assumed a statesmanlike rather than purely political role in an effort to reinforce his attention to the public rather than merely personal interest: "I speak at this Victory Dinner not only as head of the Democratic party but as representative of all Americans who have faith in political and economic democracy" (Roosevelt 1937c). Roosevelt thus tied the fate of his Judicial Reform Bill to the preservation of democracy in the United States. This was an exaggerated claim that, on the evidence, convinced no one.

It was something of an improvement that in this address Roosevelt also connected his desire to reorganize the judiciary to the Supreme Court's penchant for invalidating New Deal legislation. For Roosevelt, the New Deal was to provide the salvation and preservation of democracy in the United States. When the Supreme Court struck down that legislation, it struck at the heart of democracy. The phrase, "neither individually, nor as a party can we postpone or run from that fight on advice of defeatist lawyers" (Roosevelt 1937c) recurred throughout the March 4 address. He sought to define the terms of conflict as Roosevelt and the American people against the "nine old men" on the Court.

He followed the same theme in a Fireside Chat delivered the next week. By then, it was clear that the bill lacked congressional support. The March 9 Fireside Chat was an attempt to mobilize public support and force congressional acquiescence on its strength.

This time Roosevelt (1937d) again connected the composition of the Court to the policies it espoused: "The change of one vote would have thrown all the affairs of this great Nation back into helpless chaos." This chaos would be the result of a Court that neglected its proper role in the constitutional order of things. "The Courts, however, have cast doubts on the ability of the elected Congress to protect us against catastrophe by meeting squarely our modern social and economic conditions" (Roosevelt 1937d). Roosevelt thus became the defender not of the executive branch, nor of the New Deal programs that the chief executive favored, but of congressional authority.

Roosevelt here attempted to turn the rhetorical tables on the Court. He had been accused of exceeding the constitutional limits of his office. Now he made essentially the same charge against the Court: "This plan of mine is no attack on the Court; it seeks to restore the Court to its rightful and historic place in our system of Constitutional Government and to have it resume its high task of building anew on the Constitution 'a system of living law'" (Roosevelt 1937d). If that charge stuck, Roosevelt's actions in attempting to reorganize the judiciary would have been potentially reinterpreted as an attempt to save the Constitution and American democracy from the depredations of the Court. Unfortunately for Roosevelt, this rhetorical ploy came after the doubts and criticism concerning his motives had wide public circulation. His imputations against the Court, not likely to be persuasive under any circumstances, thus utterly lacked credibility.

On April 12, the Supreme Court declared the Wagner Act constitutional. Although Roosevelt (1937e) declined public attribution, he told reporters, "off the record and just in the family, I have been chortling all morning." Roosevelt clearly indicated that he believed the threat of judicial reorganization was the catalyst behind the favorable decision.

Roosevelt's final word on the subject of judicial reform came on May 18, 1937. When asked how Justice Van Devanter's resignation from the Court would affect "your program in connection with the Court program," Roosevelt (1937f) responded curtly, "I don't think there is any news in that." Clearly, Roosevelt saw no advantage in pursuing the issue.

His immediate problem with the Court may have been solved, but the failed strategy surrounding the Judicial Reform Bill created an environment that fostered suspicion concerning Roosevelt's motives and concern over his intentions. Roosevelt's attempt to pack the Court began his second term inauspiciously; this beginning led to further controversy as Roosevelt attempted to purge Congress, an attempt that indicates how little Roosevelt learned as a result of the Court battle (see Chapter 3).

Discussion

Roosevelt may have been able to argue more effectively for the Judicial Reform Bill by starting sooner, pursuing a more consistent effort, and basing his appeal on principle, combining policy substance with democratic procedure. There is little doubt that the substance of the bill would have created problems no matter how FDR approached the issue. Whenever presidents seek to formally aggrandize the executive at the expense of one of the other branches, they can expect resistance. Presidents do much better to increase the power of their office on what appears to be a temporary and informal basis. By attempting to stretch the prerequisites of the role, presidents risk damaging the public perception of their character.

By approaching the Supreme Court controversy in the way that he did, Roosevelt created a situation In which "the issue became not 'efficiency' as Roosevelt had emphasized, but rather the president's disingenuous way of meeting the Court's conservative philosophy" (Winfield 1990: 136). Once the issue became the president's tactics and behavior and the bill became labeled "court packing," Roosevelt's defeat was practically guaranteed.

Roosevelt was the victim of his own overconfidence and arrogance. Roosevelt seemed to assume that, as a Democratic president with a Democratic majority in Congress following a very successful reelection campaign, he was automatically empowered to take whatever action he considered necessary to insure the public interest as he chose to define it. As events proved, this was not a good assumption. Congressional dignity and public sensibilities demand that presidents at least go through the motions of working for congressional support and public approbation. Neither Congress nor the public will welcome being treated with arrogance and neglect.

That a politician as sensitive to congressional relations and public politics as Roosevelt could have pursued a strategy that was almost certain to cause problems is powerful evidence for the importance of overreaching as a communicative peril that affects otherwise successful presidents. Just as the successful presidential campaign of 1936 helped to create the overconfidence and bland assumption of success that contributed to Roosevelt's difficulty with the Judicial Reform Bill, Harry Truman's miraculous victory in the 1948 presidential election helped set the stage for his humiliation after he seized the steel mills during the Korean War.

HARRY S. TRUMAN AND THE STEEL MILL SEIZURE

The Political and Institutional Context

Harry Truman's presidency is a difficult one to evaluate, for it was a checkerboard of dramatic successes and spectacular failures. Admired for his personal honesty yet castigated for his ties to machine politics; respected for his forthrightness, but criticized for his quick temper and tendency to "shoot from the hip"; Truman was fiery, impetuous, and blunt (Underhill 1981). Above all, however, Truman was a staunch defender of the presidential office, its power, and its prerogatives.

As a former Senator, Truman understood that as president he could not simply command legislation. He knew that he was neither eloquent nor capable of the "strong personal leadership" that characterized FDR (Phillips 1966). Truman's conception of the office was primarily institutional, not personal. He felt that he had authority not as Harry Truman, but as President of the United States. He thus sought institutional means of acting and of aggrandizing the office (Pemberton 1989).

Like Roosevelt, Truman brought a strong sense of moral obligation to the presidency; like Roosevelt, Truman combined that moral sense with a talent for building political coalitions. Regarding the issues of civil rights and Palestine, for example, one Truman biographer noted: "In both cases [Truman had] an attitude of decency and fairness that accorded with the courses offering the greatest political advantage. . . . What was humane, in other words, was also good politics, although risky politics in some ways" (Donovan 1977: 332). Truman thus ordered desegregation of the military and recognized Israel.

Although Truman was capable of political courage, he was also capable of obstinence and foolhardiness. He had in his administration men known for their integrity and ability such as George C. Marshall, Dean Acheson, and James Forrestal, but the White House staff contained people open to criticism on ethical and legal grounds rather than experienced policymakers or able administrators (Hamby 1988). With political influence increasingly focused in Washington and specifically within the executive branch, this preference for old friends caused numerous problems for the Truman administration (see Chapter 1).

With the exception of his decision to drop the atom bomb on Japan, no single event of Truman's presidency created as much controversy as his handling of the Korean War. When communist North Korea invaded the South June 25, 1950, Truman's first action was to call on the United Nations. By bringing in the United Nations, Truman avoided giving the United States complete responsibility for the war. Under the aegis of the United Nations, the United States took command, supplied most of the money, and sent most of the soldiers. But the participation of other United Nations countries kept the war from being a single United States' effort. The degree of international support involved in Korea may have complicated the prosecution of the war, but not only did Truman thus avoid having to ask Congress for a declaration of war, the emphasis on international cooperation greatly simplified the political position of the United States within the international community.

Korea was not a simple war (even if such things as simple wars exist). On the one hand, South Korea represented a small polity struggling against a communist invasion. In the context of the cold war, American responsibility was clear. On the other hand, however, there was considerable debate over whether Asia or Europe ought to be the focus of American attention. Truman and many in his administration believed that Europe was the most important area of American concern (a belief manifested in the Marshall Plan). The Republican party generally and General Douglas MacArthur particularly were advocates for a strong American presence in Asia (Gosnell 1980).

This was an extremely complicated situation, for MacArthur, a World War II hero, was the Supreme Commander of the forces stationed in Korea. Although there were persuasive reasons for Truman's desire to limit the war (such as China's proximity and American unwillingness to become embroiled in another large-scale war so soon after World War II), MacArthur wanted to engage the enemy on their own ground and carry the war to the North. The issue became extremely volatile and culminated when Truman relieved MacArthur of his command in late March 1951.

MacArthur returned to the States, determined to defend his position and discredit that of Truman. He gave a speech before Congress that drew enormous public attention and acclaim. Congress immediately opened hearings on the administration's Korea policy. Truman was eventually vindicated at the hearings on the principle of civilian control of the military rather than because of widespread agreement with his conduct of the war. MacArthur had challenged the president's authority, and even though the challenge was ultimately unsuccessful, it had been very public. Credible and public challenges of a president are very damaging to that president's status and reputation. Truman's professional reputation, never really high, suffered considerably after his firing of MacArthur.

The Korean War, although dominant, was not the only issue on American's minds during the late 1940s and early 1950s. At home, the economy dominated the agenda, and the relationship between labor and management dominated all other economic issues. The coal miners, led by the charismatic John L. Lewis, engaged in several strikes and near strikes in an effort to better miners' living conditions. Other industries, including steel, followed suit. During the Korean War, the government instituted wage and price controls to manage the war economy, thus complicating the picture.

Of all American industries in the 1950s, steel was the most central. Steel formed the backbone of the automobile and defense industries, which were the basis of American economic prosperity. Steel strikes and the resulting steel shortages had repercussions throughout the domestic economy. Consequently, by the early 1950s, "Collective bargaining became a kind of three-party chase around the maypole: the union pursuing the companies for wage boosts, the companies hounding the government for approval to raise prices to cover the wage hikes, and the government . . . dashing after the union to obtain strike restraint (as well as labor votes)" (Hoerr 1988: 105). Such was the situation in late 1951 when Harry Truman's troubles with the steel mills began.

The Steel Mill Seizure

On December 31, 1951, five months after peace talks began with North Korea, the contract between the United Steel Workers (USW) and the major steel companies expired. Both sides encouraged and participated in collective bargaining, but the process resulted in frustration and stalemate. Truman personally requested that USW members continue on the job despite the lack of a contract as the nation was not only at war, but was at a crucial period in peace talks, and Truman desperately wanted to avoid even the appearance of American incapacity. The workers agreed.

Truman then referred the dispute to the Wage Stabilization Board (WSB), a section of the Office of Defense Mobilization. The WSB was composed of equal parts labor, management, and public members.

Its job was to manage wage control and "allied functions" for the duration of the Korean War (Neustadt 1990). In peacetime, labor disputes were handled through the mechanisms provided for in the Taft-Hartley Act, which included an 80-day moratorium on strikes. Truman was much criticized for not invoking Taft-Hartley. In his memoirs, he defended the decision to refer the dispute to the WSB because it had been set up specifically for industries related to the war effort (Truman 1956). The idea that the war provided extenuating circumstances justifying extraordinary presidential action was crucial to Truman's later actions.

War provides unusual circumstances. War is very hard on the traditional procedures of a democracy. War demands speed, secrecy, decisive action, and quick response. These are singularly difficult to reconcile with the democratic process as it has evolved in the United States. Consequently, democracy as a procedure suffers during wartime. The presidency as an institution, however, gains immeasurably. As Commander-in-Chief, the president has access to military information and is intimately involved with the prosecution of most wars. As the nation's chief political leader, the president decides how much of that information to share with Congress and the American people. Given the exigencies of war, the president is generally granted an impressive degree of leeway in deciding what constitutes "necessary" action and how much information to share. Presidents are rarely slow in availing themselves of this leeway.

In early 1952, therefore, Truman felt that he had a choice between treating the steel dispute as just another labor problem to be handled as outlined in Taft-Hartley, or as an incipient crisis potentially affecting both the war effort and the progress of the peace talks. Like most presidents (Windt 1990), Truman preferred to define the dispute as a potential crisis and thus bolster his own authority.

The WSB began hearing the case on January 10, 1952. The hearings lasted until February 26. During that time, the USW twice postponed strikes, both times at Truman's request. They set a third strike date for April 9.

On March 20, the WSB, after much internal debate among members, agreed to terms and informed the president of their recommendations. The terms involved a wage increase for the steel workers and some price relief to help the industry offset its cost. The union immediately and enthusiastically endorsed the WSB recommendations. The steel company did not.

Truman was caught in a bind. The WSB was part of an exceedingly complex bureaucracy charged with governing the wartime economy. A rise in the price of steel could easily upset the careful balances the government was seeking to maintain. Truman had to support the Board;

it was part of his administration. He wanted to support labor; personal inclination as well as political expedience dictated that preference. He considered the wage increase fair and thought that steel profits could absorb them without price relief (Truman 1956). But he could not afford to alienate the steel mill owners. The Pentagon feared that a steel strike and resulting shortages could precipitate an enemy offensive in Korea. But Truman could not budge the representatives of the steel industry, who insisted on price relief as compensation before they would agree to the wage increase.

To make matters worse, Charles Wilson, Truman's Director of the Office of War Mobilization, the WSB's parent bureaucracy, publicly criticized the WSB's recommendations at a press conference, thus alienating labor and weakening the president's bargaining position with the industry (Gosnell 1980). Wilson resigned on March 29, 1952, but the damage had been done. The administration was not sending out consistent messages, which undermined the president's strategic position.

After Wilson's resignation, the White House became even more directly involved in mediating—or attempting to mediate—the dispute. The WSB's recommendations were tabled, and collective bargaining was again attempted. A settlement, however, remained elusive.

Truman was informed by then Attorney General Tom Clark (who as a Supreme Court Justice would later vote against the president's action) that there was "no reasonable doubt as to the President's authority" to seize the mills (Murphy 1969: 328). Two hours before the April 9 strike deadline, Truman ordered a federal seizure of the steel mills. Workers continued on the job as federal employees. The mills were administered by the Secretary of Commerce. The mill owners accepted the seizure but went immediately to court, claiming that Truman had "acted without statutory sanction," and that the seizure was therefore illegal (Neustadt 1990: 15). The government's attorneys argued that the seizure was necessary to the national defense and was justified in terms of "inherent" presidential power. While citing national defense as justification and explanation for presidential excesses was a time-honored presidential tactic, the assertion of "inherent" presidential power was not. Truman himself repudiated this claim, a fact that failed to lessen the acrimony heaped on Truman by the courts, members of Congress, and newspaper editorials (Neustadt 1990: 15).

The acrimony was intense. *Newsweek* characterized Truman's actions as "demagogic, intemperate, and full of distortions" (Hazlitt 1952); Republican members of Congress called for investigations and/or impeachment (Egan 1952); and the *Wall Street Journal* (1952) foresaw imminent danger to the republic:

But if this doctrine which the President asserts and gives substance by this deed is true, the doctrine that the powers of the Presidency are limited only by what the holder thinks is the country's welfare, then we cannot long keep government by law. The provocations for power will grow as fast as the precedents. We may continue to have a good and just government. But make no mistake about it—it will be a government by men.

On April 29, a district judge decided in favor of the steel industry, declaring that the president had, in this instance, exceeded his authority. The USW called a strike effective the same day.

Three days later, an appeals court paved the way for the case to be heard before the U.S. Supreme Court. With this news, workers began to return to work at the mills. At Truman's request, workers and management agreed to meet at the White House to attempt a settlement. The talks, however, never got off the ground. On May 3, the Supreme Court took jurisdiction of the case. The Court ordered a freeze on wages pending a decision. There was thus nothing for the workers to negotiate, and the White House-sponsored talks collapsed.

On June 2, the Supreme Court upheld the original ruling on the seizure, declaring that Truman had exceeded his authority. That, however, was almost all that the Justices could seem to agree on, as they presented "a set of opinions so diverse as to establish nothing except the outcome" (Neustadt 1990: 16). The outcome, from Truman's point of view, was more than enough. The Court agreed that the president could, at least potentially, exceed the strict limits of constitutional authority during a crisis, but they were not persuaded that a steel strike constituted a significant enough crisis to make such presidential excess imperative.

Tom Clark, now an Associate Justice, voted with the majority, despite his earlier advocacy of the president's decision. In an oral history interview, Clark (1972: 216) remembered the vote:

It wasn't based on a strict construction of the statutes involved. It just said that the President ought to follow the rules that the Congress had laid down, as I saw them. Such instances there were statutes in the books that the President was obliged to follow; that was my point.

Truman immediately returned control of the steel mills to private hands. Again, a strike ensued. The steel mills remained closed for 53 days. On July 24, 1952, collective bargaining, along with White House capitulation on the issue of compensatory price relief, produced a settlement. The USW got a little less than they would have under the original WSB plan. The steel companies were the big winners, getting vastly more price relief than the government originally offered. Harry Truman, rebuked by the Court and reviled by the press, was the big loser.

Following the Supreme Court decision, for instance, a typical editorial read:

> Americans were assured by the United States Supreme Court yesterday that, in fighting totalitarianism abroad, they will not have to surrender basic liberties at home. The majority opinion of Justice Black rejects out of hand the amazing contention that an emergency confers upon the President of the United States inherent powers that transcend those given him in the Constitution. (*Journal of Commerce* 1952; see also *New York Times* 1952; *U.S. News and World Report* 1952)

Truman was an astute politician, well able to assess a variety of political situations. He was not immune, however, to the consequences of bad advice (Newcomb 1977). It is likely that he saw the steel dispute as a no-win scenario. In Truman's eyes, the country could not afford a steel strike. His administration could not afford divisive action following the WSB recommendations. Despite these imperatives, he lacked the power to force the steel mill owners to come to terms with their workers.

A large part of presidential communication involves knowing when to be quiet, when not to invest a problem with so much presidential attention that it becomes perceived as a crisis demanding presidential control. Crises only work well for a president when they are relatively controlled and relatively brief. Continued stalemate or episodic minor crises serve only to remind the electorate of presidential powerlessness. Truman was unwilling or unable to recognize and act on this fact.

Worse, Truman's actions appeared to be based not on the public interest, but on a personal desire for power. He had become involved in the strike, had risked the prestige of the office on its outcome, and had taken personal control when the outcome was not to his liking. For a president as invested in the institutional aspect of leadership as Truman, this was an easily avoidable mistake.

Truman's Strategy

Truman's main strategic failure during the steel seizure was his failure to adequately prepare the electorate for the seizure. As with Roosevelt and the Judicial Reform Bill, Truman's actions came as a surprise to much of the relevant audience. Presidents seeking approval for (or at least acquiescence to) unconventional action, particularly when it means an increase in the power of the office, do not gain public sympathy or support through surprises.

Truman had ample opportunity for such preparation. Foreign policy speeches formed a large part of his public speech, and the Cold War played an important role in Truman's foreign policy. In November 1951, for example, Truman said, "Fighting is going on in Korea, and the threat of communist aggression hangs over many other parts of the world. To meet this situation, the United States is now rapidly building up its armed forces. . . . We are doing this because we must."

Truman could have expanded on this theme to underline the importance of the American defense industry and the steel on which it depended. But Truman was unwilling to sound unnecessarily belligerent, and he apparently did not see the need for preparation because he sought until the end to avoid presidential action (Neustadt 1990).

As desirous as he was of avoiding taking the initiative, Truman (1952c) helped to place himself in an untenable position by stressing the importance of the war within the context of Soviet aggression and the consequent importance of the defense industry. The theme of his 1952 State of the Union Address, for instance, hinged on the importance of military preparedness (Truman 1952a).

Although this theme served Truman's purposes in helping him to maintain public support for the Korean War, stressing the need for military preparedness indirectly strengthened the hands of both sides in the steel dispute and thus may have contributed to the stalemate. The workers could threaten to shut down production by striking, and management could argue for increased prices. Both labor and management could base their arguments on the vital nature of the steel industry; both had the government in the middle; both these facts were bolstered by the president's insistence on military preparedness.

On April 8, as Truman prepared to order the seizure of the steel mills, he gave a public address explaining and justifying his action. He argued that the threat of a steel strike precipitated a crisis that necessitated governmental action. That action, which would normally be unacceptable, was justified in this case because "these are not normal times. These are times of crisis" (Truman 1952b).

This strategy of defending the seizure on the basis of a crisis had two main deficiencies. First, it was not clear that there really *was* a crisis. The steel mills had not yet shut down, the troops in Korea had not yet suffered from lack of munitions, the enemy had not yet exploited that lack, the United States' economy had not yet been undermined, and it was not obvious that all or indeed any of these potential disasters were inevitable. Preventing a disaster is considerably less dramatic than resolving one; claiming power to do so is thus considerably more difficult.

This problem could have been at least partially ameliorated by an effective public relations campaign. Truman aide Harold Enerson

(1952) recommended such a campaign long before the mills were actually seized. He said, "The government has, or should have, a sound position. It can win only if the public sees the real issues. A public hearing is one of several devices for mobilizing opinion. . . . Continued indecision and vacillation by government will surely promote a crisis." Unfortunately, Truman disregarded this advice.

Second, Truman's persuasive task was made more difficult by his rhetorical style (Stuckey 1991). Since assuming the presidency, Truman had emphasized one crisis after another. Although presidents often make effective use of crisis rhetoric to bolster their assumption of power, overuse of that rhetoric had, in Truman's case, the effect of "crying wolf" and diminished its utility. He referred to "grave threats," "tremendous tasks," "burdens and responsibilities," and a plethora of "critical situations" (Truman 1945a, 1945b, 1946a, 1946b, 1947). Truman found, and the country survived, crises so often that it was difficult to fully credit Truman's claim for yet another earth-shaking disaster. If there is not widespread consensus on at least the existence, if not the nature, of a crisis, no president will be likely to muster support for action based on that "crisis." Furthermore, the threat of a steel strike was a domestic rather than a foreign crisis, and domestic crises are less likely to result in an increase of presidential power (Windt 1990).

Truman further undermined his already weak strategic position by refusing to make arguments in favor of the seizure. Initially, he was constrained from speaking by the fact of Wilson's differences with the WSB; Truman had no desire to expose the rift within his own administration. Later, he felt inhibited because the case was before the courts. Truman's refusal to comment and offer his interpretation of events did not similarly bind either the steel industry or the news media, all of whom had plenty to say. In his *Memoirs*, Truman (1956: 476) said:

> I have always believed that the way our newspapers sometimes comment on matters pending in the courts is an unethical attempt to influence a judge in deciding a case. Certainly in the steel case every effort was made to present a slanted view of situation and to color the atmosphere. The public relations experts for the companies skillfully shifted public attention from the price demands of the industry to the supposedly abnormal and unprecedented act of the president.

Truman may have taken what he considered to be an ethical stance in refusing to communicate his point of view on the steel dispute, but it was hardly an effective persuasive strategy. Truman's silence meant that the public heard only criticism of the president. The Court's decision notwithstanding, Truman was inevitably hurt in public opinion. In the face of so much negative press, this would have been true even had the Court supported the steel mill seizure (Gosnell 1980).

When Truman was asked about the seizure at an April press conference, he responded by assuming what Dan Hahn and J. Justin Gustainis (1987: 54) call the role of the "omnipotent hero [who] is the only one who can see clearly, [and] thus is the logical one to define exaggeration." By assuming this role, Truman attempted to discredit his opponents' arguments without offering any of his own. As with Roosevelt's statement, that "there is no news" in his court-packing defeat, Truman's attempted deflection did not work.

Throughout the steel dispute, Truman appeared to assume that his status as "omnipotent hero" would be sufficient to make his case. He relied on his position as president to make his argument for him. Knowing that presidents are accorded more discretion during times of crisis, and having little personal authority of his own, Truman defined too many situations as crises and weakened the application of the crisis label in any one case. He failed to prepare the electorate for the seizure and, once the seizure was disputed in the courts, he refused to publicly defend or explain his action. Although he put this refusal down to principle, it was also an example of presidential arrogance. As president, Truman expected to be allowed to take whatever action he deemed necessary. He expected that the presidential assertion of necessity would be sufficient, and that he would not be called on to elaborate or defend his actions. He was, as events proved, wrong.

Truman's actions undermined his ability to perform the presidential role and called into question his fitness as president. Clarence B. Randall (1952), President of Inland Steel, made this explicit in a nationally broadcast address of his own:

> I have a deep sense of responsibility as I face this vast audience of the air. I am here to make answer on behalf of the steel industry to charges flung over these microphones last night by the man who then stood where I stand now. I am a plain citizen. He was the President of the United States. Happily we still live in a country where a plain citizen may look the President in the eye and tell him that he was wrong, but actually, it is not the President of the United States to whom I make answer. It is Harry S. Truman, the man, who last night so far transgressed his oath of office, so far abused the power which is temporarily his, that he must now stand and take it. I shall not let my deep respect for the office which he holds stop me from denouncing his shocking distortions of fact. Nor shall I permit the honor of his title to blind the American people from the enormity of what he has done.

From the president's point of view, there could be no more damning accusation, no more complete rebuke, than to have his character so far separated from the presidential role.

Discussion

Presidents have a tendency to assume that their point of view is the definitive one. Presidents have more information and a broader perspective on issues than most people in or out of government. But that does not guarantee the rightness of their perspective, nor does it relieve presidents of their persuasive burden. Presidential action—especially unorthodox presidential action—without adequate presidential explanation will have little chance of meeting public approval. Presidents do not get their definition of events accepted automatically. Whether or not they want to, they must argue for that definition. Refusal to do so is a sign of the arrogance that accompanies overreaching. Presidents who feel that they do not have to explain their actions are presidents who have lost sight of the nature of their power. They are also presidents who are likely to be called to account for that in the near future.

Richard Neustadt (1990) sees the steel case as an instance illustrating the inadequacy of command. For Neustadt, "Command is but a method of persuasion, not a substitute, and not a method suitable for every day employment" (28). Although Truman himself understood the presidency as primarily a persuasive office, he chose to ignore that in the steel case.

As Roosevelt assumed that his personal stature would suffice to ensure success in his conflict over the Judicial Reform Bill, Truman acted as if his institutional status as president during a war would suffice to ensure that his seizure of the steel mills would stand. Both presidents had some basis for these beliefs: Roosevelt had just won a national election by a huge majority, and Truman had not previously hesitated to command what he could not achieve through legislation (as in the executive order providing integration of the military). When Congress fought Truman in 1947-1948, he fought back and won a surprise victory. Such events do not teach humility.

Past political experience led both Roosevelt and Truman to believe that their goals lay well within the boundaries of their legitimate political and institutional prerogatives. To his credit, Truman tried very hard to avoid seizing the steel mills. Direct action on his part was clearly a last resort. Like many last resorts, however, it was poorly planned. Truman's example should serve as a warning on the importance of keeping presidential options open. Sometimes, no matter how skillful the executive, the last resort may become the only resort. Presidents who want to limit the damage caused by this circumstance would be well advised to plan ahead; they need to prepare the public and themselves for such an eventuality.

Truman was not the first president who found himself doing that which he would have liked to avoid. Neither was he the first president who felt impelled to do things he hoped to avoid as a result of war. He was certainly not the last. For Lyndon Johnson, however, the consequences would be infinitely more serious.

LYNDON JOHNSON AND THE VIETNAM WAR

The Political and Institutional Context

Lyndon Johnson became president following John F. Kennedy's assassination in November 1963. Kennedy, who had won the presidency in 1960 by a narrow margin, had spent a frustrating thousand days in office. Once elected, he faced the problems engendered by ambitious national goals and a lack of congressional support. Stymied on domestic issues, Kennedy, like many other presidents, turned to foreign affairs.

"Foreign policy" in the early 1960s meant the American relationship with the Soviet Union and the Cold War generally. Kennedy's initial dealings with world communism were disastrous. In April 1961, he blundered into the Bay of Pigs. That June, during a summit in Vienna, Nikita Khrushchev threatened him with a blockade of Berlin. Kennedy badly needed a way to assert American power and his personal strength as a leader in response. He chose Vietnam (Davidson 1988; Westmoreland 1977).

War had been ravaging Vietnam for decades. The French had been driven out in 1954, and the country divided along the 17th parallel. Communists in the North, however, sought reunification under Communist leadership, and a civil war ensued. The Viet Cong steadily increased both the size and improved the effectiveness of their attacks on the South in 1959. By 1960, South Vietnamese President Diem was nearly overthrown. By early 1961, the situation was rapidly deteriorating. The Communist involvement in Diem's troubles encouraged American response.

That response was necessarily limited however. Although it was important, in American thinking, not to "lose" Vietnam the way China had supposedly been "lost," working against that myth was an equally powerful belief that a large-scale ground war in Asia could not be won. Furthermore, the extent of American military involvement was limited by the belief that both China and the Soviet Union had an interest in protecting North Vietnam, and that excessive force by the United States would bring either or both nations into the war. The situation was further complicated by the fact that all three nations—the United States, China, and the USSR—had nuclear capabilities.

These beliefs helped to create the trap that ensnared American policymakers: It was important not to "lose" South Vietnam to Communist forces, but it was equally important to avoid any action that would precipitate a response by either China or the Soviet Union. American policy thus became defined in negative terms: do not lose, but do not come so close to winning that China and the USSR become involved (Davidson 1988). The war thus became one of protracted, but limited American involvement (FitzGerald 1972).

No other aspect of John Kennedy's legacy was to prove as troubling to Johnson as Vietnam. Johnson's primary political expertise lay in domestic policy; lacking foreign policy experience, he was dependent on advisers (Turner 1985). As a former vice president, Johnson was also bound by what "he thought John Kennedy would have done and what Kennedy's top advisors were now pressing him to do" (Woodward 1991: 9; see also Califano 1991). This burden was not lifted by Johnson's spectacular landslide in the 1964 presidential election. Although now president in his own right, Johnson was neither freed from Kennedy's ghost nor from Vietnam. In July 1965, Johnson made the fateful decision to escalate the war, and thus made it his own (Berman 1982).

Social policies, labeled together under the rubric of the Great Society, would merit less and less of the president's attention as the war consumed more and more of his time. Johnson thought that he could juggle programmatic increases at home along with an increasingly expensive war abroad; that he could, with his vaunted political skill, have both his guns and the people's butter. He was wrong.

As Johnson's term progressed, the tension between his domestic goals and the imperatives of maintaining the war increased. Racial riots began in 1964 and continued sporadically through 1967 and 1968. By 1967, protestors against the war were creating spectacles of their own, culminating in the fiasco surrounding the 1968 Democratic National Convention.

All this conflict in the ghettoes, on college campuses, and in the streets was covered on national television. All the violence, the chaos, and the confusion were brought into American living rooms every evening. For the first time in history, war came into living rooms too. Night after night, Americans absorbed footage straight from combat in all of its horrific reality.

That reality was made even more horrific by the nature of the Vietnam War. World War II had been fought as a war of attrition between equally modern armies. War technology provided a distinct advantage, as the bombing of Hiroshima and Nagasaki proved. Vietnam was a very different war, and different rules of warfare applied (Lansdale 1977; Shaplen 1971), although American policymakers tended to try to use World War II as a guide for policymaking in Vietnam (Warnke 1969). It was hard to make sense of this war, fought as it was in a place so few Americans understood, where technology could not provide the decisive edge (FitzGerald 1972). Given this confusion and lack of understanding among the public, the task of interpreting the war fell to the president and to the media (Turner 1985).

It was the media that Lyndon Johnson consequently came to hate most (Goldman 1969; Valenti 1975). Johnson had always given his loyalty to those in high office (so long as that office was higher than his own). As John Kennedy's vice president, Johnson had been loyal to Kennedy. Now, as the leader of a nation at war, Johnson expected to get the unswerving loyalty of that nation (Berman 1988). Any criticism from the press was, to Johnson, evidence of disloyalty. In the waning years of his presidency, Johnson was to find plenty of evidence for such disloyalty. Always preoccupied with his public image, Johnson began to carry copies of his public opinion polls with him (Manatos 1969) and would pull them out and cite them at the slightest opportunity.

The war increasingly dominated the national agenda. Politically, Johnson was in the difficult position of alienating liberals by fighting the war at all and alienating conservatives by not fighting it vigorously enough. Those whom Johnson considered himself to have helped the most—Blacks, students, the poor—were disproportionately affected by the war and were screaming obscenities at him, burning the nation's cities, and engaging in all manner of violent and nonviolent protest (Windt 1990). In trying to maintain himself and the nation in the untenable position of a prolonged but limited war, Johnson finally lost his balance and fell from power.

A Chronology of American Involvement in the Vietnam War

This is not the forum for a complete history of American involvement in Vietnam, especially as that task has been done admirably elsewhere (Berman 1982, 1989; Davidson 1988; FitzGerald, 1972). But a brief history of the major events is essential to an understanding of Johnson's strategic failure regarding Vietnam.

U.S. involvement in Vietnam began in 1950, with financial aid to the French. In 1954, following a series of military defeats, the French left Vietnam, and the United States assumed responsibility for protecting the democratic South Vietnam from the invading communist forces from the North. The rationale behind the assumption of this burden lay in America's perception of its role in the world (Lomperis 1984). Following

World War II, the United States assumed a leadership role in international affairs as "the policeman of the world," defending "good" international citizens from communist "thugs." Anticommunism had long been a mainstay of American foreign policy, and it was now used to justify American military involvement in a wide variety of geographical locations (Hinds and Windt 1991).

One of the keystones of institutionalized anticommunism was the "domino theory," which held that in a given region, once communists take over one country, that country would be used as a base for further incursions into its neighboring nations. Give the communists a single nation, this theory holds, and its neighbors will fall one by one, as a standing row of dominoes. As a result of adherence to this theory, small nations of little apparent concern or obvious relevance to American national interest assumed a tremendous significance as pawns in the international chess game between the United States and the Soviet Union (Westmoreland 1977).

After the U.S.-sanctioned overthrow and subsequent assassination of South Vietnamese President Diem on November 1, 1963, American involvement became even more entrenched, for now the United States had accepted responsibility for the internal government of South Vietnam as well as for protecting it from external threat.

Lyndon Johnson did not inherit merely a small problem in a faraway nation. He inherited a beachhead in the war against communism, a war that for two decades had assumed a primary place in American ideology (Hinds and Windt 1991). For Johnson to accept defeat in Vietnam he would also have to accept the logical consequence of that defeat as predicted by the domino theory—the "loss" of Asia to communism:

> The credibility of the President of the United States at a moment of crisis and the fidelity of the United States to its security treaties are both of the utmost importance in maintaining peace in the world. . . . So the issue in Southeast Asia is not just Vietnam, it's not even just Southeast Asia. It has the maintenance of peace in a system in which the United States has security treaties with more than fifty nations. (Rusk 1969b: 5)

This was not a responsibility that Johnson could easily abrogate. The question was how much he would invest in upholding it. Paul Warnke (1969: 9), Johnson's Assistant Secretary of Defense, said, that the argument was "not over principle at all. The argument is over price."

This is not to imply that Johnson had no real choices concerning Vietnam, however, for he clearly did. As Johnson adviser George Ball (1971: 13) said:

There was always a time when a basic change could have been made. I never myself subscribed to the belief that we were ever at a point when we couldn't turn around. What concerned me then as it did much more intensely even later was that the more forces we committed, the more men we committed to Vietnam, the more grandiloquent our verbal encouragement of the South Vietnamese was, the more costly was any disengagement.

There is evidence that American public opinion regarding the war was negatively affected as early as 1963, when Buddhist monks began to burn themselves in the streets of Saigon in protest: "When that picture of the burning bonzes appeared in *Life* magazine, the party was almost over in terms of the imagery that was affecting the American public opinion" (Colby 1981: 30).

Whenever he was faced with a choice, however, Johnson decided in favor of escalation. There is no doubt that Johnson's conception of the presidency contributed to his decision: "You see, as far as Vietnam is concerned, Johnson was his own desk officer. He was actually the Commander-in-Chief" (Rusk 1969a: 38). As far as Johnson was concerned, his position as president, and the credibility of the entire United States was on the line in Vietnam. He was the United States, and the war became his as well.

Johnson may well have felt trapped by the requirements of his role, yet his public character was one that constrained him from making these issues matters of public debate and, consequently, public consensus. He had to play the role of Commander-in-Chief; he could also have chosen to be a consensus builder. Instead, he continually escalated the war and attempted to keep the facts from the American public, apparently believing that he had the political skill to act as a war leader without ever really admitting to prosecuting a war.

Sometimes Johnson went to extremes of manipulation and dishonesty in justifying that choice and attempting to prevent the fragile consensus supporting the war from falling apart. The most famous instance of this manipulation took place in the Gulf of Tonkin in August 1964.

In the early days of August, reports came in to the White House stating that two American ships stationed in the Gulf of Tonkin had been fired on by the North Vietnamese. The exact circumstances surrounding the attack were confusing and unclear. It is not certain that enemy fire was involved (Berman 1987; Davidson 1988). Johnson, however, acted as though American troops had sustained an unprovoked and unwarranted attack (Cherwitz 1987). He asked Congress to sanction enough military support to protect American troops already in the region. On August 10, 1964, after very little debate, Congress passed the Southeast Asia Resolution, better known as the Tonkin Gulf Resolution, which essentially gave Johnson full authorization to expand American involvement in the war, by a vote of 416-0 in the House and 88-2 in the Senate.

At this point in the war, there was a general feeling among Johnson's military advisors that they either had to begin to deescalate and disengage from the war or "do something a lot more substantial" (Cooper 1979: 10). Yet, the United States could not increase involvement without apparent reason because of the potential for domestic and international negative reaction. On February 7, 1965, Viet Cong forces struck at a U.S. airbase in Pleiku, resulting in extensive injuries (137 Americans were wounded, 9 died, 76 had to be evacuated) and serious damage to American equipment (Davidson 1988; Fitzgerald 1972). LBJ ordered reprisals. The program of bombing selected targets as a response to action by the North Vietnamese (Operation Flaming Dart) signaled increased American involvement in the war.

On February 10, the Viet Cong attacked Qui Nhon. Again, Johnson ordered bombing, although this time there was no attempt to link the targets of the bombing with the forces that attacked Qui Nhon. This signaled a new approach to the war, a program of "measured and limited air action," nicknamed Rolling Thunder (Davidson 1988: 336). Later that month, LBJ approved the dispatch of two marine battalions to Da Nang. Although it was not seen at the time as the first step in a troop build-up, it meant the Americanization of the war (FitzGerald 1972).

Although the bombing was theoretically ordered strictly as reprisals for North Vietnamese action, the Johnson administration "seemed unable to pull its socks up and figure out just exactly what the bombing of Vietnam was supposed to accomplish" (Cooper 1979: 15-6). The retaliatory nature of the bombing developed into a problem of how to achieve parity and which acts were worthy of retaliation; eventually, the rationale changed from one of retaliation to one of trying to force Hanoi to negotiate (Cooper 1979) and/or to interdict the flow of men and material from the North (Taylor 1969). A tactic that had begun as punishment ended as a means to entirely different ends.

Johnson's next major decision concerning the war came in July 1965. By this point, it had become clear that the military situation called for either an increase in American military forces or a North Vietnamese victory (Berman 1982; Davidson 1988). Johnson chose to commit U.S. ground forces to the war. This decision was a turning point. The American mission had changed from one of protection to "a more active role" in the prosecution of the war. Despite the obvious significance of this change, Johnson and his staff sought to minimize it in terms of public discussion (Berman 1982):

> What we did not do was to take steps to create a war psychology in
> the United States. . . . One of the important things to reflect upon, as
> far as Vietnam is concerned, is that we were trying to do a kind of
> police job to fend off this aggression against South Vietnam, but to
> do it calmly, and, in effect, in cold blood. (Rusk 1969a: 42)

The attempt to avoid a larger war apparently led the Johnson administration into a position in which they could not amass support for even a
small effort.

The change was even more important given the degree of internal doubt about the wisdom of the new policy. As General Maxwell
Taylor (1969: 5) said, "I had no reservations about recommending the
bombing. I did have reservations about the introduction of ground
forces because it was quite apparent that once we started, no one could
predict what would be required—how far we would go." Yet Johnson
chose to minimize both the doubt regarding his policy and the truth
about the events of the war.

This inconsistency between the military reality of the war and
the war as Johnson chose to portray it created what became known as
the "credibility gap." The credibility gap was a shorthand phrase that
originated among the troops stationed in Vietnam (who wore buttons
claiming that they had been "ambushed at credibility gap"). It first
appeared in the American media in a December 1965 article in the
Washington Post and became a definitive part of the American political
vocabulary when it was picked up and used by Scotty Reston of the *New
York Times* in January 1966 (although at least one Johnson aide believes
that Johnson inherited credibility problems along with an "undefined by
fairly strong commitment" to Vietnam from the Kennedy administration; Cooper 1979). The phrase denoted the lack of confidence that the
troops—and eventually the public—came to feel in the president's public pronouncements on the war.

Although prosecuting a war in an unfamiliar place made the
public more dependent on the president for information (Logue and
Patton 1987), the president was not the only source of information on the
war. When the president's interpretation conflicted with the images seen
nightly on the national news, the result was an undermining of presidential interpretive status (Turner 1985).

This was never more clear than in the days following the Tet
offensive. Tet, the Vietnamese New Year, takes place on January 31. In
1968, it was the occasion for an enormous offensive into the South on the
part of the North Vietnamese. Several key cities were attacked; for a
brief period even the U.S. embassy in Saigon was held by a small group
of North Vietnamese soldiers. Despite this, the Tet offensive was a decisive military defeat for the North, who were beaten back on every front,

and who took enormous casualties. Tet was, however, a major public relations victory for the North, and represented a blow that eventually led to the end of American involvement in the conflict (Lomperis 1984; White 1969).

Americans were shocked and frightened that North Vietnamese forces could have penetrated so deeply into American defenses. It was equally disheartening that the war of attrition seemed to be stalemated. The United States could not fully mobilize an effort against the North Vietnamese—both world opinion and the threat of the Chinese army's potential involvement kept American numbers low. No matter how many troops the United States committed, the North Vietnamese matched that commitment, believing that their best hope for victory lay in protracted stalemate (Berman 1989; Lansdale 1977; Shaplen 1971). As Richard Nixon was quoted as saying, "The Communists . . . had a total commitment to victory. We had, at best, a partial commitment to avoid defeat. If this situation continued, in the end, they would win" (Lomperis 1984: 74-5).

Events proved Nixon correct. On February 27, 1968, Walter Cronkite, reviewing the events of Tet, announced to the television audience that the war in Vietnam was stalemated. With this announcement, made by the man Americans told pollster after pollster that they most trusted, it became clear that the battle for American public opinion had been lost by the president. Two weeks later, Senator Eugene McCarthy, the "peace candidate," did surprisingly well in the New Hampshire presidential primary. Three days later, Robert Kennedy declared his candidacy for President of the United States. On March 31, 1968, Lyndon Johnson, in a televised address, announced both a unilateral cessation of the bombing in Vietnam and his decision not to seek another term as president.

Johnson's handling of the war in Vietnam cost him his presidency, crippled the Great Society, and created a division in the country that is still being felt more than two decades later. As a result of Vietnam, Lyndon Johnson is the most reviled American president in modern times (Woodward 1991). Johnson was not alone in falling into the trap of trying to maintain a limited war over a long period of time, but, as president, he alone bears the responsibility (Berman 1982).

It is possible that there was no way to successfully fight a War on Poverty at home and a war against communism abroad. Certainly, accomplishing victories in both would have been an impressive achievement. A less ambitious president might have made a choice between domestic programs and a foreign war and fully committed the nation to that choice. However unpalatable that choice, a more realistic president might have made it. Lyndon Johnson refused to choose, believing that as a politician he had the skill, and as president the authority, to successfully commit American resources both at home and abroad. For Johnson and for the nation, this turned out to be a tragic miscalculation.

Johnson's Strategy

The single most important fact about Johnson's strategic decisions regarding the public understanding of the conflict in Vietnam is that he wanted to avoid a national debate on the war (Berman 1982; Davidson 1988). In attempting to structure political communication such that national consideration of the war was preempted, Johnson precluded the possibility of developing a national consensus in support of the war. Without such a consensus, Johnson faced a continual communicative battle, always on the defensive, always justifying his actions, never sure who he could depend on for support. This created a situation in which the president's communicative confidence was undermined, and his effectiveness as a communicator correspondingly suffered (Summers 1981). In a democratic context, presidents do much better when they appear to be leading debate rather than attempting to foreclose it. This was understood and accomplished with courage in Johnson's domestic policies. That understanding and courage failed him with regard to Vietnam:

> Once he decided to fight the war, his greatest tactical error as a *political* leader came when he rejected the advice of civilian and military advisors on the question of mobilizing the nation's resources. In deciding *not* to mobilize the Reserves, *not* to seek a congressional resolution or declaration of national emergency, *not* to present the program in a prime-time address to Congress or the nation . . . and *not* to disclose publicly the full extent of the anticipated military call-up, the president's credibility soon became unraveled. (Berman 1982: 147; emphasis in original)

Strategically, Johnson needed to define himself as a war leader, and he needed to define the United States as a nation at war (Turner 1985). Franklin Roosevelt, for instance, accomplished this task when he became "Dr. Win-the-War." Roosevelt put his entire presidency and the entire nation into the war effort and thus constructed a national consensus in favor of the war. Johnson, apparently believing that he already had such a consensus, but also aware of its fragility, did not take the measures necessary to create and sustain public support for the war in Vietnam.

Johnson's refusal to encourage public debate did not mean that he was insensitive to the importance of American public opinion. Quite the contrary. Johnson was extremely sensitive to and interested in affecting the nuances of public opinion. The same logic that led Johnson to apply the model of World War II to Vietnam militarily led him to suggest ways that Americans might be induced to support the war: "We should have some colorful general like MacArthur with his shirt neck open to go in and say [the stalemate issue] is pure propaganda. . . . We have no songs, no parades, no bond drives and we can't win the war otherwise" (Berman 1989: 59).

Johnson appeared to see the war effort as one in which the United States could counter military stalemate with parades and "a colorful general." Communicatively, he had little choice. The United States, symbol of industrial might and technological prowess, was being stalemated by the denizens of a small, impoverished, and agrarian nation. Johnson's task was to somehow contrive the situation such that the United States could continue to believe in its innate morality. As the bombing became synonymous with the war in the eyes of the media and in the mind of the public, this task became increasingly difficult (Berman 1989).

Johnson's most successful attempt to justify the Vietnam War came on April 7, 1965, at Johns Hopkins University in Baltimore, just three months before he made the decision to commit U.S. ground forces to the fighting. In this speech, Johnson relied on a "progression from force to reason, war to peace, stick to carrot" (Turner 1985: 128). Throughout, Johnson (1965) was at his presidential best, assuming that he had support instead of asking for it and assuming the task of educating the audience about the war instead of berating them for their lack of understanding:

> I have come here to review once again with my own people the views of the American Government. Tonight Americans and Asians are dying for a world where each people may choose its own path to change. . . . We fight because we must fight if we are to live in a world where every country can shape its own destiny. And only in such a world will our own freedom be finally secure. This kind of world will never be built by bombs or bullets. Yet the infirmities of man are such that force must often precede reason, and the waste of war, the works of peace. We wish that this were not so. But we must deal with the world as it is, if it is ever to be as we wish.

Johnson skillfully interwove the principles Americans had long understood as legitimate justification for war with the necessity of Southeast Asia. Effective presidential communication generally follows the pattern Johnson displayed here, moving from abstract principle to the practical policy being advocated.

Johnson (1965) connected the Vietnam War to both American principles and American self-interest: "The confused nature of this conflict cannot mask the fact that it is the new face of an old enemy. Over this war—and all Asia—is another reality: the deepening shadow of Communist China. The rulers in Hanoi are urged on by Peking." By holding up the specter of world communism, Johnson provided a powerful justification for the war, and one, within the context provided by the cold war, that was not likely to be lightly dismissed.

At Johns Hopkins, Johnson (1965) also made it clear that the war was not of his choosing, and that he would prefer alternatives short of war: "We often say how impressive power is. But I do not find it impressive at all. The guns and the bombs, the rockets and the warships, are symbols of human failure. They protect what we cherish. But they are witness to human folly." Johnson would prefer "a dam built across a mighty river [or] . . . electrification of the countryside" to war, but the choice was not given him. Here, Johnson united his public character as a man known to prefer the building of schools to the bombing of families, with the role of the president as keeper of the national conscience. He spoke of both the necessity and the limits of power. Later, when he forsook the role and relied exclusively on the character, both suffered.

The Johns Hopkins speech was powerful, moving, and effective. One of Johnson's best speeches about the war, it was also one of his few speeches on the war. In July 1965, for example, Johnson tried to minimize the war. He announced the decision to commit ground forces, a decision that signified a major shift in American policy, during a noon news conference at which he also announced his nomination of Abe Fortas to the Supreme Court and his appointment of NBC's John Chancellor to Voice of America. Both the timing and the context implied that the news on Vietnam was routine (Turner 1985). As opposition to the war mounted, Johnson became increasingly entrenched. The administration's message was passed on to the public via surrogates for the president rather than by the president himself.

On September 29, 1967, Johnson delivered a televised address on the war in Vietnam before the National Legislative Conference in San Antonio, TX. Johnson (1967) now made defense of American security interests the central argument justifying the war:

> We cherish freedom—yes. We cherish self-determination for all people—yes. We abhor the political murder of any state by another, and the bodily murder of any people by gangsters of whatever ideology. And for 27 years—since the days of lend-lease—we have sought to strengthen free people against domination by aggressive foreign powers. But the key to all that we have done is really our own security. At times of crisis—before asking Americans to fight and die to resist aggression in a foreign land—every American President has finally had to answer this question: Is the aggression a threat—not

only to the immediate victim—but to the United States of America and to the peace and security of the entire world of which we in America are a very vital part?

Americans thus were not "fighting the war Asian boys ought to fight" (Johnson 1964), but were fighting the war American boys ought to be fighting—they were fighting to defend the United States.

As with the Johns Hopkins address, the San Antonio speech was well received by the media (Turner 1985). The media's reaction to these speeches should have indicated to Johnson that he stood to gain from making clear and cogent public arguments for his administration's policies in Vietnam. But Johnson mistrusted the media, refused to believe that he would be treated fairly, and was, in any case, poorly equipped to lead an all-out public relations blitz, even if he could be persuaded of the necessity and value of one (Berman 1988; Stuckey 1991).

Rhetorically, Lyndon Johnson found himself in an invidious position. He could not, as Senator Aiken (D-VT) suggested, "declare victory and come home" without "losing" South Vietnam—and in his mind therefore all of Asia—to the communists. He could not escalate the war further without risking a land war with China. He could not defend a limited war to the American public as "hawks" demanded much more and "doves" demanded much less. Worst of all, Johnson could not explain and defend the rationale for American involvement in a short, memorable phrase. Americans had remembered the Alamo and the Maine, had attempted to make the world safe for democracy, and had fought the evil of fascism. But the nature of the cause that kept the United States mired in the Vietnamese quagmire was less reducible to sloganeering.

Vietnam was not a crusade, but an instrument of policy: "So if enduring peace can ever come to Asia, all mankind will benefit. But if peace fails there, no where else will our achievements really be secure" (Johnson 1966b). By the Vietnam era, it was much harder for audiences to see South Vietnam as vital to U.S. security interests than it had been for them to see France and Great Britain in a similar light 30 years earlier (Barrett 1989). The Axis, by invading one country after another, by breaking one treaty after another, lent plausibility to the argument that American security depended on their defeat. The imperialist ambitions of the North Vietnamese, however, were, in the late 1960s and early 1970s, far more difficult to substantiate. Although Johnson was capable of speaking passionately about the war, he spoke to a different audience, one that was embedded in a changed political situation. Within that new context, Johnson was left without a powerful and clear moral argument; all he had was the instrumental appeal.

This instrumental understanding of the war was connected to a rhetorical lack of purpose, an absence of a vision of victory. During World War II, Roosevelt offered the hope of a new, moral order, a structure for the preservation of peace. During Vietnam, Americans were offered only a respite from disaster, a continued stalemate through continued containment. Roosevelt gave the public a fear to run from and a hope to work toward. Johnson (1966a) offered only the fear:

> Tonight the cup of peril is full in Vietnam. . . . The conflict is not an isolated episode, but another great event in the policy that we have followed with strong consistency since World War II.

Combined with a steady increase in troops and continual expansion of the war, the lack of rhetorical purpose and commitment characteristic of Johnson's war-related rhetoric helped to create an ambiguous situation. In 1965, Johnson said, "In that region, there is nothing that we covet. There is nothing that we seek. There is no territory or no military position, or no political ambition" (Wicker 1968: 274). If this was true, what then of the "domino theory"? If we were not there to halt the communist expansion in Asia, why were we there? The confusion was not lessened by Johnson's decision to change the mission of the troops in Vietnam from defensive to offensive positions while attempting to limit public disclosure (and public discussion) of this change (Berman 1982; Davidson 1988).

As Theodore Windt (1990: 92) noted:

> Johnson had no real fall-back position other than the claims that aggression had to be stopped and that America would not be defeated in Vietnam. This lack of specific goals in Vietnam remained a persistent rhetorical and policy problem. . . . Johnson gave little direction on where the United States intended to go in Vietnam, but at the same time, he was closing the back door, leaving no honorable escape from the conflict there.

Lacking an honorable escape from Vietnam, Johnson was forced to seek one from the presidency. On March 31, 1968, after Eugene McCarthy's surprise showing in New Hampshire and Robert Kennedy's decision to challenge him for the Democratic presidential nomination, Johnson conceded defeat. He ordered a bombing halt and announced his decision not to seek another term as president:

> With America's sons in the fields far away, with America's future under challenge right here at home, with our hopes and the world's hopes for peace in the balance every day, I do not believe that I

should devote an hour or a day from my time to any personal partisan causes or to any duties other than the awesome duties of the office—the Presidency of your country. Accordingly, I shall not seek, and I will not accept, the nomination of my party for another term as your president. (Johnson 1968)

Johnson's decision did not end either the war or the national division and civil strife it fomented. It did end Johnson's political career, a career that combined stellar domestic achievements with spectacular foreign policy failure.

Discussion

Like Harry Truman during the steel crisis, Lyndon Johnson in Vietnam exerted what power he could as the president of a nation at war. Presidents are always powerful; presidents at war are even more so. But even during wartime, presidents do not have the power to act unilaterally over long periods of time without reckoning with Congress and the American public.

For Truman, the Supreme Court was the key battleground. Politics had changed by the time that Lyndon Johnson took office, and, for him, it was the court of public opinion that mattered most. Knowing this, Johnson was still unable to respond effectively to the public. He realized that arguing for the prolongation of a limited war was difficult rhetorically, and he therefore decided to stop arguing for the war rather than stopping the war.

At least one lesson may be derived from the example set by Lyndon Johnson: If a president cannot make a convincing argument for a desired course of action, then it is certainly possible that the course of action is not all that desirable. It is an error for presidents to assume that they know best and that their knowledge is a sufficient basis for action. They may well know best; certainly those who elect them hope so. But knowledge is not enough. Persuasion is a large part of the president's leadership task, and the act of persuading is an important part of public expectations for the presidential role. Whether their actions are eventually judged as right or wrong, in their own time presidents who ignore the communicative and persuasive aspects of the office will be punished.

Lyndon Johnson inherited the Vietnam War. He wanted the Great Society. But he and his staff reasoned that his role as president dictated that they had an obligation to

go where the trouble is. In other words, we didn't pick this place. This is where the crisis occurred. It either had to be met there, or not at all. If it hadn't been met at all, then Thailand would have gone. Laos would have long since followed, and I suspect the Communists would still be in charge in Djakarta. (Taylor 1969: 10)

This makes pretty unconvincing reading in the aftermath of the Cold War, and it was pretty unconvincing to many people then. But it was not unconvincing to the man who was president, who felt that he had to risk his Great Society for the demands of his role as Commander-in-Chief. As Berman (1982: 150) wrote:

Lyndon Johnson's greatest fault as a political leader was that *he chose* not to choose between the Great Society and the war in Vietnam. Instead he sought a pragmatic guns-and-butter solution for avoiding what he believed would surely have been a divisive national debate in order temporarily to protect his Great Society. (emphasis in original)

The problem was that Johnson could only protect the Great Society temporarily. The war eventually drove the Great Society programs off of the national agenda as it drove Johnson from office. Johnson apparently believed that he could have it all—domestic programs and a foreign war. He relied on his famous personal and political skill and his institutional authority as president to parlay his domestic policy consensus into support for the war without having to do so overtly. In so acting, Johnson not only overreached his power, he also led the nation into a turbulent and divisive war.

CONCLUSIONS

Presidents stake their places in history on specific programs, specific ideas, and specific definitions of themselves and the polity that they govern. They spend enormous amounts of time and considerable energy enacting those programs, promoting those ideas, and propagating those definitions. But they are embedded in a governmental structure designed to thwart the most ambitious of those programs and ideas. Presidents are consequently continually frustrated.

Frequently, presidents respond to that frustration by swearing, gritting their teeth, and settling for what they can get, realizing that "politics is the art of the possible," and that "half a loaf is better than none." On occasion, however, they decide that the rules of "business as usual" do not apply to them, that this program is too important, or that idea is too basic, to settle for only a piece of what they want. Or they decide that this time, just this once, the environment is right, and by pushing their luck, they can get what they want.

Sometimes the gamble pays off. Franklin Roosevelt passed his New Deal and his Second New Deal. Harry Truman won in 1948. Lyndon Johnson got his Great Society. Presidents win against the odds just often enough so that they know such winning is possible. Furthermore, they believe that they know what made the winning possible. They know that it was not the context, for the structure of government is remarkably effective at blocking and stalling presidential initiatives. So they come to believe that it is them: their skill, their vision, their personal ability, the power of their public character. Believing that, they try it again. But this time, they try it differently. Overreaching is caused by the arrogance born of past success. So instead of approaching things cautiously, consulting with advisors, remembering the lessons of past political experience, they assume that all they have to do is act. They are generally wrong.

Overreaching tends to occur when presidents decide that their frustration is not a product of their official place in the institutionalized system, but instead is somehow personal. Had Roosevelt not felt personally thwarted by the Supreme Court's rejection of his New Deal, he might not have allowed his personal rage to interfere with his political judgment. Had Truman felt less personally responsible for resolving the steel dispute, or Johnson less personally committed to the war in Vietnam, their political instincts may have suggested alternative courses of action. They may not have felt such a burden of necessity had they been less personally involved.

The lesson of this chapter is that one recipe for presidential strategic failure contains equal parts arrogance and oversensitivity. When blended well, the result is not palatable. The arrogance is the product of past political success. The sensitivity is the product of the modern presidency as a personalized institution, in which the focus tends to be on the individual who is president rather than on the presidency as an institution. Overreaching is thus the flaw of successful presidents. Neustadt (1990) noted that the office is no place for amateurs. The evidence presented here indicates that there are no guarantees for professionals either.

Conclusion

PRESIDENTIAL PLANS

Presidents are held responsible for practically everything that occurs during their administrations. Consequently, they seek to control as much of their environment as possible. This need for control causes presidents to approach the office strategically, calculating how their actions will affect not only the issue under immediate consideration, but their future standing in the office as well. Approaching the office strategically, however, does not, in itself, guarantee success. Presidents are as prone to miscalculation as anyone else; the consequences of their strategic calculations, however, are more public in their effects than are those of private citizens.

Strategic miscalculations affect presidents both instrumentally, in that they fail to accomplish a specific goal, and ethically, in that strategic failures affect the public perception of the president and the presidency. Failure thus has an impact on the public construction of the presidential character. As a personalized office, the presidency is dependent on the character of the individual who is president. The public construction of that character is therefore vital to the performance of the office.

The process of publicly constructing presidential character has changed over time, although all presidents have been concerned about their images and the political consequences resulting from them (Pessen

1984). Presidents governing in the modern era, however, have faced unique pressures and difficulties. The most important of these pressures are those that stem from the increased complexity of the federal government and the incursion of the media into the presidency.

Since the inception of the New Deal, the federal government has grown tremendously, often beyond its ability to organize itself. The president now sits atop a vast organization of differing, sometimes competing, bureaucratic structures. Attempting to push policy through those structures can be, and often is, a source of intense frustration for the president (Buchanan 1978). The president has, however, many resources that can be brought to bear in the endeavor to accomplish policy goals and two main sources of support—Congress and the mass public.

Presidents at least since Roosevelt have sought an increased role for the president and the presidency in the American polity. The public images of presidents and presidential aspirants are largely created by their standing with the public, rather than their standing with other professional politicians. Their relations with the mass public are also powerful sources of influence with other political elites (Edwards 1989).

In terms of negotiating with Congress, presidents have fairly routinized patterns of interaction that can be generally relied on. That routinization can work both to presidents' advantage and to their disadvantage. The refusal to follow set patterns can confuse Congress and upset the normal pattern of behavior. Presidents may well be able to take advantage of this confusion and obtain the legislation they want. On the other hand, refusing to follow or otherwise ignoring congressional needs is assuming a risk, no matter how calculated.

As the federal government has grown in size and complexity, presidents have sought ways to cope with that growth. Often these coping mechanisms have resulted in some increased latitude for action, while at the same time constraining the president. For example, even though the mass public are now a source of presidential influence with Congress, they are also a constraint, for presidents must appease that public and, at the same time, compete with members of Congress for that influence.

This has become even more difficult as the media have become increasingly important in the governmental process. The media have become the dominant agenda setters of the national government (Cantril 1991), and presidents who are not cognizant and respectful of the media's organizational and structural requirements are presidents who are likely to suffer (Bennett 1988; Kellner 1990).

PRESIDENTIAL FAILURES

Presidents operate in a complex environment. That complexity urges presidents toward attempting to control whatever they can and pretending to control even more than they can. That pretense of control in turn increases the public expectations of the office and forces the president to respond to those expectations. Presidents thus face an extraordinarily difficult strategic task every time they set out to accomplish anything. Given the difficulty of that task, it is remarkable that there are not more presidential failures, and that they do not damage more presidencies more severely. That they do not is a result of the inherent conservative bias in the American system, a bias that resists change as it resists rash action.

However, there is little doubt that these changes in the American political context have not worked to the president's advantage. Strategic mistakes are more easily made and less easily recovered from in this environment. An emphasis on quick results and immediate analysis robs both the president and the public of a sense of perspective, a more balanced lens for viewing the president's performance of the presidential role. Bill Clinton in particular has been perceived as poorly adapting to the challenges of the presidency. The themes of this book take on particular resonance when applied to his experience in the Oval Office.

STRATEGIC MISCALCULATIONS AND THE CLINTON PRESIDENCY

Bill Clinton entered the White House with several major disadvantages: He had fought a bruising campaign, in which the "character issue" refused to be resolved, the third-party presence of Ross Perot helped to provide him with a very narrow margin of victory, and the political climate of the early 1990s was anything but favorable to politicians in Washington.

Partially as a result of the campaign and the prevailing political climate, Clinton would have faced some serious questions about his character and his fitness for the presidential role. He compounded his problems, however, by making several key mistakes early in his administration, mistakes that have largely defined that administration.

Slippage in the Clinton Administration

Bill Clinton entered the White House after a campaign in which accusations of corruption and mismanagement in government played an important role. Yet he was not free from doubts concerning his character. There was something unusually personal in the animus Clinton created, prompting one journalist to compare the anger that follows Clinton to that which followed both Franklin Roosevelt and Richard Nixon into the White House (Perry 1994). From Gennifer Flowers to draft dodging and the questions surrounding his use of marijuana in college, Clinton as "Slick Willie" lacked maneuvering room should his character come under attack (Bennett 1995).

Attacking the character of political opponents, however, has become a widely used, if not widely accepted, tactic. Clinton was the object of many such attacks from his inauguration forward. Clinton's "honeymoon" with the national media was the shortest on record, and he was on the defensive from very early on in his administration. Two issues in particular have caused serious slippage problems for the president: his sexual past and Whitewater.

Clinton's sexual behavior became a key issue of the 1994 campaign, as allegations of extramarital affairs became public. Clinton and his wife Hillary effectively ended fidelity as a campaign issue after a post-Super Bowl appearance on *Sixty Minutes*. The issue stayed with Clinton, however, for after the election, Arkansas law enforcement officials told of using state police cars to escort Clinton's women friends to and from the Governor's Mansion. Some evidence later surfaced casting doubt on the credibility of the witnesses, and the issue temporarily disappeared. The next year, however, Clinton was accused of sexually harassing a young aide, who brought suit against the president. There is some question as to whether a sitting president can be sued for actions that occurred before he assumed office, and the issue is currently before the courts.

The amount of damage these allegations have caused is hard to measure. What is clear is that these allegations feed into doubts concerning the president's character and whether he can adequately perform the presidential role. Sexual misconduct is less inflammatory now than it has been in the past. Yet, although not sufficient to destroy a presidency, the imputations made against Clinton do contribute to a certain unease regarding his character. This is particularly true as there appears to be a nearly constant stream of such allegations, and once one is forgotten, another takes its place.

Clinton could probably survive allegations of marital infidelity with little difficulty; they are important primarily because they remind people of doubts concerning his character. Those reminders are especially important when there is evidence of other sorts of improprieties. Those other allegations do exist. Since the early days of the Clinton administration, his dealings with the Whitewater land development project have generated headlines and headaches for the president.

The details of the Whitewater scandal, involving as they do accusations of relatively arcane financial dealings, are less important here then their consequences. Beginning with a series of articles in the *New York Times* during the 1992 presidential primaries, and continuing with the appointment of a Special Prosecutor, Whitewater has made intermittent headlines during the entire Clinton administration. No specific evidence of culpability on Clinton's part has been unearthed, yet Clinton has been unable to rid himself of the suspicion that such evidence does exist. Whitewater has indirectly led to other accusations, some involving Hillary Clinton's brief but profitable experiment in commodities trading, and others related to the Clinton's relations with the owner of Tyson foods. Clinton's Secretary of Agriculture, Mike Espy, was forced to resign after it was discovered that he had accepted favors from Don Tyson, and his Secretary of Commerce, Ron Brown, has been accused of financial improprieties as well.

One analyst explains the persistence of Whitewater stories by blaming pack journalism "regional bias and cultural condescension," believing that the allegations indirectly feed stereotypes about the South and Southern politics (*Harper's* 1994; Lyons 1994). The implication is that people expect Southern politicians to be crooked; consequently, it is easy to believe that Clinton is indeed guilty of something, and it does not much matter what. Southerners are by definition, in this analysis, less suited than those from other regions to adequately fulfill the presidential role. This being the case, a Southern politician like Bill Clinton has an extra imperative for insuring that his character is above reproach. This Jimmy Carter generally managed to achieve. The existence of other worries about Clinton's character has made it considerably more difficult for Clinton.

Regardless of the reasons, the accusations concerning Clinton's sexual and financial dealings have combined to keep Clinton on the defensive, forcing him to defend an image of his character rather than to design one on his own terms. Even the employment of image specialist David Gergen has served more to highlight Clinton's character problems than to ameliorate them (Kelly 1993). This has fed into other areas of his presidency as well.

Singularity in the Clinton Administration

With a character so poorly understood by the American people upon entering office, and one that has been under constant attack since his inauguration, Clinton's appointments were particularly important as a source of information about the character of the president and how he understood the presidential role. His difficulties with early appointments provide more evidence that this president was being defined in all the wrong ways.

Clinton's troubles began with his apparent selection of Judge Kimba Wood as his initial nominee for Attorney General. Both she and his next choice, Zoe Baird, were eventually forced to withdraw after it was revealed that they had hired illegal immigrants. Although Commerce Secretary Ron Brown also admitted to similar tax problems, he was allowed to remain in office, prompting allegations of sexist treatment by the Clinton White House. For a man who had promised in his campaign to run an efficient, diverse, and ethical administration, it was not an auspicious beginning.

In addition to trouble with initial appointments, Clinton had a stream of problems associated with his Cabinet and staff. Ron Brown again made headlines as he drew fire concerning potentially improper meetings with Japanese businessmen under investigation by a federal grand jury (Johnston 1993). Clinton fired the entire White House travel staff and called for a Justice Department investigation, then had to reinstate five of the seven employees he had terminated. Attorney General Janet Reno was sharply criticized for the handling of the standoff with Branch Dividians in Waco, Texas. His first Surgeon General Jocelyn Elders seemed to career from one controversy to another until her resignation; Clinton's nominee for her replacement currently faces a rough confirmation battle because of his past history of performing abortions, a history that Clinton seemed unaware of until it became an issue in the confirmation hearings.

The list of Clinton's difficulties with staffing seem endless. Although no single controversy, impropriety, or mishandled nomination was sufficient to do Clinton lasting harm, together they form an impression of Clinton as an administrator that is hardly flattering. Although Clinton came to Washington with a clear and possibly controversial agenda, the clarity has been lost in favor of seemingly continuous controversy. The pattern is one that does not appear to indicate an administration that has learned from its mistakes; unnecessary problems crop up time and again, with little or no recognition of the effect staff has on the public perception of the president.

Clinton's problems with singularity went well beyond the issue of staff, however, and focused eventually—and unfortunately—on his wife Hillary.

The position of a first lady is an extremely difficult one. Even women who have been considered unambiguously "traditional" have experienced serious difficulties with the role. As the definition of the "proper" role for women in society as a whole has become increasingly controversial, first ladies have suffered accordingly. Whereas Barbara Bush and Nancy Reagan were chastised for being too passive as political actors, Betty Ford and Rosalyn Carter were often castigated for their outspokenness and refusal to be neatly pigeon-holed as "designated wife." And to the extent any of the modern first ladies have had a role in the activities of the West Wing, they were sharply and consistently criticized.

No modern first lady has had the professional qualifications of Hillary Clinton. Clearly, she is qualified for a policy role in any White House. The question has not centered on her qualifications, however, but on the appropriateness of using them. Presidential power does not extend to the spouse; yet no president can be separate from his wife. This was a serious issue during the Reagan administration, when Nancy Reagan was widely perceived—and widely reported—to be "interfering" in political and policy matters that were not properly her concern.

Hillary has considerably more of a problem than did Nancy, however, for whereas Nancy had a relatively low public profile, Hillary's has been much more noticeable. The reception given her famous remark during the campaign that it was "a two for the price of one" candidacy, as well as her statement that she "could have been home making tea and baking cookies," should have provided a warning that Hillary's style posed some potential pitfalls for the perception of that of her husband.

If a president is partially defined by his staff, he is even more defined by the actions of his wife. Yet it was less any action Hillary took than the fact that she was authorized to act at all that affected the public perception of the president's character and ability to play his presidential role.

In both his handling of the appointments process and in the role assumed by his wife, Clinton has absorbed into his character the public perception of others' characters. Everything Hillary Clinton does rebounds onto her husband—both the positive and the negative. In a similar way, the actions of the Clinton nominees, especially those viewed as marginally ethical or politically unacceptable, are perceived as extensions and reflections of the presidential character.

Mismangement in the Clinton Administration

One of Clinton's earliest actions was to advocate the inclusion of gays in the military. This was, by itself, a controversial and politically risky endeavor. It is conceivable that the Clinton team had decided that he could afford a show of political courage, that such a show would disarm his opponents who had accused him of "waffling" on major issues, and that this issue would serve to highlight the nature of the new administration. It is even conceivable that a well-managed effort to change military policy regarding homosexuals may have accomplished some or all these things.

However, Clinton's efforts to change military policy were not, in fact, well managed. Clinton made his announcement without consulting key Democrats, such as Sam Nunn (GA), chair of the powerful Senate Armed Services Committee. He did not consult with the Pentagon, and he did not consult with his own entire staff (Clymer 1993).

He made a promise that he could not keep to a controversial constituency, and, in the process, he brought his "honeymoon" to an abrupt—and early—end, increased doubts about his judgment and ability to lead Congress, and undermined his standing with the public.

Had Clinton's problems been confined to gays and the military, he would have fared better. But the early days of the Clinton administration (as well as the middle days) were characterized by a lack of focus, a "scattershot" style, and a poorly organized staff (Ifill 1993). These are all seen as directly stemming from the character of the president; a perception that provides little hope for a presidential recovery.

Final Thoughts on the Clinton Administration

Bill Clinton has certainly made his share of strategic errors in his short time in office. As with all the other presidents discussed here, however, it is important to note that a focus on failure is not likely to make any president look good. Clinton does risk having his administration judged—at least in the short term—as a failure because strategic failures have characterized public definitions of his character as he has adapted to the presidential role. If Clinton gets little credit for that which he does accomplish, it is, at least partly, due to the standard of error that he himself has set. If he is being defined as a failure, it is at least partially because he has allowed himself to be defined by his failures. As Clinton himself has said:

> I really thought that if I got to be President, I would be able to speak directly to the American people, and my image would not be twisted, and I would not be able to be turned into a cardboard cutout of myself on talk radio or negative news reports or anything like that. I was wrong about that. I mean, heck, half the time when I see myself on the evening news, I think, "Gosh, if that's all I knew about that guy, I wouldn't be for him either." (Maas 1995: 6)

Clinton's experience points to the cumulative perils of strategic failures. Once a president is perceived as ill suited to the roles required by the office, criticism will become sharper as it also becomes more credible. The persistence of a plethora of concerns about Clinton's pre-presidential behavior, including the possibility of sexual harassment as well as the Whitewater scandal, are testament to this dynamic.

If Clinton is to overcome the definitional problems that have plagued his administration, it will require a combination of factors, including a changed political environment and an issue or set of issues that resonate with the public. The Republican victories in the 1994 congressional elections and the set of issues comprising their "Contract with America" may provide Clinton with the circumstances he needs to redefine himself nationally. If Clinton can use the Republican agenda as a way of defining himself, and if he can do so in a way that resonates with the electorate without feeding into the image of Clinton as an unprincipled opportunist, then he may be able to salvage the remainder of his administration as well as his hopes for reelection.

His biggest concern is that any redefinition will carry overtones similar to those caused by Richard Nixon's perpetual reincarnations. When the fact of having designed an image becomes part of a president's image, it may be nearly impossible to build trust based on character. Clinton must therefore concentrate on fulfilling the expectations for the presidential role, paying scrupulous attention to the details involved in the policy and the appointments processes, keeping his ceremonial profile high and perhaps allowing the Republicans to dominate the news. In this way, he may be able to slowly rebuild his character through careful attention to the expectations of the role.

CONCLUSIONS

As Clinton's example indicates, presidential strategic failures are important both theoretically and as a matter of practical politics. Practically, presidents face the difficulty of trying to lead in a system that is designed to prevent leadership. They call on whatever resources they can in order to facilitate this task. Sometimes those resources can work against a president. It is important for presidents to know what they can control and what lies beyond their reach; it is equally important that the electorate begin to understand that there are limits to what a president can accomplish.

Theoretically, it is important to understand that presidential strategic mistakes are patterned, and that presidential communicative behavior is as much the product of situation and political climate as of individual choice. Separating the institution from the individual has always been one of the key problems in presidential research; it is, to some degree, unsolvable. A close examination of the patterns of presidential behavior, however, will lead to a deeper understanding of both presidential character as an individual phenomenon and the institutions affecting the presidential role.

References

Abraham, H. 1985. *Justices and Presidents: A Political History of Appointments to the Supreme Court*, 2nd ed. New York: Oxford University Press.

Alger, D. 1989. *The Media and Politics*. Englewood Cliffs, NJ: Prentice-Hall.

Arnson, C. 1989. *Crossroads: Congress, the Reagan Administration, and Central America*. New York: Pantheon.

Ball, G. 1971. Oral history, July 8. Lyndon B. Johnson library, Austin, TX.

Ball, W. 1987. Memo to the president, September 30. White House central files. Ronald Reagan library, Simi Valley, CA.

Barber, J. 1977. *The Presidential Character: Predicting Performance in the White House*, 2nd ed. Englewood Cliffs, NJ: Prentice-Hall.

Barilleaux, R. 1988. *The Post-Modern Presidency: The Office After Reagan*. New York: Praeger.

Baroody, W. 1975. Memo to the President, January 4. Robert Hartmann files, WIN campaign—general (3); Box 22, Gerald R. Ford library, Ann Arbor, MI.

Barrett, D.M. (1989). "The Mythology Surrounding Lyndon Johnson, his Advisors, and the 1965 Decision to Escalate the Vietnam War." *Political Science Quarterly* 103(4): 637-63.

Bass, H. 1992. "The National Chairman Becomes President: George Bush as Party Leader." In *Leadership and the Bush Presidency: Prudence or Drift in an Era of Change?*, eds, R. Barilleaux and M. Stuckey. New York: Praeger.

Bell, D. 1951. Memorandum to Mr. Murphy, re scandals in the Bureau of Internal Revenue, October 30. B file: The Truman Scandals. Box 1, 39. Harry S. Truman library, Independence, MO.

Bell, G. 1971. Memo to Charles Colson on the opponent's list. March 29. Colson, Box 38; Black list folder. National Archives, Nixon papers project, Washington, DC

Bennett, L. 1988. *News: The Politics of Illusion*, 2nd ed. New York: Longman.

Bennett, L. 1995. "The Cueless Public: Bill Clinton Meets the News American Voter in Campaign '92." In *The Clinton Presidency: Campaigning, Governing, and the Psychology of Leadership*, ed. S.A. Renshon. Boulder, CO: Westview.

Berman, L. 1979. *The Office of Management and Budget and the Presidency, 1921-1979*. Princeton, NJ: Princeton University Press.

Berman, L. 1982. *Planning a Tragedy: The Americanization of the War in Vietnam*. New York: Norton.

Berman, L. 1987. *The New American Presidency*. Boston: Little, Brown.

Berman, L. 1988. "Lyndon B. Johnson: Paths Chosen and Opportunities Lost." In *Leadership and the Modern Presidency*, ed. F. Greenstein. Cambridge, MA: Harvard University Press.

Berman, L. 1989. *Lyndon Johnson's War*. New York: Norton.

Berman, L., and B. Jentleson. 1991. "Bush and the Post-Cold War World: New Challenges for American Leadership." In *The Bush Presidency: First Appraisals*, eds. C. Campbell and B. Rockman. Chatham, NJ: Chatham House.

Bernstein, C., and Woodward, B. 1974. *All the President's Men*. New York: Simon and Schuster.

Biddle, F. 1951. Letter to the president, November 30. Papers of Harry S. Truman, official file, Corruption in government service. Box 875, 252S-252U, Misc. Harry S. Truman library, Independence, MO.

Biskupic, J. 1989. "FBI Background Investigations Draw Intensified Scrutiny." *Congressional Quarterly Weekly Report* April 1: 699.

Bitzer, L. 1980. "Functional communication: A situational perspective." In *Rhetoric in Transition: Studies in the Nature and Uses of Rhetoric*, ed. E.E. White. University Park, PA: Pennsylvania State University Press.

Blumenthal, S. 1980. *The Permanent Campaign*. New York: Touchstone.

Blumenthal, S. 1990. *Pledging Allegiance: The Last Campaign of the Cold War*. New York: Harper-Collins.

Bonafede, D. 1987. "Scandal Time." *The National Journal* 19(January 24): 199-200, 205-207.

Bond, J., and R. Fleisher, 1990. *The President in the Legislative Arena*. Chicago: University of Chicago Press.

Bowles, N. 1987. *The White House and Capitol Hill: The Politics of Presidential Persuasion.* New York: Oxford University Press.

Bradlee, B. 1988. *Guts and Glory: The Rise and Fall of Oliver North.* New York: Donald I. Fine.

Briefing Material. 1978. *Organizations and Companies Actively Opposing the Natural Gas Compromise.* White House files, Chief of Staff, Jordan; Box 45. Energy 1978 folder. Jimmy Carter library, Atlanta, GA.

Bronner, E. 1989. *Battle for Justice: How the Bork Nomination Shook America.* New York: Norton.

Brooke, E. 1969. Letter to the President, October 1. White House central files, Ehrlichman, Box 34; Supreme Court Haynsworth nomination [2 of 2] folder. National Archives, Nixon papers project, Washington, DC.

Brown, J. 1970a. Memo to Herb Klein, April 2. White House central files, confidential files, Box 22; Supreme Court of the United States folder. National Archives, Nixon papers project, Washington, DC.

Brown, J. 1970b. Memo to Herb Klein, April 2. White House central files, confidential files, Box 22; Supreme Court of the United States folder. National Archives, Nixon papers project, Washington, DC.

Buchanan, B. 1978. *The Presidential Experience: What the Office Does to the Man.* New York: Prentice-Hall.

Buchanan, B. 1991. *Electing a President: The Markle Commission Research on Campaign '88.* Austin: University of Texas Press.

Buchanan, P. 1969. Briefing book, September 26. White House central files, Buchanan, Box 12. National Archives, Nixon papers project, Washington, DC.

Buchanan, P. 1973. Memo to Haig, Zeigler, on news topics, June 26. Zeigler, Box 17; Watergate II 1/2 junk [2 of 2] folder. National Archives, Nixon papers project, Washington, D.C.

Buchanan, P. 1986. Memorandum to the President, weekly issues update—communication and constituent concerns, December 5. Ronald Reagan library, Simi Valley, CA.

Burke, K. 1966. *Language as Symbolic Action.* Berkeley: University of California Press.

Burns, J. 1956. *Roosevelt: The Lion and the Fox.* New York: Harcourt, Brace.

Burns, J. 1978. *Leadership.* New York: Harper and Row.

Bush, G. 1989a. "Inaugural Address." In *Public Papers of the Presidents of the United States.* Washington, DC: U.S. Government Printing Office. January 20.

Bush, G. 1989b. "The President's News Conference." In *Public Papers of the Presidents of the United States.* Washington, DC: U.S. Government Printing Office. February 6.

Bush, G. 1989c. "Remarks and a Question-and-Answer Session with Reporters Prior to a Meeting with William J. Bennett." In *Public Papers of the Presidents of the United States*. Washington, DC: U.S. Government Printing Office. February 8.

Bush, G. 1989d. "The President's News Conference." In *Public Papers of the Presidents of the United States*. Washington, DC: U.S. Government Printing Office. February 21.

Bush, G. 1989e. "Statement on the Failure of the Senate to Approve the Nomination of John Tower as Secretary of Defense." In *Public Papers of the Presidents of the United States*. Washington, DC: U.S. Government Printing Office. March 9.

Butterfield, A. 1971. Memo to the president's file on color reporting on president's meeting with key dairy industry personnel, March 23. Bull, Box 3; anecdotalist [color reporter] folder. National Archives, Nixon papers project, Washington, D.C.

Califano, J. 1991. *The Triumph and Tragedy of Lyndon Johnson: The White House Years*. New York: Simon and Schuster.

Cameron, C., A. Cover, and J. Segal. 1990. "Senate Voting on Supreme Court nominees." *American Political Science Review* 84(2): 525-34.

Campbell, C. 1986. *Managing the Presidency: Carter, Reagan, and the Search for Executive Harmony*. Pittsburgh: University of Pittsburgh Press.

Campbell, C. 1991. "The White House and the Presidency Under the 'Let's Deal' President." In *The Bush Presidency: First Appraisals*, eds. C. Campbell and B. Rockman. Chatham, NJ: Chatham House.

Cantril, A. 1991. *The Opinion Connection: Polling, Politics, and the Press*. Washington, DC: CQ Press.

Carter, J. 1977a. "The Energy Shortage." In *Public Papers of the Presidents of the United States*. Washington, DC: U.S. Government Printing Office. January 29.

Carter, J. 1977b. "Report to the American People." In *Public Papers of the Presidents of the United States*. Washington, DC: U.S. Government Printing Office. February 2.

Carter, J. 1977c. "The President's News Conference." In *Public Papers of the Presidents of the United States*. Washington, DC: U.S. Government Printing Office. February 8.

Carter, J. 1978. Letter from Jimmy Carter to Senator Riegle. Chief of Staff, Jordan, Box 45, Energy folder. Jimmy Carter library, Atlanta, GA.

Cherwitz, R. 1987. "Lyndon Johnson and the "Crisis" of Tonkin Gulf: A President's Justification of War." In *Essays in Presidential Rhetoric*, eds. T. Windt and B. Ingold. Dubuque, IA: Kendall-Hunt.

Christie, A. 1952. Letter to Harry S. Truman, April 5. b file: The Truman scandals. Box 1, 39. Harry S. Truman library, Independence, MO.

Clark, T. 1972. Oral history interview, Washington, DC, October 11. Harry S. Truman library, Independence, MO.

Clymer, A. 1993. "Lawmakers Revolt Over Plan to Lift Ban on Gay Service; Peril to Clinton Agenda; Fierce Opposition in Congress is Threatening to Sidetrack Democratic Legislation." *New York Times* January 27: A1.

Cohen, W., and G. Mitchell. 1988. *Men of Zeal: A Candid Inside Story of the Iran-Contra Hearings.* New York: Viking.

Colby, W. 1981. Oral history, June 2. Lyndon B. Johnson library, Austin, TX.

Cole, K. 1969. Memo to Herb Klein, October 2. White House central files, confidential files, Box 22; Supreme Court of the United States folder. National Archives, Nixon papers project, Washington, DC.

Colson, C. 1972. Memo to Bruce Kehrli on Nixon's habits of watching football, January 14. Howard, Box, 3; [staff secretary] action memos, [Sept. 27, 1971-May 18, 1972] [2 of 3] folder. National Archives, Nixon papers project, Washington, D.C.

Colson, C. 1988. Oral history interview, June 18. National Archives, Nixon papers project, WasHington, DC.

Cooper, C. 1979. Oral history, July 9. Lyndon B. Johnson library, Austin, TX.

Crovitz, L.G., and J. Rabkin, Eds. 1989. *The Fettered Presidency: Legal Constraints on the Executive Branch.* Washington, DC: American Enterprise for Public Policy Research.

Culvahouse, A., and T. Griscom. 1987. Memo to the president, September 23. White House central files. Ronald Reagan library, Simi Valley, CA.

Davidson, D. 1988. *Vietnam at War.* Novato, CA: Presidio Press.

Davis, E. 1979. "Legislative Liaison in the Carter Administration." *Political Science Quarterly* 95: 289.

Davis, J. 1987. *The American Presidency: A New Perspective.* New York: Harper and Row.

Dean, J. 1977. *Blind Ambition.* New York: Simon and Schuster.

DeFrank, T. 1989. "Bush Risks his Chips on Tower: The President Could Suffer a Heavy Setback." *Newsweek* 113(February 20): 19.

Denton, R. 1989. *The Primetime Presidency of Ronald Reagan: The Era of the Television Presidency.* New York: Praeger.

Denton, R., and D. Hahn. 1986. *Presidential Communication: Description and Analysis.* New York: Praeger.

Denton, R., and G. Woodward. 1990. *Political Communication in America,* 2nd ed. New York: Praeger.

DiClerico, R. 1990. *The American President,* 3rd ed. Englewood Cliffs, NJ: Prentice-Hall.

Donovan, R. 1977. *Conflict and Crisis: The Presidency of Harry S. Truman, 1945-1948*. New York: Norton.

Duffy, M. 1988. "John Tower's Hesitation Blues: He Says He's a New Man, But Will Bush Give Him the Pentagon?" *Time* 132 (December 12): 23.

Dunar, A. 1984. *The Truman Scandals and the Politics of Morality*. Columbia: University of Missouri Press.

Edwards, G. 1980. *Presidential Influence in Congress*. San Francisco: Freeman.

Edwards, G. 1983. *The Public Presidency: The Pursuit of Popular Support*. New York: St. Martin's Press.

Edwards, G. 1985. "Measuring Presidential Success in Congress: Alternative Approaches." *Journal of Politics* 47: 667-85.

Edwards, G. 1989. *At the Margins: Presidential Leadership of Congress*. New Haven, CT: Yale University Press.

Edwards, G. 1991. "George Bush and the Public Presidency: The Politics of Inclusion." In *The Bush Presidency: First Appraisals*, eds. C. Campbell and B. Rockman. Chatham, NJ: Chatham House.

Egan, C. 1952. "Inquiry Sought on Steel Seizure." *New York Times* April 13. Papers of Harold l. Enerson. Box 4, White House central files. Steel negotiations clippings, March 7-April 22, 1952. Harry S. Truman library, Independence, MO.

Enerson, H. 1952. Memorandum to Dr. Steelman, re Next steps in the steel dispute, January 9. Steel strike of 1952 [1 of 3], Papers of David H. Stowe, Box 14, Subject file, 1947-1953. Harry S. Truman library, Independence, MO.

Entman, R. 1989. *Democracy Without Citizens: Media and the Decay of American Politics*. New York: Oxford University Press.

Erickson, P. 1985. *Reagan Speaks: The Making of an American Myth*. New York: New York University Press.

Fenno, R. 1978. *Home Style: House Members in their Districts*. Boston: Little, Brown.

Ferrell, H. 1983. *Harry S. Truman and the Modern American Presidency*. Boston: Little, Brown.

Fisher, L. 1987. *The Politics of Shared Power: Congress and the Executive*, 2nd ed. Washington, DC: CQ Press.

FitzGerald, F. 1972. *Fire in the Lake*. Boston: Little, Brown.

Fly, R., H. Gleckman, D. Harbrecht, and D. Griffiths. 1989. "Who's Afraid of George Bush? Not Congress." *Business Week* February 20: 30.

Ford, G. 1974. "Remarks upon Taking the Oath of Office." In *Public Papers of the Presidents of the United States*. Washington, DC: U.S. Government Printing Office. August 9.

Hart, R. 1987. *The Sound of Leadership: Presidential Communication in the Modern Age*. Chicago: University of Chicago Press.

Hartmann, R. 1974. A dispassionate evaluation passionately argued. Robert Hartmann files, WIN campaign—general (1); Box 22, Gerald R. Ford library, Ann Arbor, MI.

Hartmann, R. 1980. *Palace Politics: An Inside Account of the Ford Years*. New York: McGraw-Hill.

Hawley, E. 1991. "The Constitution of the Hoover and F. Roosevelt Presidencies During the Depression Era, 1930-1939." In *The Constitution and the American Presidency*, eds. M. Fausold and A. Shank. Albany: State University of New York Press.

Hazlitt, H. 1952. "It is Happening Here." *Newsweek* April 21. Papers of Harold l. Enerson. Box 4, White House central files. Steel negotiations clippings, March 7-April 22, 1952. Harry S. Truman library, Independence, MO.

Hechler, K. 1982. *Working with Truman: A Personal Memoir of the White House Years*. New York: G.P. Putnam's Sons.

Henderson, P. 1988. *Managing the Presidency: The Eisenhower Legacy— From Kennedy to Reagan*. Boulder, CO: Westview.

Hertsgaard, M. 1989. *On Bended Knee: The Press and the Reagan Presidency*. New York: Schoken Books.

Hess, S. 1976. *Organizing the Presidency*. Washington, DC: Brookings.

Hinckley, B. 1990. *The Symbolic Presidency: How Presidents Portray Themselves*. New York: Routledge.

Hinds, L., and T. Windt. 1991. *The Cold War as Rhetoric: The Beginnings, 1945-1950*. New York: Praeger.

Hodgson, G. 1980. *All Things to All Men: The Promise of the Modern American Presidency*. New York: Simon and Schuster.

Hoerr, J. 1988. *And the Wolf Finally Came: The Decline of the American Steel Industry*. Pittsburgh: University of Pittsburgh Press.

Hoff-Wilson, J. 1988. "Richard M. Nixon: The Corporate Presidency." In *Leadership in the Modern Presidency*, ed. F. Greenstein. Cambridge, MA: Harvard University Press.

Ifill, G. 1993. "Clinton Sees Need to Focus his Goals and Sharpen Staff." *New York Times* May 4: A1.

Johnson, H. 1980. *In the Absence of Power: Governing America*. New York: Viking.

Johnson, L. 1964. "Address at Eufola, Oklahoma." In *Public Papers of the Presidents of the United States*. Washington, DC: United States Government Printing Office. September 25.

Johnson, L. 1965. "Seeking Peace Without Conquest in Vietnam." In *Presidential Rhetoric* (1961-to the present), 4th ed., ed. T. Windt. Dubuque, IA: Kendall-Hunt.

Johnson, L. 1966a. "Annual Message to Congress on the State of the Union." In *Public Papers of the Presidents of the United States.* Washington, DC: U.S. Government Printing Office. January 12.

Johnson, L. 1966b. "Remarks to the American Alumni Council on U.S. Asian Policy." In *Public Papers of the Presidents of the United States.* Washington, DC: U.S. Government Printing Office. July 12.

Johnson, L. 1967. "Address Before the National Legislative Conference, San Antonio, Texas." In *Presidential Rhetoric* (1961-to the present), 4th ed., ed. T. Windt. Dubuque, IA: Kendall Hunt.

Johnson, L. 1968. "Televised Address to the Nation." In *Presidential Rhetoric* (1961-to the present), 4th ed., ed. T. Windt. Dubuque, IA: Kendall Hunt.

Johnston, D. 1993. "White House Defends Brown in Jury Inquiry." *New York Times* September 28: A1.

Jones, A. 1992. "Kinder, Gentler? George Bush and Civil Rights." In *Leadership and the Bush Presidency: Prudence or Drift in an Era of Change?*, eds. R. Barilleaus and M. Stuckey. New York: Praeger.

Jones, C. 1988. *The Reagan Legacy.* Chatham, NJ: Chatham House.

Jones, C. 1988. *The Trusteeship Presidency: Jimmy Carter and the United States Congress.* Baton Rouge: Louisiana State University Press.

Jones, C. 1994. *The Presidency in a Separated System.* Washington, DC: Brookings.

Jordan, H. 1981. Miller Center Interview (including Landon Butler). Carter presidency project, vol VI. November 6. Jimmy Carter library, Atlanta, GA.

Journal of Commerce. 1952. "A Magna Carta for 1952." June 3. Papers of Harold l. Enerson, Box 4. White House central files. Steel negotiations clips. Harry S. Truman library, Independence, MO.

Karp, W. 1985. "Liberty Under Siege: The Reagan Administration's Taste for Autocracy." *Harper's* November: 53-67.

Kellerman, B. 1984. *The Political Presidency: Practice of Leadership from Kennedy through Reagan.* New York: Oxford University Press.

Kellner, D. 1990. *Television and the Crisis of Democracy.* Boulder, CO: Westview.

Kelly, M. 1993. "David Gergen, Master of the Game." *New York Times Magazine* October 31: 62-71, 80, 94, 97, 103.

Kenski, H. 1992. "A Man for All Seasons? The Guardian President and His Public." In *Leadership and the Bush Presidency: Prudence or Drift in an Era of Change?*, eds. R. Barilleaux and M. Stuckey. New York: Praeger.

Kernell, S, 1986. *Going Public: New Strategies of Presidential Leadership.* Washington, DC: CQ Press.

King, A., (ed.). 1983. *Both Ends of the Avenue: The Presidency, the Executive Branch, and Congress in the 1980s.* Washington, DC: American Enterprise Institute.

Klapp, O. 1964. *Symbolic Leaders.* Chicago: Aldine.

Klein, J. 1989. "Bush League: The Preppy Stumbles." *New York* 22 (March 13): 16.

Koenig, L. Ed. 1956. *The Truman Administration: Its Principles and Practice.* New York: New York University Press.

Koh, H. 1990. *The National Security Constitution: Sharing Power After the Iran-Contra Affair.* New Haven, CT: Yale University Press.

Korologos, T. 1974. Memo to William Seidman and William Baroody, December 17. William Timmons files, Whip Inflation Now (3), Box 12; Gerald R. Ford library, Ann Arbor, MI.

Krogh, E. 1970. Memo to Bryce Harlow, on briefing of Senators on the Carswell nomination, January 20. White House central files; Krogh, Box 2, Memos, January 1970 folder. National Archives, Nixon papers project, Washington, DC.

Kutler, S. 1991. *The Wars of Watergate: The Last Crisis of Richard Nixon.* New York: Knopf.

Kymlicka, B., and J. Matthews, eds. 1988. *The Reagan Revolution?* Chicago: Dorsey.

Lansdale, E. 1977. "Contradictions in Military Culture." In *The lessons of Vietnam*, eds. S. Thompson and D. Frizzell. New York: Crane, Russak, and Co.

Lasky, V. 1977. *It Didn't Start with Watergate.* New York: Dell.

Ledeen, M. 1988. *Perilous Statecraft: An Insider's Account of the Iran-Contra Affair.* New York: Charles Scribner's Sons.

Lee, M. 1952. Letter to the president, January 22. Papers of Harry S. Truman, official file, Corruption in government service. Box 875, 252S-252U, Misc. Harry S. Truman library, Independence, MO.

Leuchtenberg, W. 1983. *In the Shadow of FDR: From Harry Truman to Ronald Reagan.* Ithaca, NY: Cornell University Press.

Light, P. 1982. *The President's Agenda: Domestic Policy Choices from Kennedy to Carter.* Baltimore: Johns Hopkins University Press.

Logue, C., and J. Patton. 1987. "From Ambiguity to Dogma: The Rhetorical Symbols of Lyndon B. Johnson on Vietnam." In *Essays in Presidential Rhetoric*, eds. T. Windt and B. Ingold. Dubuque, IA: Kendall-Hunt.

Lomperis, T. 1984. *The War Everyone Lost—and Won: America's Intervention in Vietnam's Twin Struggles.* Baton Rouge: Louisiana State University Press.

Lowi, T. 1979. *The End of Liberalism: The Second Republic of the United States*, 2nd ed. New York: Norton.

Lowi, T. 1985. *The Personal President: Power Invested, Promise Unfulfilled.* Ithaca, NY: Cornell University Press.

Lyons, G. 1994. "Fool for Scandal: How the Times got Whitewater Wrong." *Harper's* October: 55-63.

Maas, P. 1995. "I think We've Learned a Lot." *Parade Magazine* February 19: 4-6.

Malecha, G., and D. Reagan. 1992. "Bush and Congress: The Question of Leadership." In *Leadership and the Bush Presidency: Prudence or Drift in an Era of Change?*, eds. R. Barilleaux and M. Stuckey. New York: Praeger.

Manatos, M. 1969. Oral history, August 25. Lyndon B. Johnson library, Austin, TX.

Mayer, J., and D. McManus. 1988. *Landslide: The Unmaking of the President 1984-1988*. Boston: Houghton-Mifflin.

Mayhew, D. 1974. *Congress: The Electoral Connection*. New Haven, CT: Yale University Press.

Mayhew, D. 1991. *Divided we Govern: Party Control, Lawmaking, and Investigations 1946-1990*. New Haven, CT: Yale University Press.

McGuigan, P., and D. Weyrich. 1990. *Ninth Justice: The Fight for Bork*. Washington, DC: Free Congress Research and Education Foundation.

Milkes, S. 1984. "Presidents and Party Purges: With Special Emphasis on 1938." In *Presidents and their Parties: Leadership or Neglect?*, ed. R. Hamel. New York: Praeger.

Moen, M., and K. Palmer. 1992. "'Poppy' and his Conservative Passengers." In *Leadership and the Bush Presidency: Prudence or Drift in an Era of Change?*, eds. R. Barilleaux and M. Stuckey. New York: Praeger.

Mollenhoff, C. and Buchanan, P. 1969. Briefing book, October 16. White House central files, President's personal file, Box 186, material removed from the president's desk, 1969-1974; Haynsworth folder. National Archives, Nixon papers project, Washington, DC.

Muir, W. 1988. "Ronald Reagan: The Primacy of Rhetoric." In *Leadership in the Modern Presidency.*, ed. F. Greenstein. Cambridge: Harvard University Press.

Mullen, W. 1982. "Perceptions of Carter's Legislative Success and Failures: Views from the Hill and the Liaison Staff." *Presidential Studies Quarterly* Fall: 522-34.

Murphy, C. 1969. Sixth oral history interview, Washington, DC, July 15. Harry S. Truman library, Independence, MO.

Nathan, R. 1975. *The Administrative Presidency*. New York: Wiley.

Nathan, R. 1975. *The Plot that Failed: Nixon and the Administrative Presidency*. New York: Wiley.

Nathan, R. 1982. *The Administrative Presidency*. New York: Wiley.

National Security Archive. 1987. *The Chronology*. New York: Warner Books.

Nessen, R. 1974. News conference, #51, October 17. Ron Nessen files, 10/17/74 (51), Box 2. Gerald R. Ford library, Ann Arbor, MI.

Nessen, R. 1988. "The Ford Presidency and the Press." In *The Ford Presidency: Twenty-two Intimate Perspectives on Gerald R. Ford*, ed. K. Thompson. Latham: University Press of America.

Neustadt, R. 1960. *Presidential Power: The Politics of Leadership*. New York: John Wiley and Sons.

Neustadt, R. 1990. *Presidential Power and the Modern Presidents: The Politics of Leadership from Roosevelt to Reagan*. New York: Free Press.

New York Times. 1952. "Steel Before Congress." June 11. Papers of Harold l. Enerson, Box 4. White House central files. Steel negotiations clips. Harry S. Truman library, Independence, MO.

New York Times. 1966. Obituary of Howard J. McGrath. Papers of Harry S. Truman. Vertical file; name file; Howard J. McGrath. Harry S. Truman library, Independence, MO.

New York Times. 1974. *The End of a Presidency*. New York: Bantam.

New York Times. 1975. "Penn State to Wear WIN buttons." January 1, p. 12. White House Central Files, Oversize attachments, 7667-C Promoting the WIN campaign; Box 7667, Gerald R. Ford library, Ann Arbor, MI.

Newcomb, R. 1977. Oral history interview, Washington, DC, August 6. Harry S. Truman library, Independence, MO.

Nimmo, D., and D. Swanson. 1990. "The Field of Political Communication: Beyond the Voter Persuasion Paradigm." In *New Directions in Political Communication: A Resource Book*, eds. D. Nimmo and D. Swanson. London: Sage.

Nixon, R. 1969. "Inaugural Address." In *The Public Papers of the Presidents of the United States*. January 22.

Nixon, R. 1969a. "Inaugural Address." In *Public Papers of the Presidents of the United States*. Washington, DC: U.S. Government Printing Office. January 20.

Nixon, R. 1969b. "Remarks at an Informal Meeting with Members of the White House Press Corps on Judge Haynsworth's Nomination to the Supreme Court." In *Public Papers of the Presidents of the United States*. Washington, D.C: U.S. Government Printing Office. October 20.

Nixon, R. 1970a. "The President's News Conference." In *Public Papers of the Presidents of the United States*. Washington, DC: U.S. Government Printing Office. January 30.

Nixon, R. 1970b. "Exchange of Letters with Senator William B. Saxbe on the Nomination of Judge G. Harrold Carswell to the Supreme Court." In *Public Papers of the Presidents of the United States*. Washington, DC: U.S. Government Printing Office. April 1.

Nixon, R. 1970c. "Remarks to Reporters about Nominations to the Supreme Court." In *Public Papers of the Presidents of the United States.* Washington, DC: U.S. Government Printing Office. April 9.

Nixon, R. 1970d. "Statement About Nominations to the Supreme Court." In *Public Papers of the Presidents of the United States.* Washington, DC: U.S. Government Printing Office. April 9.

Nixon, R. 1971. Memo to H.R. Haldeman. Haldeman, Box 5; "Mr. Haldeman" folder. National Archives, Nixon papers project, Washington, DC.

Nixon, R. 1973a. "The President's Press Conference." *The Public Papers of the Presidents of the United States.* January 3.

Nixon, R. 1973b. "Address to the Nation on the Watergate Investigations." In *The Public Papers of the Presidents of the United States.* August 15.

Nixon, R. 1973c. "The President's Press Conference." In *The Public Papers of the Presidents of the United States.* August 20.

Nixon, R. 1973d. "The President's Press Conference." In *The Public Papers of the Presidents of the United States.* September 5.

Nixon, R. 1974a. "Remarks at a National Prayer Breakfast." In *The Public Papers of the Presidents of the United States.* January 31.

Nixon, R. 1974b. "Remarks at a Luncheon of the National Citizens' Committee for Fairness to the Presidency." In *The Public Papers of the Presidents of the United States.* June 9.

Nixon, R. 1974c. "Address to the Nation Announcing the Decision to Resign the Office of President." In *The Public Papers of the Presidents of the United States.* August 8.

Nixon, R. 1978. *The Memoirs of Richard Nixon.* New York: Grosset and Dunlap.

Noonan, P. 1990. *What I Saw at the Revolution: A Political Life in the Reagan Era.* New York: Random House.

O'Brien, D. 1988. "The Reagan Judges: His Most Enduring Legacy?" In *The Reagan Legacy: Promise and Performance,* ed. C. Jones. Chatham, NJ: Chatham House.

O'Neill, T., and W. Novak. 1987. *Man of the House: The Life and Political Memories of Speaker Tip O'Neill.* New York: Random House.

O'Neill, W. 1971. *Coming Apart: An Informal History of America in the 1960s.* New York: Quadrangle Books.

O'Neill, W. 1986. *American High: The Years of Confidence, 1945-1960.* New York: Free Press.

Ornstein, N. 1981. "Assessing Reagan's First Year". In *The New Congress,* ed. N. Ornstein and T. Mann. Washington, DC: The American Enterprise Institute.

Paletz, D., and R. Entman. 1981. *Media-Power-Politics.* New York: Free Press.

Pechatnov, V. 1987. "Franklin D. Roosevelt and the Democratic Party." In *Franklin D. Roosevelt: The Man, the Myth, the Era, 1882-1945*, ed. H. Rosenbaum. New York: Greenwood.

Pemberton, W. 1989. *Harry S. Truman: Fair Dealer and Cold Warrior*. Boston: Twayne Publishers.

Perry, J. 1994. "Like Roosevelt and Nixon Before Him, Clinton Stirs Passionate Hatred in Many of his Critics." *Wall Street Journal* February 7: A18.

Pertschuk, M., and W. Schaetzel. 1989. *The People Rising: The Campaign Against the Bork Nomination*. New York: Thunder's Mouth Press.

Pessen, E. 1984. *The Log Cabin Myth: The Social Backgrounds of the Presidents*. New Haven, CT: Yale University Press.

Petty, R. 1974. Public service announcement. White House Central Files, Oversize attachments, 7667-C Promoting the WIN campaign; Box 7667, Gerlad R. Ford library, Ann Arbor, MI.

Pfau, M., and H. Kenski. 1990. *Attack Politics: Strategy and Defense*. New York: Praeger.

Pfiffner, J. 1988. *The Strategic Presidency: Hitting the Ground Running*. Chicago: Dorsey.

Phillips, C. 1966. *The Truman Presidency: The History of a Triumphant Succession*. New York: Macmillan.

Polsby, N. 1976. *Congress and the Presidency*, 3rd ed. Englewood Cliffs, NJ: Prentice-Hall.

Polsby, N. 1984. *Political Innovation in America: The Politics of Policy Initiation*. New Haven, CT: Yale University Press.

Porter, R. 1988. "Gerald R. Ford: A Healing Presidency." In *Leadership in the Modern Presidency*, ed. F. Greenstein. Cambridge, MA: Harvard University Press.

Press Secretary. 1986a. Press release, November 2. Ronald Reagan library, Simi Valley, CA.

Press Secretary. 1986b. Press release, November 25. Ronald Reagan library, Simi Valley, CA.

Press Secretary. 1986c. Press release, December 5. Ronald Reagan library, Simi Valley, CA.

Press Secretary. 1986d. Press release, December 16. Ronald Reagan library, Simi Valley, CA.

Price, C., and J. Boskin. 1966. "The Roosevelt "Purge": A Reappraisal." *Journal of Politics* 28: 660-70

Pritchard, A. 1983. "Presidents do Influence Voting in the U.S. Congress: New Definitions and Measurements." *Legislative Studies Quarterly* 8: 691-711.

Randall, C. 1952. These are the facts, Mr. President. Radio and television address. Files of Charles S. Murphy. Steel strike, April 1-15. Box 28,

Correspondence and general file. Harry S. Truman library, Independence, MO.

Ranney, A. 1983. *Channels of Power: The Impact of Television on American Politics.* New York: Basic Books.

Reagan, R. 1980a. "Address to the National Maritime Union." Manuscript available from the Republican National Committee. October 9.

Reagan, R. 1980b. Remarks to the Los Angeles World Affairs Council. Manuscript available at the Hoover Institution for War, Revolution, and Peace, Stanford University. December 14.

Reagan, R. 1983. "Address to the Republican National Convention." In *Ronald Reagan Talks to America.* Old Greenwich, CT: Devin-Adair.

Reagan, R. 1986. "Address to the Nation on Iran-United States Relations." In *The Public Papers of the Presidents of the United States.* November 13.

Reagan, R. 1987a. "Address before a Joint Session of Congress on the State of the Union." In *The Public Papers of the Presidents of the United States.* Washington, DC: U.S. Government Printing Office. January 27.

Reagan, R. 1987b. "Remarks at a Luncheon of the Conservative Political Action Conference." In The *Public Papers of the Presidents of the United States.* Washington, DC: U.S. Government Printing Office. February 20.

Reagan, R. 1987c. "Address to the Nation on the Iran Arms and Contra Aid Controversy." In *The Public Papers of the Presidents of the United States.* March 4.

Reagan, R. 1987a. Statement by the president, July 1. White House central files. Ronald Reagan library, Simi Valley, CA.

Reagan, R. 1987b. "Remarks at a White House Briefing for Members of the National Law Enforcement Council." In *Public Papers of the Presidents of the United States.* Washington, DC: U.S. Government Printing Office. July 29.

Reagan, R. 1987c. "Address to the Nation on the Iran Arms and Contra Aid Controversy and Administration Goals." In *Public Papers of the Presidents of the United States.* Washington, DC: U.S. Government Printing Office. August 12.

Reagan, R. 1987d. "Remarks on the Supreme Court Nomination of Robert H. Bork to Law Enforcement Officials in Los Angeles, CA." In *Public Papers of the Presidents of the United States.* Washington, DC: U.S. Government Printing Office. August 28.

Reagan, R. 1987e. "Remarks at the Annual Convention of Concerned Women for America." In *Public Papers of the Presidents of the United States.* Washington, DC: U.S. Government Printing Office. September 25.

Reagan, R. 1987f. "Remarks at a White House Briefing on the Nomination of Robert H. Bork to be an Associate Justice of the Supreme Court of the United States of America." In *Public Papers of the Presidents of the United States.* Washington, DC: U.S. Government Printing Office. September 30.

Reagan, R. 1987g. "Informal Exchange with Reporters on the Supreme Court Nomination of Robert H. Bork." In *Public Papers of the Presidents of the United States.* Washington, DC: U.S. Government Printing Office. October 1.

Reagan, R. 1987h. "Radio Address to the Nation on Voluntarism and the Supreme Court Nomination of Robert H. Bork." In *Public Papers of the Presidents of the United States.* Washington, DC: U.S. Government Printing Office. October 3.

Reeves, R. 1976. *Old Faces of 1976.* New York: Harper and Row.

Regan, D. 1988. *For the Record: From Wall Street to Washington.* New York: Harcourt, Brace, Jovanovich.

Riker, W. 1985. *The Art of Political Manipulation.* New Haven, CT: Yale University Press.

Rivers, D., and N. Rose. 1985. "Passing the President's Program: Public Opinion and Presidential Influence in Congress." *American Journal of Political Science* 29: 183-96.

Rockman, B. 1984. *The Leadership Question: The Presidency and the American System.* New York: Praeger.

Rockman, B. 1991. "The Leadership Style of George Bush." In *The Bush Presidency: First Appraisals,* eds. C. Campbell and B. Rockman. Chatham, NJ: Chatham House.

Rodota, J. 1987. Memorandum to Pat Buchanan on media coverage of the Iran scandal, January 28. Ronald Reagan library, Simi Valley, CA.

Rohde, D., and D. Simon. 1985. "Presidential Vetoes and Congressional Response." *American Journal of Political Science* 29: 397-427.

Roosevelt, F. 1937a. "Three Hundred and Forty-Second Press Conference." In *The Public Papers and Addresses of Franklin D. Roosevelt.* Washington, DC: U.S. Government Printing Office. February 5.

Roosevelt, F. 1937b. "Three Hundred and Forty-Fourth Press Conference." In *The Public Papers and Addresses of Franklin D. Roosevelt.* Washington, DC: U.S. Government Printing Office. February 12.

Roosevelt, F. 1937c. "Address at a Democratic Victory Dinner." In *The Public Papers and Addresses of Franklin D. Roosevelt.* Washington, DC: U.S. Government Printing Office. March 4.

Roosevelt, F. 1937d. "Fireside Chat Discussing the Plan for Reorganization of the Judiciary." In *The Public Papers and Addresses of Franklin D. Roosevelt.* Washington, DC: U.S. Government Printing Office. March 9.

Roosevelt, F. 1937e. "Three Hundred and Sixtieth Press Conference." In *The Public Papers and Addresses of Franklin D. Roosevelt*. Washington, DC: U.S. Government Printing Office. April 13.

Roosevelt, F. 1937f. "Three Hundred and Sixty-Seventh Press Conference." In *The Public Papers and Addresses of Franklin D. Roosevelt*. Washington, DC: U.S. Government Printing Office. May 18.

Roosevelt, F. 1938a. "Fireside Chat on Party Primaries". In *The Public Papers and Addresses of Franklin D. Roosevelt*. New York: Macmillan. June 24.

Roosevelt, F. 1938b. "Dedication of Gettysburg Battlefield Memorial." In *The Public Papers and Addresses of Franklin D. Roosevelt*. New York: Macmillan. July 3.

Roosevelt, F. 1938c. "A Message to the Conference on Economic Conditions of the South." In *The Public Papers and Addresses of Franklin D. Roosevelt*. New York: Macmillan. July 4.

Roosevelt, F. 1938d. "Address at Oklahoma City, OK." In *The Public Papers and Addresses of Franklin D. Roosevelt*. New York: Macmillan. July 9.

Roosevelt, F. 1938e. "Informal, Extemporaneous Remarks at Pueblo, CO." In *The Public Papers and Addresses of Franklin D. Roosevelt*. New York: Macmillan. July 12.

Roosevelt F. 1938f. "Address at Barnesville, GA." In *The Public Papers and Addresses of Franklin D. Roosevelt*. New York: Macmillan. August 11.

Rose, R. 1978. *Managing Presidential Objectives*. New York: Free Press.

Rowe, J. 1978. Oral history interview, July 12. Franklin D. Roosevelt library, Hyde Park, NY.

Rozell, M. 1990. "President Carter and the Press." *Political Science Quarterly* 105(3): 419-34.

Rusk, D. 1969a. Oral history, July 18. Lyndon B. Johnson library, Austin, TX.

Rusk, D. 1969b. Oral history, September 26. Lyndon B. Johnson library, Austin, TX.

Ryan, H. 1988. *Franklin D. Roosevelt's Rhetorical Presidency*. New York: Greenwood.

Sabato, L. 1991. *Feeding Frenzy: How Attack Journalism has Transformed American Politics*. New York: Free Press.

Safire, W. 1969. Memo to H.R. Haldeman, June 20. White House central files, Haldeman, Box 177; Supreme Court confirmations folder. National Archives, Nixon papers project, Washington, DC.

Savage, S. 1991. *Roosevelt: The Party Leader 1932-1945*. Lexington: Kentucky University Press.

Schlesinger, A., Jr. 1973. *The Imperial Presidency*. Boston: Houghton-Mifflin.

Schlesinger, J., and F. Moore. 1978. Memo on national energy plan congressional strategy, April 4. White House files, Chief of Staff, Jordan; Box 45. Energy 1978 folder. Jimmy Carter library, Atlanta, GA.

Schwab, L. 1991. *The Illusion of a Conservative Reagan Revolution*. New York: Transaction Books.

Segev, S. 1988. *The Iranian Triangle: The Untold Story of Israel's Role in the Iran-Contra Affair*. New York: Free Press.

Seidman, H. 1970. Oral history interview, July 29. Harry S. Truman library, Independence, MO.

Seligman, L., and C. Covington. 1989. *The Coalitional Presidency*. Chicago: Dorsey Press.

Shaplen, R. 1971. *The Road from War: Vietnam 1965-1971*. New York: Harper and Row.

Sinclair, B. 1991. "Governing Unheroically (and Sometimes Unappetizingly): Bush and the 101st Congress.I In *The Bush Presidency: First Appraisals*, eds. C. Campbell and B. Rockman. Chatham, NJ: Chatham House.

Skowronek, S. 1988. "Presidential Leadership in Political Time." In *The Presidency and the Political System*, ed. M. Nelson. Washington, DC: CQ Press.

Smith, J. 1992. *George Bush's War*. New York: Henry Holt.

Smith, M. 1969. Letter to the President, September 30. White House central files, Ehrlichman, Box 34; Supreme Court Haynsworth nomination [2 of 2] folder. National Archives, Nixon papers project, Washington, DC.

Speakes, L. 1986a. Press briefing, #1917, November 5. Ronald Reagan library, Simi VAlley, CA.

Speakes, L. 1986b. Press briefing, #1921, November 10. Ronald Reagan library, Simi Valley, CA.

Speakes, L. 1986c. Press briefing, #1926, November 14. Ronald Reagan library, Simi Valley, CA.

Speakes, L. 1986d. Press briefing, #1932, November 20. Ronald Reagan library, Simi Valley, CA.

Speakes, L., with R. Pack. 1988. *Speaking Out: Inside the Reagan White House*. New York: Charles Scribner's Sons.

Staff Secretary. 1969. Memo to the Attorney General, October 16. White House central files, confidential files, Box 22; 1969-1974, Supreme Court of the United States folder. National Archives, Nixon papers project, Washington, DC.

Stelzner, H. 1987. "Ford's War on Inflation: A Metaphor That Did Not Cross." In *Essays in Presidential Rhetoric*, 2nd ed., eds. T. Windt and B. Ingold. Dubuque, IA: Kendall-Hunt.

Stockman, D. 1986. *The Triumph of Politics: Why the Reagan Revolution Failed.* New York: Harper and Row.

Strachan, G. 1970. Television-network news coverage. September 8-29. Box 14. National Archives, Nixon papers project, Washington, DC.

Stuckey, M. 1990. *Playing the Game: The Presidential Rhetoric of Ronald Reagan.* New York: Praeger.

Stuckey, M. 1991. *The President as Interpreter-In-Chief.* Chatham, NJ: Chatham House.

Stuckey, M. 1991a. "Anecdotes and Conversations: An Analysis of the Narrational and Dialogic Styles of Modern Presidential Communication. *Communication Quarterly* 40(1): 45-56

Stuckey, M. 1991b. *The President as Interpreter-in-Chief.* Chatham, NJ: Chatham House.

Summers, H. 1981. *On Strategy: The Vietnam War in Context.* Carlisle Barracks, PA: Strategic Studies Institute.

Talking points. 1987. Talking Points on the Release of the Iran/Contra Report. November 16. Ronald Reagan library, Simi Valley, CA.

Taylor, M. 1969. Oral history, Feb. 10. Lyndon B. Johnson library, Austin, TX.

Tebbel, J., and S. Watts. 1985. *The Press and the Presidency: From George Washington to Ronald Reagan.* New York: Oxford University Press.

Telephone records. 1987. Records of telephone calls made by Ronald Reagan to members of the United States Senate concerning the Bork nomination. October 10. White House central files. Ronald Reagan library, Simi Valley, CA.

Thompson, T. 1987. "Poll: Half in South Opposed to Bork." *Atlanta Constitution* October 1. White House central files. Ronald Reagan library, Simi Valley, CA.

Tower, J. , Muskie, E., and B. Scowcroft. 1987. *Report of the President's Special Review Board.* Washington, DC: U.S. Government Printing Office.

Transcripts of White House Conversations. 1973a. February 28. Haig, Box 40, National Archives, Nixon papers project, Washington, DC.

Transcripts of White House Conversations. 1973b. March 13. Haig, Box 40, National Archives, Nixon papers project, Washington, DC.

Transcripts of White House Conversations. 1973c. March 21. Haig, Box 40, National Archives, Nixon papers project, Washington, DC.

Truman, H. 1945a. Remarks Upon Receiving an Honorary Degree from the University of Kansas." In *Public Papers of the Presidents of the United States.* Washington, DC: U.S. Government Printing Office. June 28.

Truman, H. 1945b. "Radio Address to the American People after Signing the Unconditional Surrender with Japan." In *Public Papers of the Presidents of the United States.* Washington, DC: U.S. Government Printing Office. September 1.

Truman, H. 1946a. "Address at a Jackson Day Dinner." In *Public Papers of the Presidents of the United States*. Washington, DC: U.S. Government Printing Office. March 23.

Truman H. 1946b. "Radio Address to the Nation on Price Controls." In *Public Papers of the Presidents of the United States*. Washington, DC: U.S. Government Printing Office. June 29.

Truman, H. 1947. "Address at a Jefferson Day Dinner." In *Public Papers of the Presidents of the United States*. Washington, DC: U.S. Government Printing Office. April 5.

Truman, H. 1950a. "Address on Foreign Policy at the George Washington National Masonic Memorial." In *Public Papers of the Presidents of the United States*. February 22.

Truman, H. 1950b. "Address at Valley Forge at the Boy Scout Jamboree." In *Public Papers of the Presidents of the United States*. June 30.

Truman, H. 1951. "Radio and Television Report to the American People on International Arms Reduction." In *Public Papers of the Presidents of the United States*. Washington, DC: U.S. Government Printing Office. November 7.

Truman, H. 1951a. "Address at a Dinner of the Civil Defense Conference." In *Public Papers of the Presidents of the United States*. May 7.

Truman, H. 1951b. Letter to Congressman Bennett, July 27. Papers of Harry S. Truman, official file, Corruption in government service. Box 875, 252S-252U, Misc. Harry S. Truman library, Independence, MO.

Truman, H. 1952a. "Annual Message to Congress on the State of the Union." In *Public Papers of the Presidents of the United States*. Washington, DC: U.S. Government Printing Office. January 9.

Truman, H. 1952b. "Radio and Television Address to the American People on the Need for Government Operation of the Steel Mills." In *Public Papers of the Presidents of the United States*. Washington, DC: U.S. Government Printing Office. April 8.

Truman, H. 1952c. "The President's News Conference." In *Public Papers of the Presidents of the United States*. Washington, DC: U.S. Government Printing Office. April 24.

Truman, H. 1956. *Memoirs: Years of Trial and Hope*. New York: Doubleday.

Tulis, J. 1987. *The Rhetorical Presidency*. Princeton, NJ: Princeton University Press.

Turner, K. 1985. *Lyndon Johnson's Dual War: Vietnam and the Press*. Chicago: University of Chicago Press.

U. S. *News and World Report*. 1952. "No 'strong man' for U.S.: Any Would-Be Dictator Must Answer to Courts." June 13. Papers of Harold l. Enerson, Box 4. White House central files. Steel negotiations clips. Harry S. Truman library, Independence, MO.

Underhill, R. 1981. *The Truman Persuasions*. Ames: Iowa State University Press.

Valenti, J. 1975. *A Very Human President*. New York: Norton.

Vatz, R., and T. Windt. 1987. "The Defeats of Judges Haynsworth and Carswell: Rejections of Supreme Court Nominees." In *Essays in Presidential Rhetoric*, eds. T. Windt and B. Ingold. Dubuque, IA: Kendall-Hunt.

Waldron, A. 1973. Memo to Zeigler on Watergate editorials. July 20. Zeigler, Box 16, Watergate II 1/2 junk [1 of 2] folder. National Archives, Nixon papers project, Washington, DC.

Wall Street Journal. 1952. "Review and Outlook: Law and Men." April 21. Papers of Harold l. Enerson. Box 4, White House central files. Steel negotiations clippings, March 7-April 22, 1952. Harry S. Truman library, Independence, MO.

Wann, A. 1987. "Franklin D. Roosevelt's Administrative Contributions to the Presidency." In *Franklin D. Roosevelt: The Man, the Myth, the Era, 1882-1945*, ed. H. Rosenbaum. New York: Greenwood.

Warnke, P. 1969. Oral history, January 15. The Lyndon B. Johnson library, Austin, TX.

Wasden, W. 1969. Letter to Harry Dent, November 16. White House central files, Dent, Box 6; Haynsworth [1 of 3] folder. National Archives, Nixon papers project, Washington, DC.

Watson, J. 1979. Memo to the president, Reaction to Pat Caddell's memorandum proposing an energy strategy. White House files, Chief of Staff, Jordan; Box 44. Energy folder. Jimmy Carter library, Atlanta, GA.

Watson, J., and J. Frank. 1977. Memo to the president, October 14. Eizenstat, Box 199, Energy folder; Jimmy Carter library, Atlanta, GA.

Wayne, S. 1978. *The Legislative Presidency*. New York: Harper and Row.

Westmoreland, W. 1977. "American Goals in Vietnam." In *The Lessons of Vietnam*, eds. S. Thompson and D. Frizzell. New York: Crane, Russak, and Co.

Wexler, A. 1981. Miller Center Interview (including Michael Chanin, Richard Neustadt, John Ryor). Carter presidency project, vol I. February 12-13. Jimmy Carter library, Atlanta, GA.

White, T. 1961. *The Making of the President, 1960*. New York: Atheneum.

White, T. 1969. *The Making of the President, 1968*. New York: Atheneum.

White, T. 1975. *Breach of Faith: The Fall of Richard Nixon*. New York: Dell.

Wicker, T. 1968. *JFK and LBJ: The Influence of Personality Upon Politics*. New York: Morrow.

Williams, F. 1973. Cartoon appearing in *Detroit Free Press*, March 15. Dean, Box 20; Clawson Muskie "Canuck" letter, 1972 folder. National Archives, Nixon papers project, Washington, DC.

Wills, G. 1979. *Nixon Agonistes: The Crisis of a Self-Made Man.* New York: Mentor.

Windt, T. 1977. "Introduction." In *Presidential Rhetoric 1961 to the Present,* ed. T. Windf. Dubuque, IA: Kendall/Hunt.

Windt, T. 1987. "The Presidency and Speeches on International Crises: Repeating the Rhetorical Past. In *Essays in Presidential Rhetoric,* 2nd ed., eds. T. Windt and B. Ingold. Dubuque, IA: Kendall-Hunt.

Windt, T. 1990. *Presidents and Protestors: Political Rhetoric in the 1960s.* Tuscaloosa: University of Alabama Press.

Windt, T., and B. Ingold, eds. 1987. *Essays in Presidential Rhetoric,* 2nd ed. Dubuque, IA: Kendall-Hunt.

Winfield, B. 1990. *Franklin D. Roosevelt and the News Media.* Urbana: Illinois University Press.

Wolfskill, G., and J. Hudson. 1969. *All But the People: Franklin D. Roosevelt and His Critics 1933-39.* New York: Macmillan.

Woodward, B. 1991. *The Commanders.* New York: Simon and Schuster.

Woodward, B., and C. Bernstein. 1976. *The Final Days.* New York: Avon.

Woodward, C. 1991. "The Return of LBJ." *New York Review of Books* December 5: 6-10.

Young, D. 1971. Memo for the file, October 21. White House central files, young, Box 17; Supreme Court nomination folder. National Archives, Nixon papers project, Washington, DC.

Zeigler, R. 1973. ABC phone poll, Zeigler, Box 17; III Watergate, August 1-[1 of 2] folder.

Zinn, H. 1980. *A People's History of the United States.* New York: Harper and Row.

Author Index

201

Subject Index